# DEPRESSION

## The New Integrative Approach

Other books in The New Integrative Approach series:

*Diabetes: How to Combine the Best
of Traditional and Alternative Therapies*

*Fibromyalgia: How to Combine the Best
of Traditional and Alternative Therapies*

*Menopause: How to Combine the Best
of Traditional and Alternative Therapies*

# DEPRESSION

## THE NEW INTEGRATIVE APPROACH

### How to Combine the Best of Traditional and Alternative Therapies

MILTON HAMMERLY, M.D.

Produced by The Philip Lief Group, Inc.

Adams Media Corporation
Avon, Massachusetts

*For Joanie and Matthew,*
*my love for you is beyond measure.*

Published by
Adams Media Corporation
57 Littlefield Street, Avon, MA 02322
*www.adamsmedia.com*

ISBN: 1-58062-526-6

Printed in Canada

J I H G F E D C B

**Library of Congress Cataloging-in-Publication Data**
Hammerly, Milton
Depression : the new integrative approach / Milton Hammerly.
p.         cm.
Includes index.
ISBN 1-58062-526-6
1. Depression, Mental--Treatment.
2. Depression, Mental--Adjuvant treatment. I. Title
RC537 .H3136              2000
616.85'2706--dc21          2001033455

Many of the designations used by manufacturers and sellers to distinguish
their products are claimed as trademarks. Where those designations
appear in this book and Adams Media was aware of a trademark claim,
the designations have been printed in initial capital letters.

This publication is designed to provide accurate and authoritative
information with regard to the subject matter covered. It is sold with
the understanding that the publisher is not engaged in rendering
professional medical advice. If assistance is required, the services of a
competent professional person should be sought.

*This book is available at quantity discounts for bulk*
*purchases. For information, call 1-800-872-5627.*

# Acknowledgments

This book would not have been possible without an able team of writers and researchers that included Carol Coughlin, R.D., Carol Sorgen, Marylou Ambrose, Cindy Spitzer, and Linda DiMario, and the patience and skill of Rhonda Heisler of The Philip Lief Group, who wove together the many threads into a cohesive whole. Thanks also to the superb guiding hand of Cheryl Kimball, my editor at Adams Media Corporation.

Joanie, my wife and editor-in-residence, listened patiently and helped me sort through the innumerable ideas for this series.

I am deeply indebted to the many acupuncturists, chiropractors, herbalists, massage therapists, naturopaths, nutritionists, reflexologists, and other practitioners with whom I have been privileged to work over the years. These talented, dedicated health care providers have given me the opportunity to see medicine and the healing arts through different (nonsurgical and nonpharmaceutical) eyes.

I am equally grateful to my fellow physicians and hospital administrators who have been supportive, even when my career strayed beyond the confines of medical textbooks and double-blind–placebo-controlled research. Your goodwill has kept me going many times when I have been tempted to quit.

For all the patients who have challenged me, stretched my skills, and taught me more than medical school about the art of medicine, I am both appreciative and humbled.

Finally, for circumstances totally beyond my control, for doors closing and doors opening, and for the faith to pass through those doors, I am eternally grateful.

# Contents

# Introduction

## NOT YOUR STANDARD
## BOOK ON DEPRESSION

If you've picked up this book among all the other books on depression, you probably already have a healthy curiosity about what unconventional medicine has to offer.

In that respect you're part of a general population trend. A recent landmark issue of the *Journal of the American Medical Association (JAMA)* reported that over 40 percent of Americans had broadened their health care menu to include such out-of-the-mainstream specialties as stress-reduction techniques, massage, herbal medicine, acupuncture, and homeopathy. In the past decade, visits to nonmedical healers jumped 50 percent. In fact, Americans are spending a whopping $27 billion a year on complementary and alternative treatments, vitamins, herbs, and books—most of that out of their own pockets, since much of what's classified as "complementary" or "alternative" medicine (often abbreviated as CAM) is not covered by health insurance.

Just what's driving the move to greater use of unconventional therapies? A number of factors come into play:

- Broader access to more and (sometimes) better health care information, thanks to an explosion of media attention and now, of course, the Internet

- An ever-increasing interest in disease prevention, wellness strategies, and the quest for optimal health—exactly those areas where complementary medicine can deliver the greatest benefits

- An increase in the number of people with chronic health problems—such as allergies, asthma, chronic fatigue syndrome, diabetes, depression, fibromyalgia, and various autoimmune disorders—and their inability to find adequate or lasting relief from symptoms through conventional medical treatment

- A search for more effective pain control techniques, without the side effects that frequently accompany prescription medications

- An increasing dissatisfaction with the hurried, impersonal approach that characterizes much of health care delivery today. Under managed care, a visit to your doctor's office might involve just 10 minutes with your primary-care physician, barely enough time to do anything more than diagnose and treat your immediate symptoms. In contrast, your appointment with a complementary practitioner might last 60 to 90 minutes and take a comprehensive "whole patient" approach. Writing a prescription is the fastest way to treat symptoms, and not surprisingly, this is the most likely thing you will leave with from a 10-minute office visit with a physician. While prescription medications can certainly be helpful in depression, they do not take the place of someone who will listen to you and treat you as a unique individual. This more involved process takes time and can often identify underlying or contributing factors that need to be addressed—and which no pill will correct.

- The CAM mindset that makes a patient an empowered and active partner in his or her own health care

## DOESN'T WESTERN MEDICINE HAVE THE CURE FOR DEPRESSION?

Are all depressed patients alike? Does everyone experience depression in the same way? Should the treatment of depression be the same for all patients? If you're reading this book, you know intuitively that the answers to these questions are NO! NO! and NO! Unfortunately, for many years the medical community has been answering these questions YES! YES! and YES!

There are, admittedly, a variety of prescription antidepressants that allow for some degree of individualization in the treatment of depression. However, there are many other effective options available that, for the most part, have been ignored by the medical community. Many patients have unacceptable side effects from prescription medications, and the medical community often has little else to offer. If the depression is a symptom of something else, masking your symptoms with an antidepressant, in the long run, may not be in your best interest. Treating all patients with depression as if they had an "antidepressant deficiency" avoids the harder task of finding out what is most appropriate for a given individual.

Unfortunately, many physicians, unfamiliar with what CAM has to offer, simply tell patients that trying CAM interventions will at best be "a waste of time and money." Not only is this advice uninformed, it is detrimental to patients whose lives have been affected emotionally, financially, physically, socially, and spiritually by depression. If physicians are unable to provide solutions that are acceptable to patients, they should learn to collaborate actively with other disciplines that may have the needed answers, or at least get out of the way and not try to impede patients from seeking help elsewhere.

The fact that Western medicine does not have all the answers is not a failure. The failure of Western medicine is in not collaborating with other disciplines and not recognizing that there are answers to be found elsewhere. The theories, teachings, and biases of Western medicine are often treated as if they were more important than finding solutions for suffering patients. This "med-centric" approach is somewhat akin to the pre-Copernican misunderstanding of the universe. Thinking that the sun revolves around the earth (instead of vice versa) is not dissimilar from thinking that disease-oriented Western medicine is at the center of the health care universe and that everything else revolves around it. If the goal of medicine is to serve rather than to be served, it is obvious that the health of patients should be at the center of the health care universe.

With all of the cataclysmic changes occurring in health care (technologic advancements, skyrocketing costs, government/insurance rules, etc.), it seems that the best interest of patients is often pushed aside and forgotten. The misplaced focus on "tech-centric," "cost-centric," "rule-centric," and "etcetera-centric" approaches leads to an increasingly unbalanced, dysfunctional, and sick health care system. There is only one cure for these ailments of focus. *The patient is the cure.*

## INTEGRATIVE MEDICINE—BRIDGING THE GAPS THROUGH PATIENT-CENTERED CARE

"Integrative medicine" approaches patients with depression using a more collaborative, "patient-centric" mindset that is willing to pragmatically blend the best of what Western medicine has to offer with the best of the complementary therapies. This is done with the holistic understanding that each person is unique. We all have different emotional, physical, social, and spiritual factors that affect (or are affected by) the state of our health. Integrative medicine puts the health of the patient back in the center of the health care universe, where it belongs.

Many patients with depression have come to my office, having already tried several antidepressants that were either ineffective or not tolerated. They have been told that there aren't other options and that they have to learn to live with the side effects of the medicine. My challenge has been to check the diagnostic and therapeutic "blind spots" that Western medicine has been unwilling or unable to consider. This mere willingness to think or try something different on behalf of patients has proven to be therapeutic in and of itself. When patients understand that your approach centers around them and that your philosophy will not be an obstacle to their healing, the healing relationship can change dramatically.

This book is addressed to patients with depression who are looking for answers that the medical community has not yet been willing or able to provide. Some of these answers are found in nutrition therapies, and many belong to the world of complementary and alternative medicine. The philosophy of *integrative medicine*—which recognizes the role of body, mind, and spirit in health; favors individualized, patient-centered care; and encourages the rational and judicious combination of conventional Western medicine *and* complementary and alternative medicine, based on evidence of both efficacy and safety—undergirds all of the recommendations provided in this book. Armed with this information, patients with a tendency toward depression can take a much more proactive role in their own health care.

Historically, Western medicine and complementary and alternative medicine have had little to do with each other, except to throw stones at each other on a fairly regular basis. Guess who's been caught in the middle of this futile feud? The patients! Although more and more people are turning to complementary and alternative practitioners for at least some of their health care needs, more than 60 percent of the time they're not telling their physicians about it. Given the potential for unrecognized interactions and contraindications, not to mention the likely therapeutic benefits, it's certainly in everyone's best interest to promote collaboration and a sharing of information between CAM practitioners and conventional physicians. Combining the best of CAM with the best of Western medicine allows for better individualization of therapy, fewer side effects, and better outcomes.

## WHY WESTERN MEDICINE DOESN'T HAVE ALL THE ANSWERS YOU NEED

As a conventionally trained, board-certified family practitioner, I know as well as any physician that the accomplishments of Western medicine in surgery, in infectious diseases, and in other health crises are nothing short of amazing. But as a doctor who specializes in treating people with chronic disorders, and one who often collaborates with complementary and alternative practitioners, I also know that conventional medicine does not have all the answers.

One problem is that conventionally trained doctors generally dismiss as "unscientific," "quackery," "irrelevant," or "dangerous" any therapy that has not been proven effective in double-blind–placebo-controlled (DBPC) research. There are several problems inherent in this position, the most obvious being that a majority of Western medical interventions have not met this standard. In fact, most of the treatments conventional physicians currently recommend to their patients are based on a consensus within the medical community, rather than on sound research that has met the DBPC standard.

Should patients, as the conventional medical community suggests, ignore potentially valuable complementary and alternative therapies with centuries, if not millennia, of clinically demonstrated effectiveness just because they do not meet the methodological criteria of academicians? Or should doctors acknowledge what their patients are proving on a daily basis—that many of these interventions work? Isn't it time to look for other standards of proof?

In some cases, of course, there are excellent studies that meet the most stringent criteria and show consistent benefits from complementary interventions in well defined situations. Often, however, what's missing is a theory or mechanism that explains the outcomes in scientific terms that conventionally trained physicians understand. Many complementary and alternative therapies are based on "alternate" healing systems—some of them energy-based—that are difficult to evaluate if you've been schooled in the Western biochemical model of medicine. Often such therapies are impossible to adequately "blind" so that neither the patient nor the researcher knows who is being treated with what as data is collected.

Traditional acupuncture is an example of one such therapy. There can be no true placebo in a study of acupuncture, because acupuncture needles introduced in "sham" points still have physiologic effects. Research that compares patients treated with needles in actual acupuncture points to those with needles in sham points is actually comparing the effect of doing something with the effect doing *something different*—not the effect of doing something versus the effect of *doing "nothing"* (a placebo). Furthermore, in traditional acupuncture, needle placement is based on a highly individualized assessment of the patient. A research design that calls for the practitioner to use the same set of acupoints in treating all patients runs counter to the philosophy and theory of traditional Chinese medicine. Therefore, such a study, by its own design, actually invalidates itself.

It is ludicrous to insist that therapies such as these, which cannot be studied by DBPC methodology, are not worthy of study or are clinically worthless. To say that the only real clinical effects are what is left over after subtracting out the placebo (mind-body) effect, unfairly and irrationally slams the door shut on therapies that cannot be studied by DBPC methodology. If we were only to use therapies compatible with DBPC testing, both Western medicine and CAM would have much less to offer and the amount of unnecessary suffering would increase significantly. The intellectual orphaning of therapies that are not compatible with DBPC testing does an injustice to both science and humanity.

A second problem that creates barriers to most of complementary and alternative medicine is that conventional Western medicine assumes that all patients respond to treatment essentially the same way. We doctors are taught in medical school that basic physiology doesn't vary much from person to person. This assumption is reinforced by medical research that controls for variables and treats all patients identically. However, what we've come to understand from the human genome project and from other avenues of research is that patients are not robots or genetically identical clones. There are dramatic genetic, enzymatic, biochemical, and environmental differences among people that dictate risk factors, how well a given patient will respond to a given intervention, and possible side effects. Complementary and alternative practitioners have long recognized this fact and make highly individualized assessment and treatment the cornerstone of care.

## MODERN MEDICINE—ART OR SCIENCE, BOTH OR NEITHER?

Medicine is often described as both an art and a science. Science is the art of wrestling with what we don't know. Curiosity drives scientists to postulate a theory and then use their creativity to develop ways to test the theory to see whether it is right or wrong.

Many of the physicians who are the most vocal critics of complementary and alternative medicine call themselves "scientists" but do no research of their own. They quote liberally from other people's research and shun the unknown, saying it hasn't been studied adequately. Such doctors rarely exhibit the open-minded curiosity needed to wrestle with the unknown. This is not science; it is hiding behind science in lockstep conformity out of fear of peer rejection, professional ostracism, or litigation.

This is not to say that these same physicians fail to understand the importance of the mind-body connection. Not at all. They can even quote the research that explains how thoughts, emotions, and moods profoundly affect physiology and health. Yet they rarely incorporate this knowledge into everyday patient care.

In the first place, many physicians feel that to delve into this touchy-feely area lessens their stature as scientists. Secondly, the process of medical education is a brutal one for most doctors. It trains us to deal with cold, hard, objective facts and to deny our own needs and emotions, including the relevance of these needs and emotions to our general well-being.

It's not hard to understand how physicians, who've had their emotional sensitivity beaten out of them by conventional medical training, would have a difficult time acknowledging the mind-body connection in their own lives, much less in the lives of their patients. In this respect the art of medicine has been dealt a serious blow. There can be no art without acknowledging the heart.

And if medicine is to be practiced as an art *and* a science, physicians need both open hearts and open minds.

## WHAT YOU'LL LEARN HERE

This book takes an integrative approach to the management of depression. In doing so it presents the best conventional approaches, nutritional approaches, and complementary and alternative approaches. In no way do I wish to discount the role of conventional medicine in diagnosing and treating patients with depression. After all, as a family practitioner, my own clinical practice falls squarely within this model. At the same time, my role as director of integrative medicine for Catholic Health Initiatives (a national hospital system with its headquarters in Denver) allows me to dialogue and collaborate on an ongoing basis with CAM colleagues in Colorado and across the United States.

The opening chapters of this book cover depression and related health issues from the conventional perspective. Subsequently, the case is presented for lifestyle strategies and sound nutrition. The latter half of the book provides a brief overview of the complementary therapies and describes how to integrate these rationally with Western medicine. Specific therapies and interventions are detailed and, in the closing chapter, their individualized use is illustrated with case histories of patients with depression.

# WHY SHOULD YOU SEEK YET ANOTHER PERSPECTIVE ON DEPRESSION?

That's a good question. No single person, therapy, or discipline has all of the answers to depression. Fortunately, the perspective presented here is much more than my own. As a team of writers with expert knowledge of conventional medicine, complementary modalities, and nutrition, we pull together scientific theory and standard medical/nutritional practice with real-life experience and the clinical know-how of many CAM practitioners.

I've found that my depressed patients have been far better instructors on the realities of depression than medical textbooks and journals. In that sense, the experience and wisdom of these patients—and in some cases, their complementary and alternative care providers—are also speaking to you through the pages of this book.

*Milton Hammerly, M.D.*
*Denver, Colorado*
*www.healingpartner.com*

# 1

## Lower Than Low, Deeper Than Blue

*"It's like I'm treading water. I'm functioning at a low level but I'm never moving forward. I have to work constantly just to keep my head above water. And when life dumps on me, as it does from time to time, I'm quickly overwhelmed and down under I go. One day I'd like to swim to shore and walk on solid ground."*—Roberta, age 42

*"Each day looms vast and pointless before me, like every other—an endless desert of emptiness I can never escape, even if I had the strength to try (which I don't). It's like I'm suffocating in a thick, hot air of meaninglessness and exhaustion, with occasional gasps of fear and self-loathing. When I wake up in the morning and look at the clock, my first thought is: How many more hours until I get to go back to sleep?"*—George, age 27

We all feel sad, disappointed, or blue from time to time. But for people like Roberta and George, life can become a never-ending struggle with an invisible enemy, a quiet, internal torture that erodes energy, derails hope, and sucks the joy out of life.

Depression can be mild or severe, occasional or constant, barely interfering with daily activities or so devastating that suicide looks like the only way to end the pain. It may come on suddenly, like an unexpected rain shower, or slowly, like a creeping fog that quietly builds into an impenetrable black cloud. Depression can be a primary illness or secondary to some other psychiatric or systemic disorder. And it can be either the cause or the result of all sorts of physical maladies, from hormonal disturbances to recurrent viral infections.

To complicate matters further, depression comes in at least a dozen different varieties, each with its own set of possible causes and potential symptoms. In Chapter 3, we'll take a closer look at the most common types of depression, including:

- Depressed mood
- Adjustment disorder
- Dysthymia
- Major depression
- Bipolar disorders (such as manic depression and cyclothymia)
- Atypical depression
- Seasonal affective disorder (SAD)
- Postpartum depression

By some estimates as many as one in 10 adult Americans are mildly to seriously depressed—more than during any other time in history. Countless children also experience various forms of depression. Tragically, only about 30 percent of all depressed adults, and probably even fewer children, ever get help. Over 30,000 will take their own lives by year's end. Two thousand will be teenagers. Among 15- to 24-year-olds, suicide is now the third-leading cause of death.

But on the bright side, there has never been a better time to get help. As gloomy and hopeless as you may feel right now, take some comfort in knowing it's far easier than ever before to get properly diagnosed and find effective treatment.

Years ago, depression was thought to be an entirely moral issue—a sign of a weak will, a lack of ambition, a personality problem, perhaps even the work of the devil. In time, we began to think of depression in more psychological terms, as an emotional response to some traumatic event, an experience traceable to early childhood and now buried deep in the unconscious. Eventually, we came to understand that depression could also be triggered by stressors experienced in the adult years, like "battle fatigue," domestic violence, even childbirth.

More recently, with our growing understanding of the physiology of the brain and nervous system, we've been inching our way closer to the truth: depression may start with emotional/mental problems which lead to physical and biochemical changes; or it can start as a *biochemical* problem which leads to emotional/mental symptoms. Regardless of what causes the despair, *if you're depressed, you have a very real, biochemically based illness*. The fact that this illness expresses itself principally through mental and emotional turmoil doesn't make the illness itself less genuine. It's just as real as heart disease, diabetes, arthritis, or AIDS.

Personally, I dislike the term "mental illness." It implies that depression is something other than an illness of the body. Depression can, in fact, result from one or more underlying physical disorders. But even when depression is triggered by an emotional trauma or mental stress, eventually it manifests itself as changes in the body's complex biochemistry, specifically, imbalances of important chemical messengers in the brain. These chemical messengers, called neurotransmitters, affect nearly every aspect of our lives: how we feel and think, fight infections, sleep and wake, react to stress, move our muscles, and much more.

The abnormal biochemistry of depression may occur in a single episode (like the flu) or become chronic (like arthritis). Either way, if you're depressed, *you have a genuine medical disorder*. If you had heart disease, no one would tell you to "just snap out of it." If you were suffering from diabetes, no one would suggest you simply pull yourself together and get on with your life. Don't let anyone accuse you of being lazy, weak, or wallowing in some moral wasteland. Depression is *not* a character flaw; it's an illness—a biochemical, diagnosable, treatable illness from which you *can* recover, or at the very least, find significant, long-term relief.

Like so many Americans today, people with depression are looking for answers and coping strategies in "alternative" health care—what we call complementary/alternative medicine (CAM). The world of nontraditional medicine offers an impressive variety of noninvasive, yet effective, biochemical and mind-body approaches. Many are ideally suited for people struggling with chronic disorders like depression. Rather than focusing strictly on the specific illness and its immediate symptoms, complementary practitioners generally take a broader, more holistic approach, aiming for the balanced, healthy functioning of the whole person—body, mind, and spirit.

While conventional medicine concentrates on eliminating disease, CAM puts its greatest emphasis on prevention, on optimizing health and well-being. In the conventional model, the physician essentially calls the shots and controls access to a vast arsenal of relatively aggressive medical interventions. In the complementary/ alternative model, the patient takes a more active role. This can range from learning as much as possible about the disorder and the various treatment options, to following through on self-help measures, to coordinating care among the various members of the health care team.

But depression, with its many possible causes and symptoms, can be a particularly difficult illness to diagnose and treat. To anyone whose energy, motivation, and self-esteem have taken a nosedive, the challenges presented by depression seem like an unscalable wall. Many depressed people are simply not up to the task of actively participating in their own recovery.

Yet this is exactly what's required.

With so many alternative modalities promising relief, and so little research to indicate which complementary approaches work best under particular conditions, until now it's been hard for depression sufferers to sort through the static. And a halfhearted effort—an occasional massage, a little herbal therapy with St. John's wort—can lead nowhere and even be downright dangerous if it merely distracts you and prevents you from getting the medical help you may desperately need.

Now, for the first time, all that is changing. By taking what works from conventional Western medicine and combining those interventions with the most effective CAM strategies, we can create a powerful, new synthesis called *integrative medicine*, the best of both worlds.

As a board-certified family practitioner trained in Western medicine and highly familiar with alternative health practices, I've spent a good deal of my medical career diagnosing and treating patients with chronic disorders including fibromyalgia, chronic fatigue, autoimmune disease, diabetes, depression, allergies, and asthma, to name a few. Over the years, I've found that almost half of the patients I see also have some degree of depression. Research has consistently shown that people with chronic illness have a much higher incidence of depression than the general population. By focusing on each patient as a unique individual, taking a detailed medical history, identifying underlying associated illnesses, and discussing *both* conventional and nontraditional treatments, I can lead my patients to appreciate the advantages of integrative medicine.

There are very few patients in my practice who would not rather use less aggressive interventions with less risk of side effects, if at all possible. One of the big advantages of the integrative approach is that it preferentially uses less aggressive interventions whenever possible. Aggressive therapies are not forced on patients when not needed, nor are they inappropriately withheld when they *are* needed. While conventional Western medicine tends to match the patient to the treatment, integrative medicine matches the treatment to the patient. With the expanded options available within an integrative approach, treatment can be individualized to maximize benefits and minimize risks.

Living day in and day out with the debilitating symptoms of depression can leave you feeling like a prisoner of your own life. Using an integrative model, you and the members of your health care team—a coordinated group of providers, which might include a physician, psychotherapist, nutritionist, and CAM practitioners—can collaborate to explore your multiple paths to mental wellness. Information is power. That's what I'd like to offer you in this book: the power that comes from understanding and using the integrative approach to chart your own road out of helplessness and hopelessness.

## WHO'S DEPRESSED?

The answer is your neighbor, your boss, your family member, your friend. Perhaps even you. And in any case, probably a whole lot more people than you think.

Depression strikes people of all ages, races, genders, incomes, and educational backgrounds. According to the National Institute of Mental Health, in the United States alone, almost 10 million people struggle with major depression every year. Another 10 million experience milder depression, which can still cause serious distress and significantly disrupt normal life. More than two million Americans, about one in 100, endure the cyclical mood swings of various bipolar disorders, including manic depression. The World Health Organization calls depression the fourth most devastating illness worldwide.

Nearly twice as many women as men are diagnosed with depression. Women tend to exhibit the classic emotional signposts of depression—sadness, self-loathing, guilt, and despair. Most men, on the other hand, are conditioned from an early age to hide or deny their emotional vulnerability. Men typically express their depression differently than women. They generally keep their doubts, anger, and despair under wraps, only to have these powerful emotions erupt in dangerous, destructive behaviors involving alcohol, drugs, or violence. They may never be identified as depressed at all. Interestingly, the rate for bipolar disorder, also called manic-depressive disease, is about equal for men and women.

For reasons unknown, major depression is more common in and around cities than in rural areas. Depression of all types is widely seen among the elderly and the chronically ill. And depression is a growing problem among teenagers, even young children. Over the course of a lifetime, one in six of us will experience at least one bout of serious depression.

Left untreated, depression can utterly wreck otherwise pleasant lives. Marriages are sapped of their vitality; children grow up without adequate parenting; promising careers are sidelined. Some depressed individuals just put in an appearance in their own lives. They are physically present and function as workers, spouses, parents, children—but they never make the mark they could have made had they received treatment. Their lives are colorless, barely productive, robbed of joy.

Though the cost in human misery is impossible to calculate, depression carries an actual price tag as well. In this country an estimated $43 billion is spent annually on medications for depression, on professional care, and on missed days at work or school. What depression costs the country in terms of lost productivity on the job is much harder to estimate.

Even so, the majority of those with depression—almost three-quarters in fact—carry on despite their illness. Many take medications, perhaps supplemented by psychotherapy or some other form of treatment that keeps them functioning at work or at school.

And a diagnosis of depression does not necessarily mean that you can't go on to accomplish great things. Talk show pioneer Dick Cavett struggles with depression, as does popular TV journalist Mike Wallace. Other prominent individuals who've been in the grip of depression include Abraham Lincoln, Winston Churchill, media mogul Dick Clark, actress Patty Duke, comedians Joan

Rivers and Rodney Dangerfield, painters Jackson Pollock and Georgia O'Keefe, newspaper humorist Art Buchwald, and literary luminaries Ernest Hemingway, Mark Twain, William Styron, and Virginia Woolf.

For these people and many others, depression remains mostly a private affair. Unless their experience has been the subject of a book or they've been interviewed on the talk show circuit, few know how deeply they've suffered. Not so for Dr. Kay Redfield Jamison, a professor of psychiatry at the Johns Hopkins Medical Institutions and one of the world's leading experts on mood disorders. She recently wrote an account of her own struggle with manic depression in her book, *An Unquiet Mind*. Until Dr. Jamison came forward in print, many of her medical colleagues had no idea of her long struggle with a severe form of bipolar disorder or that she had once attempted suicide with the lithium medication that eventually preserved her sanity.

## AM I DEPRESSED?

By the time most people ask themselves this question, the answer is often yes.

Accurately diagnosing depression and establishing its type and severity requires an expert health care professional (more on this in Chapters 2 and 3). Like most disorders, depression takes various forms. Symptoms vary dramatically from person to person and can change over time. When making a diagnosis of depression and differentiating it from normal grief or a passing low mood, doctors usually look for *at least five* of the following symptoms, particularly the first two. Symptoms must be present most of the time and *last for at least two weeks*. The most common markers are:

- **Persistent feelings of sadness and emptiness**—feeling overwhelmed, hopeless, helpless, and pessimistic about the future
- **Loss of interest in or pleasure from activities you once enjoyed (anhedonia)**—including work, hobbies, school, family activities, sex, etc.
- **Changes in sleeping patterns**—including trouble falling asleep, staying asleep, or getting up in the morning. About two-thirds of depressed people experience sleep disturbances.
- **Changes in appetite or weight**—loss of interest in eating, excessive eating, or weight loss or gain
- **Extreme fatigue or lack of energy**—feeling so lethargic that even the smallest tasks seem to require enormous effort
- **Changes in physical appearance and expression**—a "flat" facial expression, hollowness around the eyes, monotonal speech, or movements that are slower than normal
- **Restlessness or decreased activity that is noticeable by others**—anxiety or irritability, dropping out of contact with friends and family. Anxiety is often a component of depression, and about 80 percent of depression sufferers are troubled by unrealistic fears and worries that increase the person's risk for suicide.

- **Difficulty in concentrating or making decisions**—slowed or fuzzy thinking, memory problems, or inability to complete a project or assignment. Some patients misdiagnosed with dementia actually have depression. When the depression is treated, their thinking and cognitive function return to normal.
- **Tearfulness for no apparent reason**
- **Physical aches and pains**—headaches, stomachaches, backaches, chronic muscle or joint pain, or constipation. About 60 percent of depression sufferers report anxiety-related physical symptoms.
- **Feelings of worthlessness or inappropriate guilt**—depressed patients sometimes believe that everyone would be better off if they were dead.
- **Engaging in dangerous or risky behavior**—abuse of drugs or alcohol, engaging in self-mutilation or unprotected sex, provoking fights, crossing the street without checking for traffic, or purposely taking other risks
- **Recurrent thoughts of death or suicide**

If you think you or someone you love may be depressed, it's imperative that you seek experienced medical help as soon as possible. Left untreated, depression can be progressive and life-threatening. Don't wait until it gets worse.

## CHILDREN AND TEENS AT RISK

The National Mental Health Association estimates that as many as three percent of children may be seriously depressed, and the rate among adolescents may be as high as 12 percent. Two-thirds of depressed children and teens don't get the help they critically need. Young people whose depression goes undiagnosed and untreated are at risk for developing a lifelong pattern of depressive disorders.

Family patterns of loss or abuse elevate risk, as does having a parent with serious depression. Growing up with a depressed parent can leave a child feeling powerless and worthless. Learned helplessness, discussed in Chapter 2, can be a behavior adopted by children who grow up in homes where depression sets the tone. Such youngsters may even assume blame or guilt for the parent's condition.

Depression in adolescents mimics adult depression, but sometimes it can be difficult to distinguish the symptoms of depression from the hormone-fueled mood swings and normal posturing of adolescence. The teen years can be a time of emotional turbulence and angst. It's hardly unusual for teenagers to wear black, alternate between periods of elation and dejection, party all night and sleep all day, retreat to their rooms in a foul mood, and generally turn their parents' world upside-down.

But adolescents are going through a volatile period, a time when they are striving toward independence in fits and starts—one minute sloughing off family ties, the next minute desperately reaching out for security. It's a time when any loss, serious or otherwise, can precipitate a deep emotional reaction. Adults must pay close attention to what teenagers do and say. Watch for signs of difficulty functioning in school, sports, and relationships with friends. Parents who are too easygoing about these years can sometimes miss the signs of serious problems by assuring themselves that their kid will just grow out of it.

For children and teens, one or more of the following symptoms may indicate the onset of depression. To qualify, the symptom must persist *for two weeks or more:*

- Poor performance in school—a drop in grades, problems with authority, absenteeism, or truancy
- Changes in eating and/or sleeping habits
- Withdrawal from activities
- Isolation from friends and family
- Changes in patterns of interaction with friends— either sad and withdrawn, or angry and aggressive
- Persistent sadness and feelings of hopelessness
- Extreme irritability
- Lack of concentration, forgetfulness
- Poor self-esteem or guilt
- Extreme reaction to criticism
- Complaints of vague ailments—including stomachache, backache, headache
- Low energy level and lack of enthusiasm
- Abuse of drugs or alcohol—watch for signs that your child is hanging out with a different crowd of friends
- Panic attacks
- Delusions or hallucinations
- Contemplating suicide or thoughts of death

# A BLACK CLOUD OVER
# THE GOLDEN YEARS

Depression is not a normal, healthy part of the aging process, although it is remarkably common. About 15 percent of older adults become seriously, often chronically, depressed. Many report persistent thoughts of death and dying. Among those who live in nursing homes, the figure is higher, about 20 percent.

Depression is often overlooked in older adults because they have other illnesses that command attention and because, as time goes on, they routinely experience so many predictable losses. Older people who live alone and don't get out much can become increasingly gloomy as they absorb each shock, especially if there's no one nearby to take an interest in them and sound an alarm.

Retirement may end a long, meaningful career. As time goes by, spouses and friends die. Chronic or catastrophic illnesses take hold. Seniors who are no longer able to drive or even live independently are cut off from rewarding activities.

It's easy to dismiss the symptoms of depression as expected or "normal" reactions to such developments. But depression doesn't have to cast a pall over the senior years, not when preventive strategies and effective treatments are so widely available.

Depression is associated with many chronic medical conditions common to old age, such as arthritis, high blood pressure, heart disease, stroke, diabetes, cancer, and Alzheimer's and Parkinson's diseases. Most of these disorders are associated with some degree of disability and/or chronic pain, and many have symptoms that overlap with depressive symptoms and can mask a depressive disorder. Some medications can even produce side effects that mimic classic depressive symptoms.

Caregivers for the elderly should be on the lookout for the telltale signs of depression, including:

- Persistent physical complaints such as chronic fatigue, weight loss, loss of appetite, disturbed sleep, and difficulty concentrating
- Social withdrawal
- A sense of failure or a feeling that one is being punished
- A wish to die
- Thoughts of suicide

Many older adults never get the help they need for depression. Some cling to the old-fashioned notion that depression is a character defect and therefore resist treatment. Explaining depression in physiological terms may be helpful in getting seniors to agree to diagnostic tests and a variety of possible drug and nondrug therapies.

## THEY DIDN'T HAVE PROZAC IN ANCIENT EGYPT

Depression is probably as old as the human race. Evidence of the disorder dates back to ancient Egypt and the Bible. We know that King Saul was despondent. The early Romans called the condition "melancholia."

Some of the early saints exhibited behavior that was downright bizarre, and undoubtedly many people who were subjected to exorcism in the Middle Ages were mentally unstable, perhaps bipolar. The prim Victorians referred to the condition as neurasthenia. But it wasn't until the late nineteenth century that doctors first began to systematically classify the symptoms of mental illness.

An early leader in this effort was Emil Kraeplin, a turn-of-the-century German physician who spent countless hours observing the mentally ill, carefully noting the behavior, signs, and symptoms of what we know today to be schizophrenia and bipolar disorder. Kraeplin's work was overshadowed by the vast contributions of psychiatrist Sigmund Freud in the early part of the twentieth century. Freud was the first to theorize that emotional and mental problems were expressions of unresolved conflicts buried deep in the unconscious mind—at the time, a truly revolutionary concept.

By the mid–twentieth century, a new branch of medicine called neuroscience focused on basic brain activity. Responding to a growing demand for improved communications among physicians, researchers, and mental health professionals and the need for rigorous standardization in the classification of mental illness, the first *Diagnostic and Statistical Manual (DSM)* was published in 1952. The manual defined various disorders on the basis of their characteristic symptoms. New editions in 1968, 1980, and 1994 provided increasingly specific criteria for diagnosing different mental illnesses. By the 1980 edition, Freud's diagnosis of "neurosis" was moved into a separate classification, known as personality disorders.

Although members of the medical community continue to disagree strongly about the various classification systems found in the *DSM,* it remains the classic reference text for assessing mental illness. The book can be misused if doctors view it as a checklist and simply run down the criteria without taking the whole patient into account. But the biggest benefit of the *DSM* is that by defining terms and establishing diagnostic criteria, it allows everyone in the medical and mental health communities to communicate more accurately, using terms that mean the same thing to everyone. The newest version of the manual, the *DSM-IV,* has become a widely used and accepted tool.

## WHAT'S AVAILABLE IN TREATMENT?

If you're depressed, just marshaling the energy to find treatment can be a challenge. But taking the first step— usually by talking to your family doctor—can open a floodgate of treatment possibilities.

Twenty-five years ago, antidepressants and psychotherapy were just about your only options. Today, you have dozens of other choices: lifestyle strategies like exercise; nutritional therapy; stress management; art, music, and laughter therapy; and CAM interventions like yoga, meditation, acupuncture, and herbal therapy.

If your depression is mild, lifestyle and CAM interventions might be all that's needed to lift your mood. For more severe depression, your doctor may recommend a combination of traditional and nontraditional approaches. The next section gives a quick overview of what's available.

## DRUGS TO THE RESCUE

Regardless of how accurately mental disorders were defined and classified, and no matter what form of psychotherapy was tried, until the mid–twentieth century, physicians and mental health professionals shared a fundamental problem: for many patients, there was no truly reliable treatment that could break the grip of serious depression. Then in 1949 an Australian psychiatrist named John Cade made a startling discovery. He found that a substance called lithium—a compound that had failed miserably a century earlier when it was tried as a treatment for cancer, diabetes, and epilepsy—had a remarkable "side effect" of practically eliminating manic depression.

At first, the U.S. medical community was hesitant to accept lithium. The drug is an alkali metal that combines with carbonate or citrate to form a salt. Earlier trials, which attempted to use lithium as a salt substitute for patients requiring a low-sodium diet, had proved disastrous. Without sodium, lithium enters the brain and becomes toxic. But by the 1960s, lithium was widely used in other countries to treat bipolar disorder, and finally in 1974 it became the drug of choice in the United States. It's used both to halt the active mania state of bipolar disorder and as a maintenance medication to prevent manic-depressive cycles.

Antipsychotic drugs traveled an equally bumpy road. Chlorpromazine (Thorazine) was originally developed for its antihistaminic properties during surgery. The drug caught French surgeon Henri Laborit's attention 50 years ago when he noticed how it calmed some of his patients. But the medical community remained skeptical. Finally in 1952, clinical trials revealed that this drug reduced the delusions and hallucinations associated with schizophrenia. The drug is still used today to treat psychosis and the manic phase of bipolar disease.

Antidepressants made the scene in the early 1950s when a Swiss pharmaceutical company tested a compound that resembled chlorpromazine, one of the antipsychotic drugs. Although the new compound failed to reduce psychotic symptoms, it did prove helpful in lifting depression. By the early 1960s, the "tricyclic" antidepressants—so-called because of their chemical structure—came into wide use. These first-generation antidepressants still have a treatment role today, although their side effects make them less desirable than some of the newer drugs.

A newer class of antidepressants, called selective serotonin reuptake inhibitors (SSRIs), of which Prozac is probably the best known, burst onto the scene in the 1980s with much fanfare, in part because they worked well, had fewer and better tolerated side effects, and weren't fatal in "overdose" amounts—a key concern when prescribing medication to people prone to suicide. You'll read more about these medications, and even newer classes of antidepressants, in Chapter 7.

## Psychotherapy

In the past psychotherapy was thought of as something for "crazy" people or only for the very rich and self-indulgent. Now we know that most people can benefit from it at some time in their lives. Millions of people have used "talk therapy" to find relief from depression. A study reported in the November 1995 issue of *Consumer Reports* noted that nearly nine out of 10 respondents who sought psychological care indicated that their condition improved significantly with treatment.

The simplest form of talk therapy involves discussing problems or feelings with your doctor, a close friend, or a family member. Sometimes, however, difficult problems can't be resolved in conversation, no matter how supportive, so it's a good idea to consult a trained mental health professional—such as a psychologist, psychiatrist, or social worker.

If you decide to undergo psychotherapy, you and your therapist will meet regularly in a confidential, supportive, nonjudgmental environment. In the course of treatment, the therapist will work with you to:

- Identify life problems that may be contributing to your depression and explore how the situation can be solved or improved
- Pinpoint negative thought patterns that may be contributing to helplessness or lack of hope
- Help you see the choices in your life and encourage you to take part in satisfying activities

Despite the high success rate, some people find it difficult to get started with psychotherapy or stay in treatment. Admittedly, it's often hard to discuss painful feelings or troubling experiences. But for those who are willing to work through difficult issues, the process often brings relief from depression and opens the door to a more fulfilling life.

We'll be focusing more attention on the various talk therapies in Chapter 6.

## DRUG-FREE APPROACHES

Standard pharmaceuticals aren't the only course of action for the person with depression. More and more people are turning to complementary and alternative therapies for ways to prevent and cope with depression. For some, antidepressant medications—even when used in conjunction with psychotherapy—have not been effective. Others may want to avoid the troublesome side effects of the antidepressant medications, or may simply prefer a more natural "whole patient" approach. Some simply want to explore every possible treatment option.

The growing popularity of CAM interventions has forced the medical establishment to initiate the rigorous testing of various treatment options to determine their efficacy and safety, the same testing formerly reserved for products in the pharmaceutical pipeline. As researchers learn which complementary therapies are most effective, they'll no doubt uncover more clues as to the causes and nature of depressive disorders.

A number of nonstandard approaches have garnered particular attention. An herbal remedy, St. John's wort, is known to be effective in relieving certain types of mild depression, and the metabolic supplement SAMe (newly available in this country, but a popular supplement for some time in Italy and Germany) holds great promise. Light therapy is clearly established as a highly successful nondrug intervention in seasonal affective disorder (SAD). Research is just beginning to probe into why an alternative therapy like acupuncture can achieve a full remission in some depressed patients, as it did in one study done at the University of Arizona.

The role of other therapies, for example in the treatment of depression, is currently under investigation, though their value in relieving stress and anxiety has been documented in countless studies.

## REASONS FOR HOPE

We live in an era of rapid scientific discovery and increased public awareness. We know now that depression isn't a sign of moral weakness, a personality problem, or a character defect, but a consequence of dysfunctional brain biochemistry. As we learn more about the biological basis for depression, as well as what triggers and relieves depression in susceptible people, the long-standing stigma associated with the disorder is rapidly fading. Meanwhile, better health insurance coverage and new legislation that protects the mentally ill from job discrimination are also helping to bring depression out of the closet.

As more people affected by depression come forward and seek treatment, increasingly sophisticated interventions are evolving. While many people still go the entirely conventional route, more and more people with depression are benefiting from an approach that brings together the best conventional therapies with nutritional therapy and complementary/alternative practices. As we'll see throughout this book, the integrative approach, coordinated by a forward-thinking physician, offers you the widest possible array of treatment options. By taking a more active role in your own care, you'll be assembling the information and tools you need to make the lifestyle changes that can optimize your long-term health, improve your overall quality of life, and help keep depression at bay.

# 2

## How Did This Happen to Me?

If you're in the grip of depression, you've probably already asked yourself, *How did this happen to me?* The short answer is that nobody knows for sure. The long answer involves a complex web of genetic, biochemical, physiological, and psychosocial factors. Most often, depression is triggered by the interplay of genetic predisposition, chemical imbalance, physical illness, and emotional or mental stress. Let's take a look at these factors.

### BIOCHEMICAL FACTORS

For some time now, scientists have been looking into the possible biochemical causes of depression. Regardless of the trigger, once initiated, depression manifests itself as an imbalance in the biochemistry of the brain. Researchers have zeroed in on the way information is transferred between the cells. Two body systems are involved: the endocrine system and the nervous system.

Within the nervous system, neurons receive electrical impulses from other nerve cells. These impulses run along the neural circuits to help us regulate mood and behavior and also help control critical functions such as thinking, sleep and wakefulness, and appetite. As these messages travel along neural pathways, they reach microscopic gaps, called synapses. Chemical transmitter molecules, called neurotransmitters, carry the impulses from the nerve cells across the synapse to the cells on the other side. Once the neurotransmitter's job is done, it's either inactivated by enzymes or reabsorbed or recycled into the part of the brain where it was originally released, a process known as reuptake. Either way, the synapse is cleared for the next chemical messenger.

Researchers have determined that severely depressed people can have an imbalance or disruption in the levels of several neurotransmitters (serotonin, dopamine, and norepinephrine). Although scientists don't completely understand the process, they've been able to develop a number of effective medications that relieve depression by modulating neurotransmitter levels.

The endocrine system has special cells that secrete hormones that travel through the bloodstream to other parts of the body, where they attach to specific receptors that are structured to respond to them. Among other functions, the endocrine system regulates the body's response to stress—the well known "fight or flight" response. Researchers at the National Institutes of Health are looking at whether one underlying cause of depression is linked to a persistent overreaction of the body's stress response system—known as the hypothalamic-pituitary-adrenal (HPA) axis. The HPA axis is implicated in such complex processes as hormone balance, sleep cycles, appetite, thirst, and emotional behaviors.

The hormone cortisol is of particular interest to investigators. Cortisol is a steroid hormone that prepares the body for defensive action when confronted by danger or prolonged stress. Scientists know that people with major depression have trouble regulating the production of cortisol.

## THE ROLE OF GENETICS

Research indicates that in some families depression is passed down from generation to generation. The genetic link is even stronger in bipolar disorders. It's likely that multiple genes are involved, and this "genetic predisposition" acts together with environmental factors to make some people more vulnerable to depression than others. It's now suspected that the tendency to have irregular levels of certain neurotransmitters may be an inherited condition.

The American Psychiatric Association notes that major depression occurs one-and-a-half to three times as often among those with a parent or sibling with a history of depression. But genetics is only part of the explanation—socialization also plays a role. If a parent suffers from the disorder, it's more likely that the children will show signs of depression, because they tend to reflect the prevailing outlook in the home.

And while only about one percent of the general population has bipolar disorder, if you have a parent or sibling who's affected, you have a 12 percent chance of developing bipolar disorder yourself. One study published in the *Journal of the American Academy of Child and Adolescent Psychiatry* (1996) focused on 14 families (including 50 children) with a strong history of bipolar disorder. Thirty-nine percent of the offspring of parents who suffered from either bipolar disorder or major depression developed one of these disorders while they were still children.

Studies of identical twins have shown that if one twin has depression, there's a 70 percent chance the other twin will develop it as well. In one study, if one identical twin had a mood disorder, there was a 67 percent chance the other twin did too, even if the twins were raised apart. Interestingly, only 19 percent of fraternal (non-identical) twins shared an affective disorder.

## DEVELOPMENTAL AND ENVIRONMENTAL FACTORS

Evidence points to the fact that young people who experience early childhood trauma, such as physical or sexual abuse, or a deep emotional loss (such as losing a parent through death or divorce) are more likely to develop depression as adults. Other causative factors include severe communication problems; deeply disturbing conflicts with family members, friends, and coworkers; and ongoing relationship problems—all of which can lead to loneliness and isolation. Ongoing life stresses—such as financial problems, serious illness, or the presence of violence in the home—may also play a major role.

## RELATIONSHIPS, MARRIAGE, AND CHILDREN

Family and friends can have positive and negative impacts on us all. Healthy relationships—those built on honesty, trust, and mutual respect, in which people have good communication skills, express feelings, and share responsibilities—help buffer us from the stress and strain of everyday life. People in such relationships generally have high self-esteem and are less likely to develop depression. On the other hand, the lack of close, supportive relationships—an acute problem among the elderly—can put one at increased risk for an assortment of mood disorders.

Animal studies point to another possible explanation: learned helplessness. In a 1967 study, shocks were administered to dogs. At first, no matter how the dogs reacted (jumping, barking), the shocks continued, until eventually the animals just gave up, lay down, and whimpered. Later, when the shocks were administered in a situation that allowed the dogs to avoid the pain by barking or jumping, the animals still just lay down and took the treatment.

When a similar experiment was attempted on humans, the people also simply gave up. What struck researchers most was the similarity between the symptoms of learned helplessness and the symptoms of depression. These studies suggest that people who absorb enough negative blows in life can lose their ability to respond because they come to feel that they can't make a difference. They give up, even though circumstances may change. If something good happens to them, they think it's only luck and has nothing to do with any positive action on their part.

## DRUGS AND DEPRESSION

While specific antidepressant medications may work wonders when given at the right time to the right patient under the right conditions, other drugs, either on their own or in combination, can actually cause depression in certain vulnerable individuals.

Many depressed people "self-medicate" by drinking alcohol or abusing controlled substances, such as narcotics or prescription sedatives and tranquilizers. They use alcohol and drugs to "take the edge off" manic feelings or to blunt feelings of despair. Some people with bipolar disorder attempt to slow down racing thoughts with alcohol or over-the-counter medications, such as Benadryl. But these substances can severely worsen a depressive episode, especially if mixed with other prescription or nonprescription drugs.

Various studies have linked alcoholism with manic depression, either as a symptom, a result, or a contributing cause. One study suggests that stimulant drugs, like "speed" and cocaine, may precipitate the early onset of bipolar disorder in persons with a pre-existing family disposition for mania. Other studies point to a link between familial disposition for depression and the abuse of alcohol and drugs.

## CHRONIC ILLNESS AND DEPRESSION

Depression is a common symptom and/or consequence of many chronic illnesses. One survey found that depression complicates the treatment of about 45 percent of heart attack victims, 42 percent of hospitalized cancer patients, 40 percent of stroke survivors and those with Parkinson's disease or multiple sclerosis, and about a third of all diabetes patients.

As most of us can appreciate, coming to terms with a chronic illness can itself be depressing. On the one hand, a physical disability or recurrent pain can limit your access to activities you used to enjoy and make you feel as though you're living under a dark cloud. Then there's the frustration of trying to locate effective treatment for commonly misunderstood or misdiagnosed illnesses, like chronic fatigue syndrome or fibromyalgia. For many of these patients, the average time between onset of symptoms and an accurate diagnosis is about five years! The patient traipses from doctor to doctor, looking for some relief, only to be told, "It's all in your head," "There's nothing else we can do," or "You just have to live with it." What a recipe for depression!

It can be somewhat tricky to prescribe antidepressants for people taking medications for chronic disorders. Dosages may have to be adjusted, and you and your physician should be wary of contraindications and the potential for adverse side effects. Given these risks, alternative and complementary therapies may be a safer bet. Always be sure to let all your doctors and CAM health practitioners know *all* the drugs and herbal remedies that you're taking.

## CANCER AND DEPRESSION

Dealing with depression in cancer patients presents its own particular set of challenges. With advances in medical technology and new drug therapies, cancer patients—even those with advanced disease—are living longer and enjoying a better quality of life. But living longer has a price tag: half of all cancer patients experience some type of psychological disorder, usually an adjustment disorder with depression.

Once a person is diagnosed with cancer, the resulting anxiety and depression may cause him to put off needed treatment, which can understandably reduce his chance of survival. The treatment itself—often an assault of chemotherapy drugs, surgery, and/or radiation therapy—will almost certainly change a person's lifestyle, limit activities, alter body image, affect relationships, and lead to debilitating side effects such as pain, nausea, vomiting, and fatigue. Physical pain alone can bring on depression.

Various factors boost the odds that a cancer patient will experience serious depression. These include:

- Social isolation
- Financial pressures

- History of mood disorders
- Alcohol or substance abuse
- Poorly controlled pain
- Side effects of some medications and treatments

Some physicians will present you with a diagnosis of cancer and then immediately tell you your odds for survival. Given that the doctor isn't God, telling you your odds of survival are low because people with your type of cancer have only a 15 percent survival rate can be incorrect and downright counter-therapeutic. Dr. Andrew Weil, a well known author and advocate of integrative medicine, calls this "medical hexing." Once the patient hears a dire prediction, it can become a self-fulfilling prophecy.

This is not to say that doctors should not be truthful or realistic when their patients develop a chronic or life-threatening illness. But neither should they go out of their way to paint a pessimistic picture. Hope is therapeutic. The mind-body connection is a two-way street. Our physiology can dramatically affect our thoughts and mood, and our thoughts can also affect our physiology for better or for worse. Recognizing and treating depression cannot only improve mood but can actually improve outcomes in the coexisting condition.

## RECURRENT INFECTIONS

There is significant evidence that the immune system and nervous system communicate with each other and that depression can gradually diminish immune function, especially in older individuals. A compromised immune system leaves you less able to fight off infection.

That said, it's critical that people prone to depression do what they can to maintain healthy lifestyles. This includes paying particular attention to diet, exercise, socialization, and sleep—especially during periods of increased stress. Research has shown that people with a strong social support system show less reduction in immune system function, even when they are depressed or under stress.

## HEART DISEASE

According to large epidemiological studies, approximately 1.5 to 3 percent of the general population can be classified as depressed at any one time. In the case of heart disease patients, this figure rises to 18 percent. A growing body of research indicates that negative emotions—such as chronic anger, anxiety, loneliness, and depression—are dangerous for people with coronary artery disease. For example:

- A study at the Montreal Institute of Health followed 200 heart attack patients and found that those who suffered from depression were four times as likely to die within six months of their heart attack. In fact, researchers concluded that *depression was just as reliable a predictor of impending death as previous heart attacks and poor heart functioning.*

- Dr. Robert Carney, a professor of medical psychology at Washington University in St. Louis, found that depressed people who had just been diagnosed with heart disease were twice as likely as nondepressed new heart patients to suffer a heart attack or require bypass surgery within 12 months of diagnosis.

- A 14-year study conducted at Johns Hopkins School of Hygiene and Public Health seems to indicate that *depression may lead to heart disease*. Researchers followed approximately 1,500 heart-healthy people and found that *those who were depressed suffered heart attacks four times more often than those who weren't*.

Why would depression be a stress on the heart? Several factors are probably at work. When people are depressed, an excess of the stress hormone cortisol keeps them in a constant state of arousal and anxiety—a condition that can continue for weeks, months, even years. Increased cortisol also shifts the production of cholesterol from "good" HDL cholesterol, which protects blood vessels, to "bad" LDL cholesterol, which damages vessels. An overabundance of the hormone norepinephrine quickens the heart rate and elevates blood pressure, stressing the blood vessels and heart even more. In addition, the heart rhythms of depressed people are often not well regulated in response to different kinds of activities, thus increasing the risk for a first or second heart attack.

## SO WHY ME AND NOT YOU?

We still don't understand why, when presented with the same set of factors, one person becomes depressed and another doesn't. Sometimes the brain chemistry malfunctions for no obvious reason, and people who've been happy, loved, and fulfilled can become seriously depressed. It appears that different individuals have different personal thresholds when it comes to depression. In some cases, an episode of depression may be triggered by a specific event or stressor; other times there is no clear trigger.

## A CALL TO ACTION

It can be a daunting task to summon up the strength and perseverance you need to cope with any serious illness—finding appropriate help, pursuing the right diagnosis, and sorting through your many treatment options. But if you're depressed, or think you might be, these complex tasks can seem downright impossible. After all, you're depressed! Who's got the energy, optimism, or drive to do all that?

The answer is *you* do.

No matter how hopeless and helpless you may feel at this moment, or how pointless life may seem, please keep one thought clearly in mind: *You are not your symptoms.* Your overwhelming feelings of sorrow, guilt, or worthlessness—no matter how debilitating—are not an accurate representation of the total you, any more than an achy knee accurately represents the totality of someone with arthritis, or high blood pressure tells the whole story about someone with hypertension. When depression strikes, it may *seem* as if that's all there is to your life, but that's not so. Like an achy knee, your despair is just an important signal telling you that something is out of whack and needs to be set right. Depression can make you feel passive and useless, but don't succumb to those feelings. Look at it as an important *call to action*.

Whether you feel mildly affected by depression or entirely trapped, *action* is your ticket out. In the next chapter and throughout the rest of the book, I offer you dozens of effective ways to get into action—and conquer your depression. By developing a take-charge attitude about getting the right diagnosis, exploring your treatment options, and committing yourself fully to recovery, you *can* get better.

# 3

## Getting the Most from Conventional Medicine: Diagnosis and Treatment

Now that we've looked at the scope of depression, the various forms of depressive illness, and what causes and triggers these disorders, it's time to focus on what matters most to you: getting an accurate diagnosis and figuring out your best treatment options. This is where you have to step up to the plate. The more active your role in this process, the better the prospects for your short-term and long-term health.

To be frank, many of my fellow physicians are still in the habit of acting as if *they* are entirely in charge of your health. For years, conventional medical doctors were systematically trained to treat patients like passive, naive children. And for the most part, patients acquiesced. So physicians got used to making many important decisions for their patients, with little discussion of options and alternatives.

Of course, in the last 15 years we've seen dramatic changes in the expectations and interests of patients, who increasingly see themselves not as victims waiting passively to be healed, but as informed consumers actively pursuing health. With this change has come growing public interest in alternative medicine and various healthy lifestyle strategies, such as nutrition and exercise. As the baby boomers continue to age (reluctantly!), they are no longer content to be simply disease-free; they want optimal health and are pursuing it with a passion—and with their pocketbooks.

Conservative by nature, conventional medicine typically ignores the passing winds of popular change. But with consumers now spending more than $27 billion on complementary/alternative health approaches, even the steadfast American Medical Association has had to wake up and smell the herbal tea.

Many doctors who only a year or two ago turned a blind eye to CAM are now willing to consider its many potential benefits. In the long run that's good news because, in my view, the rational weaving together of conventional and CAM approaches into integrative medicine provides a new, more powerful level of patient care than either approach can offer on its own.

For people with depression, the evolution toward integrative medicine means greater recognition of the biophysical nature of depressive illness, greater accuracy in diagnosis, and considerably more treatment options.

What this means to *you*, the savvy medical consumer, is the age-old adage: *Buyer beware*. Some complementary strategies—like improving your diet and exercising regularly—can benefit virtually anyone with depression. But other alternative practices—like acupuncture—are more effective at relieving certain types of depression than others. And even the modalities that worked wonders for your neighbor's depression may be inappropriate or useless—or even dangerous—for you.

Of course, the same caveats apply to certain conventional medical interventions. So ask plenty of questions, examine the pros and cons of all treatment options that are recommended to you, monitor all therapies for effectiveness, and make sure all members of your health care team know everything you're doing to conquer your depression—both standard medical and nontraditional.

While I'm the first to remind you that you're the person in charge of your health and well-being, because depression affects your ability to think clearly and objectively, it is not something you can figure out on your own. You need assistance from an experienced physician—not just any doctor, but the right doctor *for you*.

## FINDING THE BEST CONVENTIONAL PHYSICIAN *FOR YOU*

It is absolutely essential to your successful diagnosis, treatment, recovery, and long-term well-being to find a physician who is medically competent, experienced in diagnosing and treating depression, knowledgeable in or at least open to CAM, and easy to talk to. In my opinion, you really can't skimp on any one of these four requirements.

If you're lucky, your current medical doctor already fits the bill. But the odds are you're going to have to shop around. You can start your search by contacting some of the professional associations and support organizations for depression listed at the back of this book. Or ask CAM practitioners in your area to identify some local doctors who are, in their experience, open to alternative approaches. You may even be able to track down a CAM-friendly psychiatrist who can make a referral, especially if you live in or near an urban area.

Don't settle for one referral; collect a few and make appointments. Simply explain to the receptionist that you are interested in meeting with the doctor for a few minutes to get to know him or her better, and that you're not coming in for a full consultation or treatment. Most physicians do not charge for this type of visit.

## WHAT MAKES A GREAT DOCTOR?

A great doctor is a true partner. He or she is technically prepared to see you through your depression and philosophically prepared to work with you and various additional health care professionals, as you see fit. Don't just pick the first doctor in your health plan directory or someone whose office is conveniently located down the street. Take the time to find someone truly up to the job. Here's what to look for:

## Technical Competence

- *Institutional endorsement*: Did she or he graduate at the top of the class or at the bottom?
- *Peer endorsement*: Within the medical/complementary medicine communities, the names of the more respected practitioners keep coming up again and again.
- *Patient endorsement*: Word-of-mouth is sometimes the most reliable information.
- *Experience*: What results has the physician had in treating other patients with depression?

## Balanced Philosophy

- *Collaborative approach*: Is the physician comfortable working with you and with other practitioners as partners in a team? Does she or he recognize the value of using both conventional and complementary/alternative therapies? If not, there's no need to go any further.
- *Communication*: Is the physician comfortable talking with other medical doctors or CAM practitioners, sending them progress and consultation notes regarding shared patients?
- *Recognition of limitations*: Ask the physician what disorders or symptoms she or he is not comfortable treating. If the answer is none, this should be a warning. No one practitioner or discipline can successfully treat all conditions.

The bottom line is to find someone you can trust. Beyond technical competence and a balanced philosophy, your doctor ought to be the type of person you could tell the most personal, perhaps even embarrassing things, when necessary for your proper diagnosis or appropriate treatment. Your physician needn't be your best buddy. But you should have the feeling that you can count on him or her to stick with you for the long haul and go the extra mile for you.

## Your Rights as a Patient

As a health care consumer, you have certain rights, including:

- The right to ask for help
- The right to be treated as a person, not merely a diagnosis
- The right to be informed and educated about your condition
- The right to be listened to regarding your needs and concerns
- The right to receive quality medical care
- The right to be involved in medical decisions that affect you

Don't abdicate any of your rights to your doctor or anyone else. Exercising these rights as a patient is more important to your health than you may think. Studies show that taking a positive, active role in treatment can actually speed the healing process.

## Your Responsibilities as a Patient

With rights come responsibilities. Meeting these responsibilities moves you out of a passive role and can hasten your recovery. In severe situations (such as after a suicide attempt or while you are hospitalized), there may be times when you simply cannot do your part. But whenever possible, do your best to:

- Inform yourself about your condition (you're already taking a first step by reading this book).
- Provide accurate information about your medical history, current and past medications, and current symptoms. To be concise and complete, it helps to write down as much of this information as possible *before* your first visit. Even if you will fill out questionnaires in the office, bring your own notes.
- Inform your doctor of any side effects you may be experiencing as a result of medicine you are currently taking.
- Be prepared to give your doctor a list of any changes in your appetite, diet, weight, sleep patterns, sexual interest, ability to concentrate, memory, mood, or other symptoms.
- Let your doctor know of any recent stressful situation such as divorce, death of a loved one, family problems, or job-related changes.
- Actively participate in your own treatment. Ask questions, no matter how trivial they may seem to you.

- Follow through on therapies to the best of your ability. No therapy will work if it isn't implemented.
- Honestly express your concerns, feelings, and fears to your physician.

Remember, *you* are the one who ultimately decides which diagnostic tests to accept and which treatments to pursue. It's up to you to communicate to your doctor what you're thinking and feeling—including all decisions to start, alter, or discontinue treatment.

*If you are feeling desperate or have any thoughts of suicide, do not wait for a scheduled medical appointment. Go immediately to a hospital or urgent care facility, or call a crisis hotline.*

## GETTING DIAGNOSED

Whether your first-line interventions are conventional, complementary, or a blend of the two, lining up effective treatment begins with getting an accurate diagnosis. This can be tricky with depression. Not only are there more than a dozen types of depression, there are dozens of other health problems that can trigger, mask, or mimic depressive illness.

As with any other disease, in order to diagnose depression your doctor goes on a fact-finding mission.

The process consists of taking your history, performing a physical examination, and ordering laboratory tests.

## PATIENT HISTORY

The patient history is a key part of any doctor visit. During this information-gathering session, you describe your problems so the doctor has clues to use when making a diagnosis. He asks you to describe your symptoms, how long you've had them, whether they've occurred in the past, what you did to treat them, and whether the treatment was effective. He also asks how the symptoms have changed your day-to-day activities and your ability to enjoy life. Be as honest and thorough as possible—your doctor is trying to understand all the factors and stressors that might affect your health.

### Screening Questions

In the course of my clinical practice, I see mostly patients with chronic disorders ranging from hormonal imbalances, diabetes, hypertension, fibromyalgia, and chronic fatigue, to allergies, asthma, heart disease, and cancer. Close to half of these people could be diagnosed with some degree of depression.

Some of my patients tell me outright that they're feeling down, blue, lethargic, hopeless, or even suicidal. In these cases, I can make a diagnosis pretty easily, particularly if I've been treating the patient for a while.

Other patients might recognize that they're depressed, but they don't feel comfortable openly expressing their feelings. They may approach the issue indirectly by telling me about recent or ongoing stressful events in their lives, such as a death in the family, problems at work, rocky relationships, financial trials, and so on.

Still other patients are unaware that depression lies at the root of their problems. They often show up with a variety of non-specific complaints such as fatigue, sleep disturbances, trouble concentrating, changes in appetite, digestive problems, decreased libido, and aches and pains.

Sometimes when a patient I know visits me for a routine checkup, I notice a change in his usual demeanor. He may appear emotionally deadened or withdrawn, express negative thoughts, stare at the floor or avoid making eye contact, become weepy, or look disheveled or neglectful of personal hygiene. If I know that this person is normally optimistic, my inner alarm goes off. On the other hand, negative thoughts in a person who's normally pessimistic aren't necessarily a sign of depression.

If I *don't* know the patient well, but she has obvious signs of depression, I ask her some simple screening questions. While I usually ask a variety of questions related to possible indirect symptoms of depression, there is one simple question that is most effective. I simply ask: "Have you felt down, blue, or depressed lately?" Over the years I've found (and research has confirmed) that the direct approach is generally best.

Depression can still be easy to miss, especially if the patient has physical symptoms that lead me to suspect another disorder.

One clue that the patient's real problem is depression is a poor response to treatment. Or one symptom, such as a digestive problem, may clear up only to have another symptom, such as headache, take its place—a phenomenon called "symptom substitution."

If you're suffering from depression, it's likely you'll describe some of these key symptoms:

- Feelings of sadness, hopelessness, or helplessness lasting at least two weeks
- Loss of interest or pleasure in daily activities
- Changes in sleep patterns, such as inadequate or excessive sleep or waking up several times during the night
- Appetite loss or weight loss not caused by intentional dieting or increased exercise, *or* an increase in appetite with attendant weight gain
- Fatigue or lack of energy
- Feelings of worthlessness, perhaps the result of intense or inappropriate guilt
- Lack of concentration, indecisiveness
- Decreased sex drive
- Increased use of alcohol or drugs
- Thoughts of death or suicide

If this is your first visit, your doctor will ask about existing or past illnesses. This information is particularly important if you're seeing several doctors for different conditions. Your physician needs to know if you have a chronic or debilitating disease, because these ailments often lead to depression. Depression can mask or mimic other diseases with similar symptoms. Then there's the fact that depression itself can lead to physical ailments like digestive upsets, headaches, and chronic aches and pains (more on this later).

During the patient history, you also need to give your doctor a list of all the medications you're taking, including prescription drugs and nonprescription remedies such as pain relievers, vitamins, herbs, and nutritional supplements. A number of drugs can actually *cause* side effects that mimic depression. These include certain drugs prescribed for high blood pressure (for example, Serapes, Aldomet, and Inderal), as well as some drugs used to treat Parkinson's disease, arthritis, and cancer. If you're in this group, simply switching to another medication may alleviate your depression.

If your doctor suspects depression, he or she will ask you about stressors and recent major changes in your life. As we've seen, depression can be triggered by prolonged stress, divorce, the death of a loved one (including a pet), losing your job or retiring, or moving to a new town. Because depression seems to run in families, mention whether relatives—especially your grandparents, parents, or siblings—have ever been diagnosed with dysthymia (chronic mild depression), major depression, severe mood swings, or alcoholism.

Finally, the doctor will probably ask if you've ever felt so unhappy that you've thought about hurting yourself or ending your life. Don't withhold this information out of shame or embarrassment. The doctor needs to understand how serious your condition is so he or she can prescribe the right treatment. Anyone contemplating suicide needs prompt intervention—antidepressants, psychotherapy, and possibly short-term hospitalization in order to get treatment initiated.

If you don't understand your doctor's questions or instructions, or why a particular therapy is being recommended or changed, ask for clarification. Sometimes your appointment can go by so fast, you get confused. Ask questions! The only stupid question is the one you didn't ask.

### Drugs That Cause Depression

Any drug that crosses from the blood into the brain can cause depression. Many common drugs have this unfortunate side effect, including the following:

- Illicit drug Use
- Alcohol
- Accutane
- Antianxiety drugs (Valium, Xanax)
- Anticonvulsants (Dilantin, Tegretol)
- Antihistamines (Benadryl, Hismanal)

- Drugs to treat Parkinson's disease (Dopar, Sinemet)
- Cardiovascular drugs (Cardizem, Inderal, Tenormin)
- Chemotherapy drugs (Velban, Oncovin) used to shrink tumors in cancer patients
- Corticosteroids (Cortone Acetate, Deltasone) used to treat arthritis or asthma
- Female hormones (estrogen, progesterone) used for birth control, or to control menopause symptoms
- Interferon-alpha treatment (for hepatitis B and C, adult leukemia, malignant melanoma, and some kidney cancers)

## ASSESSING PHYSICAL SIGNS OF DEPRESSION

If you haven't had a complete physical examination recently, the doctor will probably perform one to rule out other medical problems that might coexist with depression or mimic it. This exam typically includes checking your blood pressure, heart rate, pulse, and weight, and then doing a head-to-toe assessment of all body systems for signs of illness. In addition, the doctor will order blood tests to check for problems like electrolyte and hormone abnormalities, vitamin deficiencies, and signs of infection or anemia. A urinalysis will indicate whether your kidneys are functioning normally. These tests are necessary before antidepressant medication can be prescribed, because antidepressants are often excreted through the kidneys and some are dangerous to patients with liver, kidney, or heart problems.

When depression is suspected, a mental status exam is critically important. During this evaluation, the doctor observes your general appearance and notes certain changes (if he or she knows you) or outward signs of depression. Common signs are:

- Disheveled, dirty appearance, inappropriate clothing
- Apathetic attitude, saying you feel helpless
- Slow or monotonous speech
- Dull or flat affect, deadpan facial expression
- Speech that jumps all around or occurs very slowly
- Inability to concentrate
- Poor memory

## Is It Really Depression?

Some well known diseases are easy to mistake for depression because they can have similar symptoms. The list includes Addison's disease, AIDS, Alzheimer's disease, anemia, brain tumor, cancer, chronic fatigue syndrome, chronic infection, Cushing's disease, diabetes, electrolyte imbalance, encephalitis, hepatitis, Huntington's chorea, hyperthyroidism, hypothyroidism, hypoglycemia, Lyme disease, mononucleosis, mercury poisoning, multiple sclerosis, Parkinson's disease, stroke, systemic lupus erythematosus, syphilis, and certain types of epilepsy.

Before diagnosing depression, the doctor needs to rule out these other disorders. Obviously, antidepressants or psychotherapy won't restore a patient to health if his symptoms are caused by another disorder. They'll only delay the correct treatment as the underlying disorder worsens and treatment becomes more difficult.

If screening tests signal the presence of another disorder or a hormonal imbalance, these health issues need to be addressed first. Depression caused by hormonal imbalance (often premenstrual, postpartum, or perimenopausal) generally responds well to standard estrogen replacement therapy or one of the natural alternatives, such as natural progesterone. Similarly, DHEA, testosterone, or thyroid medication can work wonders for elevating mood if levels of these hormones are low.

### Blood Tests That Help Diagnose Depression

Strictly speaking, you don't need a lab test to identify depression. But as we've seen, often depression doesn't appear all by itself. It's generally accompanied by other health problems. Because so many factors come into play with depression, an integrative approach often calls for even more diagnostic testing than a conventional protocol might suggest.

The following tests cannot diagnose depression, but they can help your doctor rule out other diseases and choose the safest, most effective antidepressant for you. The following tests may be used to screen patients for depression:

*Complete blood count (CBC).* This test screens for anemia (low red blood cell count) and chronic infection (high white blood cell count), either of which make you feel tired and sluggish.

*Blood chemistry panel.* This test is a common tool for assessing liver and kidney function, cholesterol counts, and levels of electrolytes. This can help the doctor rule out metabolic causes of depression.

*Thyroid tests.* Six to seven million Americans, most of them women over age 40, have an underactive thyroid gland, which can cause fatigue, sluggishness, weight gain, trouble concentrating, and increased sleeping—all symptoms that could easily be confused with depression. Although the thyroid stimulating hormone (TSH) test is ordered most often, I find the free T3 test more revealing. Free T3 is the most active form of thyroid hormone. Many people aren't adequately able to convert T4, the less active form, into T3, and as a result develop symptoms that mimic depression.

*Adrenal tests.* I check a blood DHEA-sulfate level, as well as a cortisol level. DHEA is a hormone produced by the adrenal glands that is used as a building block for a number of other hormones. People with low DHEA levels are often tired, achy, have difficulty concentrating, and some feel depressed. Elevated cortisol levels can be caused by stress or, very rarely, by an adrenal tumor. Elevated levels are associated with lower immunity and sometimes elevated sugar levels.

"Adrenal exhaustion" is a controversial diagnosis, but is the term used to describe an adrenal gland that isn't meeting the demands placed on it.

*Sex hormone tests.* In men, a low testosterone level can sometimes produce depressive symptoms. In women, hormonal fluctuations in estrogen and progesterone due to the menstrual cycle and onset of menopause may contribute to intense mood swings and/or depression.

*Infectious disease tests.* Several infectious diseases may present with some of the same symptoms as depression. These include Lyme disease, HIV infection, syphilis, herpes virus, and others.

*Allergy tests.* Allergies or environmental sensitivities can make you feel worn out and sluggish, mimicking common symptoms of depression. Skin tests or blood tests can measure the presence of antibodies, pointing to a possible allergic reaction. If specific allergens are identified, avoidance or desensitization can often improve symptoms of depression.

*Imaging technologies.* In some (rare) situations, PET scans, CT scans, or x-ray studies of various tissues or organs may be useful diagnostic tools in determining the causes or results of depression.

*B vitamins.* Low blood levels of vitamin $B_{12}$ and folate can be associated with depression. If so, this is a relatively easy problem to correct.

*Fasting amino acids.* If a fasting blood test shows significant imbalances of the amino acids (which are used to make neurotransmitters), it may be helpful to correct those imbalances through nutritional interventions.

## Diagnosing Sleep Problems

Sleep disturbances are common in depression and often resolve when depression is treated. But some sleep problems are not rooted in depression and need other treatment. Some people never get a good night's rest because of sleep apnea, a condition in which you stop breathing for several seconds, followed by a gasp for air. Each time your breathing stops, you're roused from sleep just enough to get your breathing restarted, often without your awareness. The cycle continues throughout the night, resulting in exhaustion from lack of deep (delta-wave) sleep.

A nocturnal pulse oximetry test is a useful screening tool for this condition. This noninvasive test can be performed in the privacy of your home and is usually provided free of charge or at low cost by home oxygen supply companies.

If results show an abnormality, a formal sleep study in a sleep laboratory may be warranted. In this exercise, you spend the night at the laboratory, hooked up to an EEG (electroencephalogram) machine and other types of monitoring equipment. Painless electrodes are attached to your head. Sounds restful, doesn't it? In time, when you finally fall asleep, the EEG records data regarding how long it took you to fall asleep, how long you spend in each stage of sleep, and if you experience delta-wave sleep, REM sleep, sleep myoclonus, or sleep apnea.

## Depression Can Make You Sick

Serious, long-term depression can literally make you sick. Chronic lack of sleep, poor nutrition, lack of exercise, and overuse of alcohol or other drugs all weaken your immune system, lowering your resistance to disease.

Psychological stress can also compromise your immunity. The physiology is complicated, but in a nutshell, this is how it works. Your immune system, endocrine (hormonal) system, and central nervous system are interconnected. Psychological stressors like depression can disrupt communication within this network by changing the concentration of cytokines in the blood. These "messenger molecules" produced by cells in the immune system help provoke the immune response—your body's way of defending itself against foreign substances (antigens). Depression also changes the concentration of hormones in the blood, further suppressing immune system activity.

Animal and human studies support the notion of a link between stress and infectious disease. In one investigation, humans and mice infected with the herpes virus had new outbreaks following major social disruptions. In another study, people caring for spouses with Alzheimer's disease (a high-stress responsibility) were given flu vaccine, along with a group of noncaregivers with similar medical histories. Those who were not caring for an

Alzheimer's patient fared much better during flu season. A third study compared two groups of people exposed to an upper respiratory tract infection. Those who reported a higher level of stressful life events developed more cold symptoms than the less-stressed group.

### Are Those Aches and Pains All in Your Head?

Because the mind and body are connected, talking about "physical illness" and "mental illness" is an artificial distinction. Psychosomatic illnesses are a case in point.

People who are depressed often complain of back pain, headaches, and digestive problems. These ailments aren't "all in your head," as some people believe. Your pain and other physical symptoms are genuine, even if they're triggered by psychological factors.

The process by which depression and other psychological stressors are linked is called *conversion.* It diverts your attention away from the real problem—your depression—and allows you to focus on a less daunting, more socially acceptable problem: a physical ache or pain. If you don't realize that your symptoms are caused by depression or won't admit it, you're said to have *masked depression.*

## MAKING A DIAGNOSIS

Once your doctor has heard about your symptoms, performed a physical exam, and reviewed the results of your laboratory tests, he or she can diagnose your depression and any associated health problems with greater confidence. Most physicians rely on the *Diagnostic and Statistical Manual of Mental Disorders*, referred to as the *DSM*. This book divides mental disorders into diagnostic categories, describes symptoms and behaviors, and identifies each disorder with a unique code number. The *DSM* has made the diagnosis of mental illness more precise than ever before.

The doctor will match your symptoms, behavior, and personal history with the criteria listed for a particular *DSM* diagnosis. Many disorders have overlapping symptoms, so a precise diagnosis may be difficult, but "categorizing" your disorder gives your doctor a logical starting point for treatment.

Once you are diagnosed with depression, your doctor may need to submit your treatment plan to your insurance company for approval, especially if psychotherapy is recommended. Unfortunately, many health insurance policies do not cover psychiatric illness as comprehensively as they cover physical illness. For example, some will reimburse only a limited number of visits per year to a therapist, while others cover only in-patient psychiatric care. Be sure to check your policy carefully, and if you have any questions, talk to your insurance carrier or your employer.

## SETTING PRIORITIES

With so many symptoms, dozens of possible coexisting conditions, and even more potential therapies, where in the world do you and your physician start the treatment process?

Unfortunately, too many practitioners start (and end) with whatever limited treatments they already know or are used to recommending. This is a red flag to seek another opinion. Wise physicians don't always start with their favorite treatments (which they learned in medical training many years ago); they start with each individual patient, one patient at a time.

Developing an individual treatment plan that provides real and lasting relief requires prioritizing your problems. You and your doctor should discuss which issues to tackle first and which can wait a little longer.

Healing depression is always a three-part process:

1. *Stabilize or control the immediate danger or discomfort.* If your depression or mania is severe, or you feel like ending your life, go directly to the emergency room of the nearest hospital or urgent care center. If your condition does not pose an emergency, the first priority is to lift your mood as quickly as possible. Depending on your unique situation, ways to restore the brain's chemical balance include drugs, exercise, diet changes, and psychotherapy. Whenever possible, I recommend a "less is more" approach to treatment (discussed in the following section).

2. *Return to a more functional state.* Once you're feeling stronger and better able to cope, you can turn your attention to exploring the causes of your depression and to repairing the damage that depression has done to your overall health, relationships, career, self-esteem, finances, and other aspects of your life. Psychotherapy or various types of targeted counseling can make a real difference here. Treating other illnesses and restoring overall physical health is also vitally important.

3. *Prevent future bouts of depression.* Long-term drug therapy may be indicated in some cases, perhaps supplemented by regular or occasional psychotherapy. Of course, you would also be advised to take positive steps toward healing your body and neutralizing stress. These steps might include lifestyle changes, exercise, faith-based activities, pet therapy, journaling, socialization, improved diet, stress reduction, and making the skills and insights gained in therapy a part of your daily life.

Reading over this list from your present vantage point, you may wonder how you'll ever implement all these changes (the answer is one step at a time). Or maybe you've tried some of these interventions and they didn't work. If so, discuss your concerns with your doctor. Some people are hesitant to try psychotherapy or counseling because it's expensive or they feel self-conscious or ashamed. If you feel this way, your doctor may decide that antidepressant drugs are a better option for you now. Later, when you feel stronger and better able to cope, he'll probably suggest therapy again.

## A LESS-IS-MORE APPROACH TO TREATMENT

You are not like any other patient. Your lifestyle, past experiences, physical limitations, pre-existing medical conditions, opinions about drug therapy and psychotherapy, financial situation, and home and work responsibilities must all be considered when you sit down with your doctor to decide on a treatment plan.

Severe depression, especially when suicide is a risk, calls for immediate, aggressive intervention. The first priority is to stabilize the patient, relieve intense discomfort, and prevent her from doing any harm to herself or others. In such cases, I usually refer the patient immediately to a psychiatrist. The psychiatrist will typically prescribe antidepressants and/or hospitalization, and in a small percentage of patients, electroconvulsive therapy (ECT).

In cases of mild-to-moderate depression, the diagnosis and symptoms will guide which treatments to pursue and in what order. A variety of effective treatments are available from both conventional Western medicine and complementary or alternative medicine. With appropriate treatment, 80 percent of depressed patients show an improvement in mood, usually in about three weeks.

My guiding principle in designing a successful treatment plan for a patient who is not in a dangerous or crisis situation is to *start with the least aggressive forms of treatment first*, and see if they help before progressing to more aggressive, more invasive, often riskier treatments. In other words, I start with the least I can do to achieve treatment goals and do more only if I must.

Although this sounds logical, there can be tremendous resistance to this approach. On the one hand, patients often want a quick fix, preferably in an easy-to-swallow pill form. Many physicians are happy to oblige, spurred on by their desire to do something effective as quickly as possible. Too often this combination of desires leads to premature prescriptions for medications, many of which are difficult to tolerate, and puts the patient at significant risk for adverse side effects.

For people with mild depression, I'm inclined to first try a nondrug solution. This approach has two advantages: it gets the patient actively involved in the healing process, and there are far fewer chances of side effects. The focus here is on better nutrition, regular exercise, and one or more self-help therapies. Once self-help measures are well underway, the next logical step is to choose one or more natural therapies (herbs, acupuncture, mind-body techniques, etc.), depending on test results and ongoing symptoms.

If these approaches don't lift mood and relieve other depressive symptoms within six to eight weeks—or if the depression worsens or the patient is unable to initiate or follow through on any self-help strategies—then it's time for more aggressive treatment. This could include psychotherapy, antidepressants, as well as complementary therapies chosen from the CAM side of the menu.

Be patient. Treatments for depression can be very effective, but improvement is usually not instantaneous. When you do start to see results, the changes may appear to be quite gradual. Try to hang in there and give your treatment a chance to succeed.

## EXPANDING YOUR TREATMENT TEAM

After you and your physician are reasonably confident of your diagnosis and understand what it is you are trying to treat, you may decide to bring in other medical, mental health, or complementary/alternative practitioners. These might include:

- Family physicians, general practitioners, and primary-care physicians. These doctors provide general care for adults and children. If your first point of medical contact was with a specialist, you may be referred back to a primary-care physician once your symptoms are under control.
- Physician's assistants are trained, certified, and licensed professionals who assist physicians by taking patient histories, performing physical examinations, making diagnoses, and designing treatments. They work under the supervision of a physician.

- Nurses may assist your physician by teaching you about your treatments and answering many of your questions. Doctors are not always available to return phone calls or answer questions promptly, so it's always a good idea to develop a trusting relationship with at least one nurse who knows your case.

- Clinical psychologists and psychiatrists can be essential to your short-term recovery and your long-term prospects. Read all about their role in Chapter 6.

- A nutritionist or registered dietitian can help you set up a healthy eating plan that can make a real difference in rebalancing your brain chemistry and managing your symptoms. Learn all about nutritional approaches to depression in Chapters 8 and 9.

- A variety of complementary/alternative practitioners (see Chapters 10–15), such as acupuncturists, chiropractors, herbalists, massage therapists, and so on. Learn how to find qualified practitioners in Chapter 10.

- Occupational therapists (OTs) help depressed patients cope with their symptoms at work or change jobs. An OT may also help you develop a plan for pacing yourself, living with children, or performing daily tasks in and around the house—especially if you work at home.

- Pharmacists fill your prescriptions and can explain how drugs work and their potential side effects. They advise you of possible drug interactions and answer your questions about over-the-counter medications.

- Social workers can help you explore solutions to social and financial problems related to your disorder. A social worker will be especially important if you have no health insurance or if your depression is so severe it causes you to lose your job.

## Getting a Referral

If your doctor suggests psychotherapy, he'll probably give you the name of a reputable psychiatrist, psychotherapist, clinical social worker, or psychiatric nurse. In fact, you may need to get a direct referral from your primary care doctor or use a specified provider if your insurance plan will be providing coverage. Other sources of referrals include:

- Your HMO, managed care group, or other insurer
- A friend or relative
- The department of psychiatry at an area medical school or hospital
- Physician referral programs operated by local hospitals
- The following professional organizations:
  American Psychiatric Association—
  
  202-682-6066 or *www.psych.org*
  
  American Psychological Association—
  
  202-336-5500 or *www.apa.org*
- Employee assistance programs at work

- Community health centers
- Senior citizens' centers or groups
- Your religious leader
- Support groups, such as Alcoholics Anonymous or Weight Watchers
- Guidance counselors at your school

## IF NOTHING SEEMS TO WORK

Despite the number and variety of treatments available, some people can't shake their depression no matter what interventions they try. Those who are "treatment resistant" try every antidepressant on the market, and many nontraditional approaches as well, dragging themselves from doctor to doctor, sometimes for years. A small number of them even try last-resort treatments like electroconvulsive therapy (ECT), all to no avail.

Experts tell us that about 10 percent of people who are depressed get no relief from antidepressants, and an undetermined percentage may be able to function but never recover completely or really enjoy life. Still others find temporary relief on each new drug they try, but then, inexplicably, the drug stops working—a phenomenon called "poop-out syndrome."

Unfortunately, little research has been done on this problem. No one knows why some people don't respond to antidepressants while others do. Brain structure or brain chemistry may play a role, or the patient may simply have taken the drug for too short a time or received too low a dosage. Some patients also have other problems like substance abuse, neurological conditions, or physical ailments that complicate their treatment. In addition, patients with complex psychosocial problems might not fully respond to antidepressants because what they truly need is a multidisciplinary approach— medication, psychotherapy, specialized counseling, and various complementary and lifestyle interventions.

# 4

# Finding the Road to Relief: An Integrated Approach to Treating Depression

If you or someone you're close to suffers from depression, chances are your most pressing concern as you read this book is how to get *immediate relief*. I wish I could give you a quick and simple way to escape the distressing physical, emotional, and mental symptoms of depression, but the truth is there's no magic cure that works for everyone. Because there are many types of depression, many possible causes, and many symptoms that come and go and change over time, effective treatment may require professional help, and perseverance and patience on your part.

Serious depression isn't something you can cope with alone. It's too medically complicated, and you're probably not in the best mental or emotional state to handle it on your own.

Nevertheless, it's important to keep in mind that unless you require temporary hospitalization, ultimately *you* are in charge of your own health and well-being. That includes finding the best professional help, exploring all your treatment options, giving those treatments a chance to work, and assessing your progress.

My goal for this book is to make your task as easy as possible by providing you with the information I give my own patients, including pointing you in the direction of dozens of conventional and alternative resources for further help and support. My first task is to give you an overview, a *road map,* of what it takes to cope successfully with depression. In this chapter we'll discuss:

- Knowing what you're up against
- The risk of suicide
- Recognizing the many faces of depression
- Building a treatment team
- Healing your brain
- Healing your mind

## KNOWING WHAT YOU'RE UP AGAINST

Depression is a very real and potentially life-threatening illness. Odds are, it's not going to resolve quickly on its own. And if it does, chances are good it will be back again soon. So treatment isn't just an option; it's a necessity.

Left untreated, major depression can last six months to a year. Half the people who have one episode will have another. Once you've had two, you're a sitting duck for many more, with each episode perhaps worse than the last. By the time you have three episodes of depression, your odds for a fourth shoot up to 90 percent.

Even if you never have an episode of major depression, mild depression (dysthymia) can linger for years and seriously erode your life the way a slow, steady drip of water can wear down the strongest stone. You may think you're handling it, but you're really handing over your life, in tiny bits, to an invisible enemy. In time, low-level depression colors every aspect of your life. Think of all the joy you could experience and the contributions you could make if you weren't constantly struggling to crawl up out of a bottomless pit. Left untreated, mild depression can evolve into major depression without warning.

Untreated bipolar disorders—either manic depression or the milder cyclothymic disorder—can keep you swinging from highs to lows throughout your life. Such conditions rarely vanish on their own. Typically, the highs climb higher and the lows drop lower, until the shifts become too extreme or too frequent to bear. If your disorder is still relatively mild, now is the time to take action to keep it from escalating. If you already suffer from intense mood swings, face the fact that you need help and get it *now,* while you can still do it on your own. Please don't wait until someone forces you to enter an in-patient treatment center to protect you from yourself.

Whatever your type of depression, don't delay treatment. Few people would put up with the pain of a broken finger or a terrible toothache for more than a day or two before seeking help. Isn't your mental health as important as a finger or a tooth? The sooner you seek help the more effective it will be and the sooner you can start living a happier, more productive life.

Your most important ally can be a physician with considerable experience in diagnosing and treating depression, and in Chapter 3 you learned how to find such a doctor. Under the guidance of your physician and other experienced health care professionals, pursue diagnostic testing for related conditions. Work together to develop a customized treatment plan. For mild depression, start with the simplest, gentlest, least invasive treatments: simple lifestyle changes like better nutrition, increased exercise, and so on. Pay attention to what works, and move on to a more aggressive intervention only when that treatment fails to deliver the expected relief.

*Don't be discouraged by failure!* Some therapies work beautifully for some people and don't do a thing for others. Think of failure as a vital clue that contains important information for you and your health care team. The more failures you experience, the closer you are to figuring out what will work for you.

Depression can be tough, but you're tougher than any of your symptoms. If it helps, think of yourself as a scientist, a warrior, or an explorer on a mission of discovery. You're part of a team. You can't find your own path to relief by turning your fate *entirely* over to others. Avoid the temptation to feel and act like a victim; take charge of your health and healing. Know what you're up against and be confident that, with the right help, you have what it takes to win.

## THE MOST SERIOUS RISK: SUICIDE

About 25 percent of those with serious depression try to kill themselves—that's about 2,000 suicide attempts *every day*. Suicide is the eighth leading cause of death in the United States and the third leading cause of death among teens. Each year, a quarter of a million teenagers attempt suicide. Girls are more likely to attempt to take their own life; boys are four times as likely to succeed, because they are far more likely to use firearms.

The elderly commit suicide at double the rate of any other age group. Suicide is particularly common among elderly men, who account for over 80 percent of the self-inflicted deaths in those 65 and older. Tragically, many older adults come within inches of getting help just prior to taking their own life. According to a report issued by the National Institute of Mental Health, 70 percent of those who committed suicide visited their doctor within a month of death, almost 40 percent within seven days of the suicide.

Some people incorrectly believe that anyone who talks about suicide will not actually attempt it. That is simply not true. Many people announce their intentions before acting. Take any and all talk or thoughts of suicide very seriously. Call a doctor, hospital, or suicide prevention hotline immediately.

## Warning Signs of Suicide

- Talk or threats regarding suicide
- Excessive alcohol or drug use
- Aggressive or disruptive behavior
- Increased sadness, moodiness, or irritability
- Withdrawal from friends, family, and favorite activities
- Changes in sleep patterns
- Changes in eating patterns
- Neglecting clothes and appearance
- Failing school subjects
- Giving away prized possessions
- Preoccupation with death
- Having a friend or family member who has committed suicide

# RECOGNIZING THE MANY FACES OF DEPRESSION

The *Diagnostic and Statistical Manual of Mental Disorders (DSM-IV)*, a handbook published by the American Psychiatric Association, recognizes over a dozen types of depression. I discuss the major categories of depression in the following sections. Keep in mind that the boundaries between the various depressive disorders are rarely clear-cut. Family and friends aren't always the best judges of when normal grief or a temporary adjustment disorder has become clinical depression.

You may not realize what's happening until things have gotten especially bad.

If you recognize any of your symptoms in the following descriptions, jot down some notes to discuss with your health care provider, but please don't try to self-diagnose. Get immediate professional help to determine your specific diagnosis and assess your treatment options.

## Normal Depressed Mood and Grief

Everyone experiences a normal range of grief reactions to the many losses we face in life. Such reactions may range from mild sadness and lethargy (in the case of a relatively minor setback, like missing an important opportunity at work) to intense grief, anger, and despair (in the case of a major loss, such as the death of a loved one). When the loss has been significant, such feelings can be accompanied by decreased or increased appetite, weight loss or gain, disturbed sleep patterns, obsessive thoughts, guilt, anger, even rage.

What makes all these reactions normal is that eventually people do recover. If you've lost out on a big opportunity at work, it may take a few days or weeks to bounce back. If you've lost your job due to a layoff, it may take several months to right yourself. If someone dear to you has died, it can take a year or more to recover. But given some time, you do pick up and go on. If recovery doesn't happen within a reasonable time frame, or if your reaction is out of proportion to the triggering event, you may have clinical depression, and you should see your doctor.

## ADJUSTMENT DISORDER WITH DEPRESSED MOOD

Change is part of life. But sometimes the change is more than you can absorb all at once, and you feel temporarily overwhelmed, even off-balance. This can happen, for example, when someone moves to a new city, goes away to college, or retires. If time passes and you still can't get a grip on the new reality, it can color your entire world, making you sad, resentful, and pessimistic. Bouts of tearfulness are common. You may be unable to cope with your daily responsibilities. This type of depression is referred to as an *adjustment disorder*.

Adjustment disorder is a temporary reaction to stress, and one that resolves quickly, especially with a little counseling. Typically, once you adjust to the change, you feel better. But if you display these symptoms without an appropriate triggering event, or if your reaction seems out of proportion to the event that set it off, it's time to call a doctor.

## MILD DEPRESSION (DYSTHYMIA)

*Dysthymia* (pronounced dis-THIGH-mee-uh) is characterized by a state of chronic mild depression accompanied by low self-esteem and low levels of the symptoms typically associated with major depression: sleep problems, appetite problems, lack of energy, difficulty in concentrating or making decisions, and irrational feelings of guilt, worthlessness, or hopelessness. You feel depressed and lousy most of the time, but the condition is never severe enough to keep you from functioning, going to work, and taking care of your family's basic needs. What it does do is prevent you from enjoying life. Because people with dysthymia usually don't lose their jobs or attempt suicide, they may muddle along indefinitely, never receiving the help they need. They get so used to feeling low that they never realize anything serious is wrong.

Dysthymia isn't the correct diagnosis if depression is accompanied by manic episodes—exaggerated moods of either high spirits or extreme irritability, coupled with restlessness, racing thoughts, and an inability to sleep.

Some people slip from dysthymia into a major depression. Such people are sometimes said to have "double depression."

## MAJOR DEPRESSION

Major depression, or *clinical depression,* is sometimes called unipolar disorder because the person has a single, dominant mood: despair. It's generally characterized by deep sadness, negativity, and hopelessness so profound that you lose interest in life and become incapable of feeling pleasure. As one of my patients described it: *"I feel like I'm trapped in a glass box, cut off from everyone and everything I used to enjoy, unable to break free."*

In addition to persistent feelings of despair and incapacity for pleasure, major depression also involves *at least four* of the following symptoms:

- Sleep disturbances—sleeping too little or too much
- Changes in appetite or weight

- Extreme fatigue or lack of energy that permeates every aspect of life, including work, leisure activities, and sex
- Restlessness, anxiety, or irritability
- Feelings of worthlessness or inappropriate guilt
- Difficulty in concentrating or making decisions
- Isolation from people and social situations
- Suicidal thoughts or a suicide attempt

Sometimes sufferers feel so low that they forgo food, neglect their appearance, and stay in bed for days at a time. Other times, the predominant symptom isn't low mood, but acute anxiety and extreme irritability.

Major depression can strike with or without a triggering event. That certainly compounds the frustration for the patient, as well as for relatives and friends who make every effort to understand and help.

In extreme cases, major depression may evolve into *psychotic depression,* characterized by hallucinations and delusions, the classic symptoms of psychosis. Hearing voices is common, as is the patient's insistence that something is true, despite evidence to the contrary.

## BIPOLAR DISORDERS

In bipolar disorders, the person's mood swings or cycles uncontrollably between two poles, hence the name "bipolar." On one end of the pendulum, they slump into a low-energy, depressed state; on the other end, they swing into a high-energy, euphoric state. People who swing widely from one intense state to the other suffer from *manic depression*. People who swing between lesser levels of depression and elation suffer from a milder form of bipolar disorder called *cyclothymic disorder*. Bipolar disorders are further distinguished as bipolar I, bipolar II, and cyclothymia.

## Bipolar I

People suffering from "bipolar I" have classic manic-depression: episodes of major depression alternating with episodes of major mania. They're often described as being on an emotional roller coaster, moving from points of high energy and wild elation to the depths of despair, sometimes within a very short period of time. Usually, one pole or the other dominates. Men tend to have more manic episodes and fewer major depressions, while women often have more depression and less mania.

The manic state of bipolar I disorder can be highly destructive and even life-threatening. Your mind races with irrational thoughts, unrealistic ideas, mispercep-tions, even delusions of grandeur. Because the brain is operating at hyper-speed, people in the manic state have difficulty sleeping through the night and relaxing or thinking clearly during the day. People in extreme manic states embark on love affairs they later regret, say unfor-givable things to family members, undertake impossible projects, run up huge expenses without giving a thought to how they'll pay the bills, and otherwise engage in out-rageous, inappropriate behavior that wears out their family and alienates their friends. Temporary hospitaliza-tion may be required.

The depressive phase of bipolar disorder has already been described. Since the manic phase can result in extremely destructive behavior, it's important to recognize those signs as well. Signs and symptoms of mania include:

- *Persistent high or irritable mood states*—The "high" may be a kind of euphoria or ecstasy, where you are deliriously happy, or it can be expressed as extreme irritability or anger (sometimes manifesting as a propensity for lawsuits) at everyone around you.
- *Less need for sleep*—This symptom often signals the onset of a manic episode. You may suddenly need an hour or two less sleep, then decrease sleep to only a couple of hours each night. As the episode peaks and becomes dangerous, you may cease sleeping entirely.
- *Increased activity*—You may decide to write the great American novel, compose a symphony, or redecorate your house from top to bottom. Some people go on irrational spending sprees, acquiring new cars or houses. One 50-year-old businessman literally threw money away on the streets of New York for the amusement of watching people run after $50,000 in small bills blowing in the wind.
- *Pressured speech*—In the midst of a manic state you may speak rapidly, loudly, intensely, and not allow interruptions by others.

- *Racing thoughts*—Your thoughts speed from topic to topic, and before you finish your first thought you're totally occupied by the next one. Your mind jumps from one image to another, one subject to another, and you can't seem to stop or slow the flow.
- *Loss of self-control and judgment*—Manic episodes are characterized by increased risk-taking and an unrealistic belief in your own abilities.
- *Appetite disturbances*—You may have a ravenous appetite, particularly for bizarre foods or food combinations.
- *Increased sexuality*—You may engage in more sexual activity than is usual for you, including promiscuity.
- *Excessive religiosity*—While religious activity can provide a buffer for stress, when taken to extremes religious preoccupation may signal a mood disorder.

In bipolar disorders, long periods without either mania or depression can be common, with an average of about 10 total episodes in a lifetime. Some people, called "rapid cyclers," endure four or more episodes per year and are more difficult to treat. The medication lithium, with or without antidepressants, is the standard treatment for most people with bipolar I and is essential to helping them maintain equilibrium. Anticonvulsive drugs may also be prescribed. Because antidepressants used alone can launch a manic episode in people with bipolar disorder, accurate diagnosis must always precede any treatment plan.

About one percent of Americans experience bipolar disorder each year, although some experts now estimate that up to 35 percent of all depressed people actually are bipolar—about half having bipolar I disorder and half having bipolar II. Doctors believe that as many as 15 to 20 percent of people with bipolar disorder are at serious risk, particularly those whose manic states are marked by alcohol abuse, paranoia, the hearing of voices, and delusional thoughts. Left untreated, suicide is a real possibility.

Vincent van Gogh is believed to have suffered from bipolar disorder and had several periods of institutionalization. Van Gogh's tragic life illustrates the cruel paradox of manic depression: the disorder helped fuel his enormous creativity and artistic output, giving the world some of its greatest masterpieces, until the artist ended his life with a gun at age 37.

## Bipolar II

Bipolar II is a milder form of the disorder, characterized by hypomania, literally meaning "low high." While the depression may range from mild (marked by indecision and the inability to complete projects) to major, the mania of bipolar II is far more manageable than the mania of bipolar I. In fact, the high side of this disorder can prove pleasant and highly productive for many people, who report being in an exceptionally good mood, full of enthusiasm and ideas, cheerful and optimistic, self-confident and sexy. Indeed, many great artistic, scientific, and political contributions are the product of highly creative and energized bipolar IIs on a roll, brimming with enthusiasm and accomplishing a multitude of tasks with a rush of energy and clarity.

But hypomania has a dark side as well. Impetuous judgment and reckless action may lead the super-charged bipolar II person to walk out of a job or rack up credit cards bills beyond her ability to pay. At the peak of hypomania, rapid speech, quick temper, decreased need for sleep, jumping from one unfinished project to another, and embarking on impossible tasks may become the norm.

Despite the sometimes negative consequences, the hypomania of bipolar II can feel so good, few people realize they need help until serious depression sets in.

## Cyclothymic Disorder

*Cyclothymic disorder* is a milder form of bipolar disorder. Instead of discrete episodes of depression and mania, cyclothymics generally experience chronic, low-level depression (dysthymia), interrupted by occasional, low-level mania (hypomania). Most of the time they're in a down mood, marked by indecision and an inability to complete projects. During occasional "up" periods, they can be especially cheerful, radiating energy, optimism, and self-confidence. Not surprisingly, friends and family usually call the cyclothymic person "moody."

Most cyclothymics function reasonably well, although a good deal of their behavior is self-defeating and they may not reach their full potential. As with other depressive illnesses, cyclothymic disorder may evolve into the more severe states, including major depression or bipolar I or bipolar II.

## ATYPICAL DEPRESSION

The person with *atypical depression* cycles through different mood states, feeling hopeless and helpless for a while, then all right for a short time, then anxious and irritable. Sufferers are usually highly sensitive to rejection or criticism. Such people tend to oversleep (rather than undersleep, as is more typical of other depressions) and overeat (rather than lose interest in food). The person typically craves sweets and carbohydrates and may put on weight. Mood worsens as the day wears on. The condition is chronic, and often develops without a triggering event. The gloom may lift temporarily when something goes well, but then depression returns.

## SEASONAL AFFECTIVE DISORDER (SAD)

*Seasonal affective disorder* is a mild to major depression that strikes most commonly in the late fall and winter months, when exposure to sunlight declines. Mild cases are sometimes called the "winter blahs," "winter blues," "seasonal blues," or "cabin fever." SAD's low energy and low mood predictably disappear as soon as the days lengthen in early spring. More severe forms of SAD may be associated with major depression or bipolar disorders.

Officially recognized as a form of depression in the 1987 edition of the *Diagnostic and Statistical Manual*, SAD is estimated to affect more than 10 million adults and as many as 1 million children each year. SAD occurs most often in the latitudes more distant from the equator, when there is less sunlight in winter. In the United States, for example, the condition is much more prevalent in Alaska than in Florida. An estimated 11 percent of New Hampshire residents are affected to some degree. As with other types of depression, women are more likely to experience SAD than men, and the condition does run in families. The worst months seem to be December, January, and February (in the Northern Hemisphere).

The symptoms of SAD are similar to those of major depression, but they seem to be triggered when daylight hours are short. Nobody's morale is lifted by a gray, dreary, wintry day. But most people, even those who prefer the white-hot heat of a summer beach, can get up in the morning, scrape the ice off their windshield, and go about their routine, no matter how dark and gray the day. People with SAD feel truly incapacitated in such conditions. Adults may feel their moods darken, their productivity decline, and they may start to put on weight. Some may find they can't function normally until the arrival of spring. Children may see their grades drop in school over the winter months, with a corresponding upswing as soon as the days start to lengthen.

The biochemistry behind SAD involves a malfunctioning in how the brain handles a compound called melatonin. The brain naturally produces melatonin to help induce sleep. (That's why some people who experience disturbed sleep patterns take a melatonin supplement before bedtime.) In the morning, light entering the retina of the eye signals the pineal gland in the brain to stop making melatonin so we can wake up and be alert. During the late fall and winter, less sunlight is available. This can leave an excess of melatonin in our brains during the day. Most people are not negatively affected by this extra melatonin, but people with SAD experience drowsiness, lethargy, and mild to moderate depression.

People who endure SAD every winter often crave carbohydrates (sugary or starchy foods), which tend to increase levels of serotonin in the brain and therefore help fight depression. Unfortunately, overeating often leads to weight gain, which is counterproductive. More effective relief comes from various types of phototherapy in which people are exposed to very bright, full-spectrum indoor light soon after waking. Symptoms generally begin to lift after about a week of treatment, but for lasting relief phototherapy must continue daily until spring. Read more about this treatment in Chapter 11.

## POSTPARTUM DEPRESSION

Clearly triggered by a physiological event, postpartum depression affects at least half of all new mothers, who experience a brief period of weepiness, sadness, and letdown after giving birth. This temporary period, sometimes called "the baby blues," typically occurs within five days of birth and is probably due to a combination of sleep deprivation, physical exhaustion, and the dramatic hormonal changes that accompany labor, delivery, and the period immediately following childbirth. Normal postpartum depression usually resolves within weeks without medical intervention.

About 10 to 15 percent of new mothers experience a more sustained clinical depression, during which they may find themselves unwilling or unable to care for themselves or their newborn. In extreme cases, the mother may not want to touch her baby and avoids routine care like feeding or changing. Other symptoms may include anxiety, panic attacks, anger, sleep problems, loss of interest in activities previously enjoyed, forgetfulness, and feelings of being trapped. If the new mother doesn't receive proper emotional support and medical treatment, the condition can be dangerous to both mother and child, leading to infant neglect, even to the point of death.

Once the condition is diagnosed, there are a number of treatment options. A good start is to participate in a new mother's support group, especially one focusing on postpartum depression. The group "Depression After Delivery" has dozens of chapters around the country. Hormone therapy can be effective in some women who need to boost estrogen, progesterone, or thyroid hormones after delivery. Tricyclic antidepressant medications are also prescribed in some cases, and they seem to be safe even for nursing mothers, since researchers have found that these particular antidepressants don't pass into the breastmilk.

In rare instances, about one in a thousand, the condition leads to what is termed *postpartum psychosis*, a condition in which the mother hallucinates and becomes delusional and suicidal. She may even become violent toward her own child. Obviously, this is a true medical emergency requiring immediate intervention. Crisis counseling is available through community hotlines. See the resource listings at the back of this book for more information.

## BUILDING A TREATMENT TEAM

It is difficult and sometimes impossible to overcome depression entirely on your own. A collaborative partnership involving you, your primary-care physician, one or more mental health professionals, and various CAM practitioners can help you beat depression.

Your physician is probably the key player on the team, and certainly the one to start the ball rolling. He or she will take a detailed medical history, order appropriate diagnostic tests, and oversee and help coordinate your ongoing care as you try different treatment approaches. Under the guidance and with the knowledge of your physician, you could conceivably try many different therapies, both conventional (see Chapters 4–9) and complementary/alternative (see Chapters 10–15), before discovering what works best for you.

You may need to "shop around" to find a doctor who has *both* the necessary experience in assessing and treating depression *and* is open to collaborating with you and with other health care practitioners such as nutritionists, herbalists, massage therapists, and acupuncturists. Even if your primary physician doesn't have enough firsthand knowledge to refer you to qualified CAM practitioners in your area, he or she should at least be supportive of your interest and willing to hear what other experts have to offer. If not, find a doctor who is.

Remember, it's not a personal insult to leave your regular doctor in search of someone who is more experienced with the complex diagnosis and treatment of depression. After all, you wouldn't go to a plumber to fix your car, no matter how good a job he did on your bathroom last year. You have a right to seek the health care you need, when you need it. (See Chapter 3 for more advice on finding and working with your primary physician.)

## HEALING YOUR BRAIN

As I've stated before and will remind you throughout the book, regardless of the origin of your depression, if you're depressed, you have a real, biochemical illness. Your illness manifests itself as one or more imbalances of important neurotransmitters in the brain. Other imbalances may be hormonal. These imbalances, in turn, account for nearly every other adverse symptom of depression.

Conventional medicine usually seeks to adjust the amount and activity of key neurotransmitters by prescribing various antidepressant drugs and other medications (see Chapter 7). Alternative and complementary approaches (see Chapters 10–15) offer gentler treatments, with varying degrees of effectiveness. Such treatments are typically less invasive and have fewer negative side effects.

The beauty of integrative medicine is that it gives you a framework within which you can consider *all* of your options. For example, you can start back on the road to relief with:

- Nutritious foods that promote the production of serotonin and other neurotransmitters
- Dietary supplements that stimulate the production of specific neurotransmitters or activate enzymes needed for the proper functioning of these vital brain chemicals
- Exercise, which stimulates endorphin production, along with providing numerous other health benefits
- Cognitive or cognitive-behavioral therapy, which has helped many depressed people to restructure negative, self-defeating patterns of thought and behavior
- Targeted counseling to tackle specific problems in your personal life, family life, or professional life
- Natural, highly effective mood-lifting agents, such as St. John's wort and SAMe
- Prescription antidepressants, such as Prozac, that directly promote or block brain chemicals
- Homeopathic remedies that stimulate the body to heal itself
- Massage therapy, which promotes relaxation, improves breathing and circulation, aids digestion, and stimulates the release of endorphins

- Various hormone replacement medications, when laboratory tests indicate low hormone levels
- Meditation and relaxation techniques to reduce anxiety and stress
- Nutritional supplements to promote deeply restorative sleep
- Aromatherapy, which activates the olfactory system's connection with deep brain structures
- Biofeedback, which trains the brain to reprogram certain patterns of activity
- Acupuncture, which may help restore balance and harmony to body and brain
- Phototherapy, by which bright light enters the eye, travels to the pineal gland, and alters brain chemistry

Of course, you wouldn't pursue these possibilities all at once! But you can see that with all these options to explore, you have no reason to go without help even one more day.

## HEALING YOUR MIND

It's not hard to accept the fact that brain biochemistry can affect your thoughts and feelings. But it may take a moment to get used to the idea that it works the other way, too. What you think and feel can actually alter the biochemistry of your brain. That's one of the goals of the various talk therapies, to heal the brain by healing the mind.

We explore the many types of "talk therapies" in Chapter 6. For now, as you start your journey to recovery, it's essential that you understand the enormous power of your mind. It's *your* mind and it's *your* power. No physician or psychologist can "fix" you without it.

Despite the many physical and emotional challenges of living with depression, you *can* begin to create a new, healthier, happier you. Here's how:

- *Develop a positive attitude.* You deserve a healthy, happy life. You have what it takes to learn how to cope with depression and anything else life throws your way.
- *Watch your language.* When talking to others or to yourself, stop using words and phrases that reinforce your illness. For example, instead of issuing general, negative statements like "I'm sick of being so tired," or "This depression is really killing me," try being more specific and positive (or at least neutral). Listen to the difference: "Today I'll try to relax more," or "This depression is really talking to me today." Remember, depression is not a punishment or a pointless torture; it's your body telling you that something needs attention.
- *Take action.* When you're feeling especially down or discouraged, try taking one positive, health-promoting step. Take a 30-minute walk outdoors, eat a nutritious snack, make an appointment to see your doctor, get on the Internet to learn more

about your problem, or relax with meditation or guided imagery. Any action, no matter how small, will help. If you can't think of anything, call a friend or force yourself out into the world of people. If it seems like nothing can help and you're feeling desperate, call your doctor, hospital, or crisis hotline immediately.

- *Get help.* You may be the captain of your ship, but you need a lot of experienced hands on deck if you want to get anywhere without sinking. First and foremost, you need a first mate—a physician with plenty of experience in diagnosing and treating depression. Don't put off getting professional help. Research shows that the longer you wait, the harder it is to get effective treatment. Do it *now.*

- *Ask for support.* Chronic illness can be lonely. A few of us are lucky enough to be surrounded by people eager to listen and offer support; the rest of us have to reach out for it. Friends and coworkers may not realize what you're going through and how much you need them now. If these people don't respond as you hoped, seek out new friends at support group meetings or by keeping in touch with other people facing similar health challenges (see the resource list at the back of this book). It's easier to forgive your loved ones for shortchanging you emotionally when you have an alternate support system.

- *Don't isolate yourself.* You don't have to be the life of the party—but force yourself to socialize. Go to church, the community center, or the library. Human contact is a powerful healer.

- *Do something for someone else*, someone you love or even a complete stranger. Emotional pain makes us very self-centered; thinking about another person's needs can provide a temporary distraction, maybe even pleasure.

- *Get informed and stay informed.* Information is power. Actively hunt it down wherever you can. Read books and articles, ask lots of questions, take notes, surf the Web, listen closely and ask questions during doctor visits. You don't have to get a degree in medicine, but learn what you can about depression and stay informed. No matter how many health care professionals you recruit for your team, you're ultimately in charge of your own journey. Don't travel blind.

# 5

## First Things First: Lifestyle Strategies for Positive Living

In a perfect world, we'd never have to deal with stress, insecurity, failure, or loss. If we could prevent these situations, we could also put an end to depression in many people. But since the world isn't perfect, we need to focus instead *on what we can control* in our lives—or at least learn some effective coping skills. Taking these steps can help us improve our peace of mind and boost our mood.

When I see a patient with mild depression, I generally suggest starting with self-help measures—some easy-to-implement lifestyle strategies that can help him or her through the current situation and help prevent future episodes as well. If these measures aren't enough to lift the mood within six to eight weeks, or if the patient has too much emotional inertia to implement them, or if the depression worsens, then more aggressive measures are warranted.

For patients with moderate-to-severe depression, I generally recommend self-help measures along with anti-depressants and/or psychotherapy.

A number of self-help measures can be effective in easing and preventing depression. These include sleep regulation, exercise, sound nutrition, stress management, socialization, support groups, faith-based activities, and pet therapy. Most of these activities and lifestyle changes are easy to integrate into your daily life. Some, like exercising and taking steps to regulate your sleep-wake cycle, provide immediate benefits and cost nothing. Many have a scientific basis.

To determine which therapies work best for you, I suggest you do some research. The Internet is a good place to start. You can also find books on self-help strategies at your local library, bookstore, or health food store. In addition, your family doctor probably has some literature. (For more sources, see the resource listings at the back of this book.)

As you do your research, look at the information critically. Ask how and why each intervention works. Experiment with a few no-cost or low-cost activities until you find the ones you like and give you the best results. When you decide to try a specific activity or therapy, listen to your body. Ask yourself: Am I enjoying this? Do I want to continue doing it? Do I feel better? More positive? Less preoccupied with my problems? This chapter describes several self-help therapies that have proven beneficial for people with mild-to-moderate depression.

They include:

- Sleep regulation
- Exercise
- Stress management
- Socialization
- Support groups
- Faith-based activities
- Creative expression (music therapy, art therapy, dance/movement therapy, drama therapy)
- Pet therapy
- Laughter therapy

## GET THE SLEEP
## YOU DESPERATELY NEED

Depression—and some antidepressant medications—often cause sleep disturbances, and a lack of sleep can intensify depression by making it harder for you to cope with everyday stressors. Either way, if you're always feeling down in the dumps, you could benefit from more high-quality, deeply restorative sleep.

Some people who are depressed fall asleep quickly but have difficulty staying asleep. You may wake in the wee hours of the morning, clearly exhausted but too wakeful to get back to sleep. Or you sleep and sleep and sleep, and still can't seem to get going in the morning. (People with this symptom are also more likely to overeat.)

Any step you can take toward improving sleep will begin to help you heal. Even if you can sleep only a few hours a night, make those hours count! No single solution works for everyone, but here are some suggestions worth trying:

- Go to bed at the same time every night, and get up at the same time every day.
- Limit your sleep during the day; if possible, avoid all napping.
- Develop a bedtime ritual. For example, walk the dog, lock the doors, change into your pajamas, brush your teeth, read for 15 minutes, then turn out the light and go to sleep.
- As part of your nightly routine, make a list of things you plan to accomplish the following day. Be realistic in your goals. Put the list where you can find it easily, then put it out of your mind.
- Don't exercise within two or three hours of bedtime. It will only get you revved up so you can't fall asleep.
- Avoid caffeine for several hours before bedtime. If you still can't sleep, try eliminating all caffeine from your diet. Avoid alcohol and tobacco as well—both disturb sleep.
- Don't eat a big meal before bedtime. It can make you uncomfortable or give you indigestion.
- Have a light snack or a glass of milk before turning in for the night. Milk contains tryptophan, a natural chemical that aids sleep.
- Artificial lighting can confuse your internal clock. About an hour before bedtime, dim the lights in

your home. This will reduce your energy level as a prelude to an easy slumber.

- Create a restful bedroom environment: soft colors, muted light, no clutter. Shop for a mattress that's right for you. It's worth the investment.
- Keep the bedroom cool. A hot room can keep you awake.
- Before bedtime, unwind by performing some of the relaxation techniques described in Chapter 13. They will help you release bottled-up stress.
- Ask your doctor whether prescription antidepressants, or the natural, over-the-counter herbal products might improve both the quantity and quality of your sleep.

## GET MOVING!

Researchers have conducted more than 1,000 studies on the benefits of exercise in relieving depression. Although we still aren't sure whether exercise can *prevent* depression from occurring or recurring, it's clear that it elevates mood and helps *reduce* existing depression.

In fact, studies show that regular aerobic exercise (at least three 30-minute sessions per week) is just as effective as psychotherapy in reducing mild-to-moderate depression.

The antidepressant effects of exercise were also found to increase with the length of time you exercise. Although most research has focused on the effects aerobic exercise, any type or amount of exercise has an antidepressant effect if it's more than what you've been doing in the past. Even climbing a few stairs or walking a few blocks is beneficial if you've been inactive for a long time.

Besides decreasing depression, exercise has been found to relieve anxiety, enhance appetite, improve sleep patterns, heighten sexual interest, and boost self-esteem. Aerobic exercise (like running or fast walking) improves stamina, strength, and cardiovascular fitness by increasing your heart and respiratory rate. Anaerobic exercise (like weightlifting and stretching) can improve your muscle flexibility and strength.

Exercise stimulates the production of brain chemicals called catecholamines, which stabilize mood and are often in short supply in people with depression. In addition, aerobic exercise reduces the level of stress-related hormones in your bloodstream, especially cortisol. This can make you feel better immediately after you work out.

Exercise also releases endorphins into the bloodstream, which elevate mood, relieve pain, and produce a "natural high." Twenty to 30 minutes of aerobic exercise at least three times a week keeps endorphins in your bloodstream, counteracting depression. People with seasonal affective disorder (SAD) will see significant improvement in mood if they spend 30 to 60 minutes a day exercising outdoors in the midwinter sunshine.

In short, exercise can give you a new perspective on life, making you feel freer, stronger, and better equipped to handle stress. To learn more about the benefits of exercise and for some tips on how to make exercise a regular part of your day, see Chapter 14.

## DIAL DOWN THE STRESS

Isolated stressful events, like having an argument with your spouse or getting a speeding ticket, are part of everyday life and easy to bounce back from. Stress that goes on for weeks or months is a different story. It can make you so anxious and so depressed that you act like a different person—irritable, hostile, even fearful to the point of phobia. Prolonged stress can also feed on itself by causing insomnia, digestive problems, headaches, and muscle aches—physical ailments that only make you feel more depressed.

These days, everyone seems to be "stressed out." New sources of stress surface every day, many of them out of our control. We have job downsizing, managed health care, information overload, headline news that focuses almost exclusively on disasters and tragedies, increasing dependence on computers and technologies, and worsening traffic jams. We are overcommitted at home and on the job, a situation fueled by the need to perform every task at hyperspeed. Change is the only thing that is constant and it appears to be happening faster than we can adapt. We worry about our children, about care for aging parents, about being able to afford retirement, about juggling families and careers. With the trend toward increased mobility and decreased social and family ties, the strength of our traditional social networks is compromised. Beepers, cell phones, faxes, and e-mail do little to repair our social disconnectedness. The use of these technologies often provides the digital illusion of connectedness, with all the stress and few of the benefits.

Each of these factors contributes to our sense of helplessness, and thus can contribute to depression.

If chronic stress is ruining your physical and mental health, you need to find some healthy outlets. Clinical studies show that relaxation techniques—including deep breathing, progressive relaxation exercises, guided imagery, yoga, meditation, and biofeedback—can help you decrease physical and mental tension and thereby relieve depression. Some of these techniques require practice or professional instruction before they're effective. Others are easy to learn on your own, can be put into practice almost immediately, and can be used just about anywhere when you start feeling overwhelmed.

Read more about stress management techniques in the chapter on mind-body therapies.

## SOCIALIZATION

Having a strong network of friends and family is a proven antidepressant. Studies show that people who are socially isolated actually have an excess of stress hormones in their bloodstream, predisposing them to depression, anxiety, higher blood pressure and heart rate, and compromised immune system function. On the other hand, people with strong social ties have lower levels of these hormones, a situation associated with better physical and emotional health, including the ability to cope well with stress.

Research also confirms a statistical relationship between social isolation and early death (including suicide) that's just as compelling as the link between smoking or high cholesterol and early death.

The fact is, many people become socially isolated through no fault of their own. In today's mobile society, you or your spouse may get a job transfer to another state or even another country and have to leave friends and extended family behind. If you're elderly, you'll feel increasingly isolated as your spouse, friends, and siblings die, particularly if your children live far away.

How can you keep from feeling isolated? One way is to be a "joiner." Affiliate with a group or take a class that focuses on your hobbies and interests—perhaps home improvement, photography, cooking, or gardening. This instantly connects you with a group of people with whom you have something in common. Another idea is to do volunteer work in your community. Once again, look at your interests. If you love to read, volunteer at the library or work with a literacy group; if you're an animal lover, help out at the animal shelter. It feels good to help others. Besides meeting people, you'll be building self-esteem and making a contribution to your community. For ideas on where to volunteer in your area, check the guide to human services section in your phone book.

Even though family and friends may live far away, you can still maintain close relationships with them through telephone, letters, and e-mail. Internet chat groups can also be a source of social contact, especially for housebound people. On the other hand, at least one study has shown a higher incidence of depression in people who spend more time on the computer and

Internet (probably because virtual activity ends up displacing healthier activities). The virtual world can never substitute for the value of human touch and real-life relationships.

## SUPPORT GROUPS

Participating in support groups can be very therapeutic for people with depression. There are support groups specifically for people with depression, as well as groups for people with problems related to depression, such as alcoholism, eating disorders, bereavement, and cancer and other diseases. All of these groups offer education and support; some also publish newsletters and have Internet Web sites. People in support groups can provide you referrals to psychotherapists, first hand information on antidepressants and their side effects, self-care tips, and just about any other information you need.

Most depressed people feel very isolated, and joining a support group gives them a bridge back to society through membership in a group united by a common bond. A support group helps you restore your dignity by putting you in touch with people who understand what you're going through, who can listen with empathy, and who offer advice based on their own experiences. These groups also give you a safe place to vent your anger and frustration, sparing your family and friends. (For more information on various support groups, see the resource listings at the back of this book.)

## FAITH-BASED ACTIVITIES

Research has shown that prayer and other faith-based activities can speed recovery from depression. A recent study centered on 85 hospitalized patients who had serious physical ailments as well as depression. The patients' religious values and faith were rated on a scale of 10 to 50 using the Hoge Intrinsic Religiousness Scale. Patients recovered from their depression 70 percent faster for every 10-point increase on the Hoge scale, suggesting that deep-rooted religiousness in depressed medical patients can result in faster recovery from depression. This held true even in patients whose physical condition didn't improve.

Research also indicates that deep religious faith can *prevent* depression. The National Institute on Aging studied 4,000 people and found that those who attended religious services at least once a week were depressed only half as much as those who never attended services or went less than once a week. In another study of 860 elderly men hospitalized with acute illness, those who used their religious beliefs to cope had significantly less depression.

Although hopelessness, sadness, and other *emotional* symptoms of depression are less common in people with strong religious convictions, research shows that *physical* symptoms of depression (such as weight loss, insomnia, or fatigue) aren't affected by spiritual coping and religious beliefs. This suggests that a holistic approach to preventing and treating depression may work best: psychotherapy to deal with issues of the mind; medication (or supplements), exercise, and diet to address biological causes of depression; and spiritual counseling to address spiritual issues and to provide hope. Keep in mind that prayer has no adverse effects.

## CREATIVE EXPRESSION

Numerous studies have demonstrated the physical and mental health benefits gained from creative activities such as writing or journaling, music therapy, and art therapy. The ability to see the world differently and express this creatively can be very therapeutic.

### Music Therapy

Throughout history, music has been known to have a healing influence. In the Bible, the shepherd David soothed King Saul with his harp. The ancient Greeks, Romans, and Chinese philosophers believed that music could heal body and soul. But although the healing effects of music have been recognized for centuries, and contemporary studies lend support, music therapy isn't used much today and remains controversial.

We all know that soothing music can lull you to sleep. But did you know that studies show that music can also relieve pain through distraction, lower blood pressure, normalize irregular heartbeats, promote deep relaxation, relieve insomnia, enable you to recall suppressed memories, reduce anxiety, improve mood, and help lift depression? Music can either calm or stimulate us, and its therapeutic effects depend on our health, our surroundings, whether we're tired or alert, whether we're familiar with the music used, and whether we have musical experience.

How does music affect your body and mind? Studies are inconclusive. Music may cause physical changes in the autonomic nervous system, such as lowering blood pressure, which then affects emotions. Or music may have its initial impact at higher levels in the brain where it mixes with emotions and abstract thought before causing physical changes in the body. Or these two mechanisms may work together.

Music is an orderly arrangement of sound that has a very personal and intimate meaning for each person. When a therapist uses music to treat depression, she may ask the person to actually perform the piece or just listen to music that's been carefully chosen, based on the person's condition and personality.

You probably recognize that different types of music have various effects on you. For example, bright, cheery music, like salsa, reggae, or polkas, can be a mood-elevating tonic. Music that brims with strength, courage, or faith can inspire you and make you feel powerful. Think of how uplifted you feel when listening to "Amazing Grace," "Chariots of Fire," "Ave Maria," or Beethoven's "Ode to Joy." Marches, Dixieland, bluegrass, or rock music can stimulate people who are mildly depressed. New age music, such as that performed by Yanni, can be extremely soothing.

## ART THERAPY

More than 100 years ago, European writers observed that patients in mental hospitals created artwork out of whatever materials were available. In the 1940s and '50s, the teacher and psychotherapist Margaret Naumburg and her sister Florence Cane founded art therapy in the United States. With the help of artists who volunteered in mental hospitals, the two women eventually convinced psychiatrists of the value of art therapy in treating mental illness.

As a formal discipline, art therapy combines elements of psychoanalysis and other psychological theories, art education, and human development. Because art is a form of nonverbal communication, it can help people express feelings that they might otherwise keep buried inside. The goal of art therapy is to reflect the patient's personality, conflicts, concerns, interests, and abilities. It helps people resolve emotional conflicts, develop social skills, foster self-awareness, manage behavior, decrease anxiety and depression, solve problems, increase self-esteem, and become more grounded in reality. It's a highly effective therapy for both adults and children. Your physician or therapist may recommend formal art therapy for you if you're struggling to get at the root of your depression and internal conflicts.

If you enjoy drawing, painting, or other forms of artistic expression, you can get therapeutic benefits right at home. Set aside time to express yourself on paper or canvas, then look at your work and ask, "What does it say about me?" Your artwork might provide some insight into your mood and feelings. At the very least, having a creative outlet will give you something to concentrate on besides your depression.

## Dance/Movement Therapy and Drama Therapy

Dance/movement therapy and drama therapy are formal disciplines, like art therapy or music therapy. Both have been shown to have a beneficial effect on depressed patients; however, scientific evidence is limited.

In the treatment of depression, a dance therapist uses structured exercises to help people express themselves through movement and enhance their well-being. Sessions are usually held in a group for 30 to 40 minutes once a week. (For more information, see Chapter 14.)

Drama therapists have similar goals. They use the techniques of theater—including acting, role-playing/role reversal, and improvisation—to help people express themselves, explore personal issues, and enhance self-understanding. Both interventions are conducted in small groups and on a one-to-one basis.

## PET THERAPY

Pets can play a big role in alleviating depression. Trained pets, especially dogs, are being used more and more in hospitals, nursing homes, private homes, and other settings to improve quality of life for people with physical and mental illness.

But the idea is far from new. In ninth-century Belgium, animals were used in the care of handicapped people, and in the 1800s, animals were used in a German home for epileptics. In 1860, Florence Nightingale, the founder of modern nursing, wrote: "A small pet is often an excellent companion for the sick, for long chronic cases especially." She also recommended that caged birds be used to provide companionship and pleasure to bedridden patients.

During times of major life change such as divorce, the loss of a loved one, unemployment, or major illness, pets can give comfort and support. They can reduce your sense of isolation, provide companionship, and in the case of dogs, give you an excuse to get some outdoor exercise, especially valuable for people with depression. A pet also gives you a sense of purpose and a reason to go on living.

Although research is limited, studies show that pet ownership or simply being around animals is good for your health. Just stroking a dog or a cat can lower stress, blood pressure, heart rate, and respiratory rate. Nursing home residents are less depressed when puppies are brought in weekly. Elderly people who own pets show increased alertness. People with coronary disease who own pets have better survival rates than those who don't.

For years now, companion dogs have helped the blind. More recently dogs have been trained to assist hearing-impaired and wheelchair-bound people. Not only are dogs helpful with day-to-day tasks, they also draw people to the handicapped person, reducing isolation and enhancing social contacts. The same is true for people with depression.

## LAUGHTER THERAPY

In the 1976, Norman Cousins wrote an article in the *New England Journal of Medicine* detailing his 12 years of living with a severe form of arthritis that doctors said was incurable. He described his frustration with the medical community that offered him only traditional treatments and no hope of getting better. This led him to develop his own treatment, which he called "laughter therapy."

Instead of staying in the hospital, Cousins checked into a hotel and watched every funny video he could get his hands on. He told jokes, asked people to tell him jokes, and availed himself of anything that would make him laugh. He discovered that 10 minutes of belly laughter allowed him 2 hours of pain-free sleep. Eventually his pain subsided, and he wrote a book about curing himself with laughter.

Research done since Cousins's experiment suggests that laughter really can help you fight disease by calming your nerves, taking your mind off your condition, and keeping your immune system functioning optimally.

Because chronic pain often leads to depression, laughter may be doubly beneficial. Several theories seek to explain this phenomenon. According to one theory, laughter causes the brain to produce endorphins, the body's natural pain killers. In a study of patients with spinal cord injuries, limb amputations, and other major neurological and musculoskeletal problems, 75 percent agreed with the statement: "Sometimes laughing works as well as a pain pill."

What else can laughter do? It decreases stress by giving hospitalized patients a sense of control (at least over their mood). It helps you release tension by causing the muscles in your arms and legs to contract and then relax, similar to the effect of progressive relaxation therapy. A good laugh can raise your heart rate for up to 5 minutes, providing an aerobic workout for your heart. Laughing can clear your lungs and stimulate coughing, ridding your lung passages of bacteria and mucus. Laughter releases pent-up anger and clears the way for you to discuss your real feelings and deal with conflicts. It also reduces the levels of the stress hormones epinephrine and cortisol in your blood.

Laughter is a natural resource that you can tap into at will to restore your personal power. It can help you see the glass half-full instead of half-empty, and keeps you from feeling like a victim by helping you cope with conflicts or problems. Laughter may be healing and its effects are definitely self-sustaining. So take a cue from Norman Cousins and write yourself a prescription for laughter. Devote some time each day to enjoying old comedy tapes of the Marx Brothers, Monty Python, Robin Williams, Richard Pryor, or *I Love Lucy*—whatever moves the needle on your laugh meter. The more you laugh, the happier you feel, and the happier you feel, the more you laugh.

# 6

## Talking It Out

No one is born depressed. Gaze into the eyes of a healthy infant and you'll see an innocent mix of excitement and inner peace. Look into the eyes of a seriously depressed adult and you may glimpse unspeakable despair, or worse, the eerie absence of any real feeling. Somewhere along the line, something changed.

We know from our growing understanding of the complex interplay of brain biochemistry and hormonal activity that too much or too little of this neurotransmitter or that hormone—or the right amounts made available at the wrong time—can have profound effects on our thoughts, emotions, and mood. Sometimes we seem to be transformed into someone we scarcely recognize.

But this body-mind connection is a two-way street. Not only do neurotransmitters and hormones affect how we think and feel, our thoughts and feelings can dramatically alter hormone levels and neurotransmitter activity in the brain. In other words, not only can our brains change our minds; *we can use our minds to change our brains.*

That's the idea behind many forms of talk therapy: to reprogram our brains for healthier, more productive functioning. Psychotherapy, once thought to work because it helped release unresolved conflicts buried deep in the unconscious, is now believed to be effective because, over time, it may literally restructure the biochemistry of depression in the brain.

Depression is the quintessential mind-body disease. You can attack depression from the "body" side with various herbs, antidepressants, phototherapy, biofeedback, and dozens of other treatments. Or you can approach it from the "mind" side with various stress reduction techniques and talk therapies. When depression arises from a treatable physical/biochemical condition, clearly a "body" approach is called for. When there seems to be no serious underlying physical disorder and when depression is mild to moderate, a "mind-centered" approach may be appropriate. Depending on the type and degree of the depression, many people find a *combination* of body and mind therapies to be the most powerful treatment for the relief and prevention of depressive disorders.

As we discussed in Chapter 3, the road to effective treatment begins with an accurate diagnosis—not only to "type" your depression, but to assess your overall physical health. Once you have a clear picture of your mental and physical status, you may wish to consider various talk therapy options.

## WHAT'S TALK THERAPY?

The simplest form of talk therapy is simply talking—discussing problems or feelings, past or present, with a close friend, a family member, a member of the clergy, a teacher, a neighbor, or even a complete stranger you meet on a train. The mere act of expressing yourself, telling your story, or admitting vulnerability can be very therapeutic, regardless of who's listening. That's why even talking into a tape recorder or writing letters you may never actually send can be a step on the path to healing.

On the other hand, getting stuck in a constant litany of complaints—how horrible your life is, how someone wronged you, how you can never do anything right, how no one understands you—can actually reinforce and perpetuate your problems.

Serious depression deserves professional help. In professional talk therapy, a psychologist, psychiatrist, social worker, or trained counselor listens to your thoughts and feelings, identifies issues related to your mental and emotional state, and helps you think more clearly about how you can create a more satisfying life.

For moderate to severe depression, a combination of psychotherapy and antidepressants often leads to the best outcomes. Antidepressants can help you stay focused so you get more out of psychotherapy, and psychotherapy can provide emotional support until antidepressant treatments begin to work—which can take up to six weeks or longer.

## IS TALK THERAPY FOR ME?

Say the word "therapy" and many people still imagine a self-centered patient lying on an expensive couch, droning on about his or her problems, while a bearded doctor silently takes notes. That's hardly the case these days. Psychotherapy today is really an extended conversation between a client and an attentive mental health professional. You describe your problems, symptoms, experiences, past and present thoughts, emotions, behaviors, and relationships, and your therapist offers insight and feedback. She can't solve your problems, but she can help you find sensible solutions that are right for you.

Psychotherapy can help undo some of the damage depression has inflicted on your self-esteem. You may feel dull and uninteresting, almost invisible. If you have bipolar disorder, you may feel unstable, unreliable, and out of control as you fluctuate between episodes of depression and mania. You may even begin to believe your disease defines who you are. Therapy can help turn your life around by changing the behaviors or thought patterns that created or maintained your depression, and by preventing another bout of depression. It can help you start enjoying life again.

Your primary-care physician may recommend therapy as the main treatment if you have mild-to-moderate depression that's lasted only a few weeks and hasn't occurred before. He may also suggest combining therapy with exercise, diet modifications, or alternative treatments such as the herb St. John's wort for a more natural approach to managing your depression.

Many people prefer therapy because they'd rather not take antidepressants and risk unpleasant side effects. On the other hand, some people are dead-set against therapy. They see it as embarrassing or even shameful and feel that taking a medication is more "socially acceptable." They erroneously believe that therapy is for "weak" people, and that strong people can handle their own problems and pull themselves together.

If you happen to fall into this category, here are some facts to consider. Years of research studies have proven that therapy is enormously valuable in helping depressed patients. In fact, a 1998 study in the *Journal of Consulting and Clinical Psychology* suggests that therapy may be just as good as antidepressants for certain people. Two groups with major depression were followed for eight months. Those receiving only psychotherapy improved just as significantly as those receiving only antidepressants. In a less severely depressed group, people getting psychotherapy didn't improve as quickly as those on antidepressants, but after four months of treatment, both groups showed similar improvement.

Several types of psychotherapy are effective for treating depression. How you relate to your therapist is generally more important than the type of therapy used. Experienced therapists almost always use a combination of approaches, custom-fitting the treatment to the client's style and needs.

Because depression has many potential emotional and mental causes—such as abusive relationships, past conflicts, repressed emotions, pessimistic thinking, negative behaviors, or major losses—your therapist must consider your personal situation before deciding on a particular treatment approach. How you respond to one type of therapy over another depends on your personal issues, your problem-solving style, your level of commitment to feeling better, and the strength of your personal support systems. The following information will help you understand the various types of psychotherapy and choose a therapist who's right for you.

## SHORT-TERM THERAPIES

Opponents of long-term psychotherapy argue that it can go on for years without any end in sight and with no way for the patient to know when he's "cured." Actually, long-term therapies such as Freudian psychoanalysis have largely been replaced by shorter-term therapies, which are more effective, more efficient, and less expensive. A National Institute of Mental Health (NIMH) study showed that 55 percent of mild-to-moderately depressed people felt significantly better after only 16 weeks of psychotherapy.

Managed care is another reason for the surge in short-term therapy. Managed care plans and HMOs limit the number of therapy visits per year, based on the *DSM* diagnosis. But this doesn't necessarily mean that patients are getting shortchanged. Therapists are compelled to be more efficient and develop new, effective brief-therapy programs. When problems do arise, it may be due to an inadequate number of visits or it may be that therapists are forced to fit all patients into specific therapeutic models, even when they don't conform.

Short-term therapy typically lasts between five to 20 sessions, emphasizes present rather than past problems, and sets concrete, attainable goals that require the client and therapist to actively work together. Cognitive and behavioral therapy are especially effective for the treatment of depression.

## COGNITIVE THERAPY

Cognitive therapy—also called cognitive restructuring—helps people identify and consciously change patterns of negative thinking that lead to or maintain depression. Developed in the 1970s by psychiatrist Aaron T. Beck of the University of Pennsylvania, the approach was designed specifically to treat depression. While Sigmund Freud suggested that how we feel influences what we think, Beck postulated that what we think determines how we feel. Both theories are valid.

When we engage in negative thinking—what Beck calls "cognitive distortions"—we tend to blow minor incidents out of proportion until they seem like catastrophes. If you're already depressed, this is like running your own black cloud machine.

Psychiatrist David Burns, Beck's colleague and the author of *Feeling Good: The New Mood Therapy*, looks for ten types of negative thinking, including these:

> *All-or-nothing thinking:* Perfectionism; seeing everything in terms of black and white. If you make a

mistake at work, you're a failure. If someone hurts you, they're all bad.

*Labeling:* All-or-nothing thinking taken one step further. If you lock yourself out of the house, you didn't just make a mistake, you're an idiot.

*Mental filtering:* Dwelling on the negative aspects of a situation, while ignoring the positive. If you give a speech and one person in the back row says he had trouble hearing you, you obsess over this one complaint instead of enjoying all the compliments you receive.

*"Should" and "shouldn't" statements:* If you get a B on a test, you chastise yourself, thinking "I should've gotten an A."

Such self-defeating thinking makes even small successes a struggle. Your therapist will help you restructure these destructive thought patterns into positive, realistic statements so you can say to yourself, "I made a mistake, but I learned from it. Next time I'll do better."

The cognitive therapist uses five basic techniques to turn your thinking around:

- Recognizing negative thoughts that may automatically enter your consciousness when you're feeling your worst
- Disputing negative thoughts by focusing on contrary evidence
- Applying different explanations to dispute negative thoughts

- Controlling your thoughts and avoiding rumination
- Replacing negative thoughts with more empowering positive thoughts and beliefs

Your therapist will help you rehearse new, positive thought patterns to replace habitual, negative thinking. One way she does this is by having you keep a diary of your negative thoughts and the incidents that prompted them. For example, your assignment may be to write five pages in a week. Just the act of writing down your negative thoughts is therapeutic. Putting your thoughts on paper makes it easier to see that they're irrational. Saying them aloud helps, too. As you progress in therapy, your therapist may have you go back and rewrite your negative thoughts as more positive statements or take some concrete actions.

In another tactic called "cognitive rehearsal," you imagine a difficult situation and then plan a step-by-step approach to the problem. Your therapist helps you obliterate negative "I can't" thoughts and replace them with positive "I can" ones.

Cognitive therapy takes effort. Long-standing thought patterns are hard to break. On the other hand, the steps to recovery—mainly being aware of your negative emotions and what triggers them and then making substitutions—seem too facile to some people. But simplicity is cognitive therapy's strong point. It's quick and easy once you understand how it works, and it's easy to apply in your real life.

## BEHAVIORAL THERAPY

Unlike cognitive therapy, which strives to change negative thoughts, behavioral therapy strives to change unproductive, self-destructive behavior. While other psychotherapies are geared toward increasing your awareness or helping you find the root causes of your problems, behavioral therapy helps you find the tools to actively change your life.

Behavioral therapy arose from laboratory experiments with animals that involved positive and negative reinforcement, conditioned reflexes, and other learning principles. Behavior therapy techniques are most effective in treating people with specific problem behaviors, such as eating disorders (anorexia or bulimia), alcoholism, drug abuse, smoking, anxiety, or procrastination—which often coexist with depression. However, this type of therapy is less effective than cognitive therapy for treating major depression, unless the depression involves a behavioral problem.

To change counterproductive or destructive behaviors, therapists give clients "assignments" to complete by the next session. These assignments take the form of behavior modification, systematic desensitization and exposure therapy, or assertiveness training.

- *Behavior modification* aims to break self-destructive behavior patterns by rewarding positive behavior. For example, if your problem is smoking, your therapist might ask you to buy yourself a gift if you go a week without a cigarette.

- *Systematic desensitization and exposure therapy* helps people with anxiety or phobias, which often accompany depression. If you are afraid to meet new people, for example, the therapist will ask you to gradually immerse yourself in various social situations—at first, encouraging you to go out only with people you know well, eventually working up to attending a party where you'll be introduced to strangers.
- *Assertiveness training* systematically trains you to clearly state your thoughts and feelings and stand your ground despite objections. Your "homework" might be to speak your mind when your husband says something that hurts or angers you, or to practice asking directly for something you want.

The strength of behavioral therapy is that it zeroes in on specific problems, offers concrete ways to change behavior, and provides skills that you can use after therapy is over. But the success of this short-term therapy is entirely dependent on how often and how consistently you apply the behavior modification techniques after you leave the session.

## Very Brief Therapy

A recent British study shows that very brief therapy, also called "two-plus-one" therapy, may be effective in treating mild depression. The participants—67 men and 47 women—were given the Beck Depression Inventory (BDI) to determine their degree of depression and were classified as either stressed, subclinically depressed (not yet showing symptoms of depression), or mildly clinically depressed.

Participants attended two therapy sessions one week apart and a third session three months later. Two types of therapy were tried: cognitive-behavioral and psychodynamic-interpersonal. Some patients started therapy immediately after taking the BDI; others started it four weeks later.

At the end of therapy, participants took the BDI again. All had improved significantly, regardless of when they started therapy. The subclinically depressed group fared the best, with 72 percent showing major improvement on the BDI. Sixty-seven percent of the stressed group and 56 percent of the mildly depressed group also had improved test scores.

In a follow-up study done a year later, participants receiving cognitive-behavioral therapy showed the most improvement, suggesting that this type of therapy works best in cases of mild depression.

# TRADITIONAL THERAPIES

Classical psychoanalysis and traditional psychodynamic therapy haven't proven to be as effective for depression as short-term therapies. They focus on understanding the past rather than on changing present thinking and behaviors.

## CLASSICAL PSYCHOANALYSIS

Developed by Sigmund Freud in the early twentieth century, classical psychoanalytic theory focuses on revealing unconscious conflicts and repressed feelings from your childhood. These conflicts and feelings become incorporated into your personality and may cause depression and other emotional problems that hold you back in life.

The goal of psychoanalysis is to restructure the patient's personality—nothing short of a huge undertaking. Psychoanalysis demands an enormous commitment of time, money, and emotional work. Sessions are held from three to five times a week, often for many years, with the client doing almost all the talking, saying whatever enters his mind (free association). Psychoanalysis isn't usually recommended for the treatment of depression because many depressed people need immediate help and their problems are often situational.

### *Psychodynamic Therapy*

Like psychoanalysis, psychodynamic therapy explores the roots of your problems going back to your childhood, but it isn't as intense or lengthy. In the treatment of depression, this therapy focuses on working through the problems that may be causing the depression. During treatment sessions you may recall repressed memories, conflicts, or events that happened long ago. You'll be asked to confront these memories, go through a healing process, or put them into a new perspective. Your therapist might also help you explore your dreams and the unconscious messages they deliver.

As in classical psychoanalysis, a free-association or stream-of-consciousness technique may be used where you relax, focus on a specific issue, and then talk about the first thing that comes into your mind. This type of therapy is also known as "insight-oriented" therapy.

The psychodynamic therapist is much more involved with the client than the classical psychoanalyst. The therapist and client work together to understand the onset and causes of depression by discussing childhood experiences and repressed feelings. Psychodynamic therapy can be effective for severely depressed patients, especially when combined with antidepressants.

## GROUP THERAPIES

In the following therapy models, more than one person works with a therapist or group leader. These therapies emphasize the "unit" rather than the individual and can be very effective in treating certain types of depression.

### Family Therapy

Instead of dealing with just one person, as in traditional psychotherapy, family therapy treats the family as a unit and aims to change the way members relate to each other. Depression is considered an expression of not merely one person but of a dysfunctional family. This type of therapy may be helpful in treating depression in instances where a person's depression is caused by a serious family problem (for example, marital discord or a partner's alcoholism) or where a person's depression jeopardizes family relationships.

Family therapy focuses on breaking destructive cycles of behavior, improving communication among family members, and finding more effective ways of coping with stressful family situations. It also explores ways family members can better support each other and work toward common goals, while maintaining a sense of individual independence. Although one person's depression may be the impetus for therapy, other family members should be prepared to examine their lives and behaviors, too.

Some therapists include children as young as four years old in family therapy sessions; others prefer to wait until children are at least nine or ten. Anyone living in your home may take part, including elderly parents or nonrelatives who play important roles in your family life.

Models of family therapy range from a psychoanalytic approach that examines unconscious conflicts to a behavioral approach directed toward changing family behavior patterns through positive and negative reinforcement. The most recent family therapy models were developed by Nathan Ackerman (considered the father of family therapy), Jay Haley, Virginia Satir, and others.

Ackerman was the first to suggest that therapists should actively participate and shake things up by moving the family out of predictable patterns of behavior and responding. Several interactive techniques are used, such as role reversal, in which individuals switch roles with other family members and act out a typical problem situation. Role reversal can teach communication and problem-solving skills, help people deal better with conflict, and enhance empathy.

Variations on family therapy include "network family therapy," where friends, neighbors, or even employers are involved in sessions, and "multiple family therapy," where several families meet as a group.

The length of family therapy varies. Brief therapy may take place in three to 10 sessions. In longer-term therapy, patients usually see a therapist once a week for six to eight weeks, then check back every month or two for several months. Sessions usually last an hour and a half. This therapy won't be effective unless all family members are open and cooperative. Depressed people may also require individual therapy to work on other, specific issues.

## Couples or Marriage Therapy

Like family therapy, couples or marriage therapy focuses on the family unit rather than an individual. If depression is straining your relationship to the breaking point, or if conflicts at home are causing depression, both you and your partner may benefit from couples therapy. As in family therapy, the objective of couples therapy is to confront problems, discuss underlying issues, and find better ways to resolve conflicts and relate to each other. During a session, the therapist brings up sensitive issues that you and your partner usually avoid or argue over. He may use role-playing and staged interactions to show you constructive, direct ways to express your feelings instead of destructive, covert ways like giving the silent treatment. He may even prompt one partner to do something that especially bothers the other—which, surprisingly, can prompt that person to understand his own annoying traits and change his behavior.

Couples therapy is usually held for one hour, once a week. Minor problems can be resolved in as few as three to eight sessions; major problems may take up to a year. If problems aren't resolved after a year, the couple may not be fully committed to improving the relationship, and this type of therapy may not be appropriate. On the other hand, if partners are confused about what they want from their relationship, individual therapy to explore personal goals may be preferable.

## Group Therapy

Although it's a popular form of psychotherapy, group therapy isn't recommended for a severely depressed person whose low self-esteem and low energy level prevent him from actively participating in conversation. However, once antidepressants or individual therapy begin to relieve depression, a sympathetic group where you can openly share your feelings can be a very effective way to gain a greater acceptance of yourself, learn more effective ways to cope, and find support in difficult times.

Group therapy often consists of six to 10 people meeting weekly for an hour and a half. It may continue for a predetermined amount of time, go on indefinitely, or break up when members lose interest. Participants are chosen by the therapist, and although they must all have the same goal for the group to work, they don't necessarily need to have the same problems. Mixed groups (different ages, sexes, and problems) more closely reflect the real world. Homogeneous groups (alcoholics, depressed people, couples) make it easier to share experiences.

The therapist sets the ground rules, guides discussions, and resolves conflicts. Some therapists remain neutral, while others actively promote group interaction. Members are encouraged to be frank and spontaneous. With time, they see how their patterns of interacting with others might help or hurt them in relationships outside the group.

Group therapy is especially helpful for depressed people who have concurrent problems like substance abuse or eating disorders. It can also be much less expensive than individual therapy, and sessions last twice as long. The downside is that depressed people can't focus on their own problems for the entire session (although each member is given some time to talk). Therefore, many people in group therapy choose to see an individual therapist concurrently.

## Child Therapy

When exploring depression in young children, therapists don't rely on the same approaches they use with adults. That's because children often lack the vocabulary to express their feelings adequately and may be too intimidated by adults to talk openly. Therapists must also avoid being viewed as disciplinarians.

Play therapy was developed to give children a nonthreatening way to express their feelings. The therapist uses games, dolls, and drawings to let the child express himself in safe, familiar ways, and to vent painful emotions, troubling feelings, or conflicts. Feelings such as anger, jealousy, or rejection pop out. The therapist then encourages the child to act out conflicts with puppets or other toys in an attempt to help him understand his depression and work on appropriate ways of expressing feelings. Children are usually more verbal by the age of 10 and can begin individual psychotherapy in addition to play therapy.

For depressed older children and adolescents, group therapy with kids their own age can be extremely useful in dealing with feelings of alienation, isolation, and social acceptance. At this age, children are more likely to reveal problems to, and accept solutions from, a peer group rather than an authority figure like a parent or therapist.

Often parents are asked to participate in the child's therapy. The child's problems may be related to the home situation and the way family members interact. Family therapy may also be recommended, because the child's depression may be a reflection of family stress or other difficulties, and because other family members may be feeling frustration, guilt, anger, or depression about the child's problem. Going to therapy together lets the child know how much his family cares about him and how his behavior affects others.

## SUPPORT GROUPS

Support groups are sometimes called the "lay person's group therapy." They're more informal than group therapy and usually focus on a single problem, such as alcoholism, eating disorders, or depression. Three well known support groups are Alcoholics Anonymous, Overeaters Anonymous, and Weight Watchers. There are also support groups specifically for people with depression. See the resource list at the back of this book for contact information.

Support groups can be predominantly an open discussion among members, or they can have a structured format where, for example, guest speakers present information on subjects like stress management or relationship building. They may have a permanent leader, or members may take turns performing this role. If you're depressed, joining a support group may help you turn a negative aspect of your life into a positive learning experience. As you share your frustrations and grief and offer support to others, you develop dignity, compassion, and a sense of cooperation and community. Support groups are especially helpful for people with limited family support. They're also a valuable source of information for such things as therapist referrals and tips on managing stress and depression.

Internet chat rooms are a new type of support group. They can be a lifeline for depressed people who are housebound because of illnesses or fear. Some depression chat rooms are legitimate; others are not. When in doubt, ask a mental health professional to recommend an online chat room. Some of the larger Internet support groups are included in the resource list at the back of this book.

## OTHER FORMS OF COUNSELING

Many depressed people have a variety of practical problems that need to be addressed before they can get their lives in order. These problems can contribute to depression or vice versa—it's a vicious cycle. For example, you may forget to pay your bills because you're depressed, then when you begin feeling better, realize that your credit rating is ruined. Or you may spend money frivolously, then feel depressed when you realize you've maxed out your credit cards. If financial problems are contributing to your depression, financial counseling can help you regain control, make a budget, and come up with a plan to repay your debts.

Career counseling can help you assess your interests and skills, restructure your resume, get some professional or technical training, and prepare for job interviews.

If you are overeating or undereating, which commonly occurs with depression, nutritional counseling can help you set up a healthy nutritional program. Read more about the role of nutrition in depression in Chapters 8 and 9.

## FINDING THE RIGHT THERAPIST

Studies have shown that the type of therapy a clinician uses is less important than the relationship between the therapist and client. Selecting a therapist is a very individual matter, but getting referrals from your physician, close friends, or family members is the best place to start. Word-of-mouth referrals allow you to get firsthand information about the therapist's style and approach to care. If you're not ready to discuss your depression openly, you can get a referral through a more anonymous source, such as a professional or community agency. For more options on finding referrals, see Chapter 3.

Not all licensed health professionals will be covered by your insurance plan. Check with your insurance carrier before beginning treatment. It's very difficult to begin treatment and then be told that your insurance won't pay for a therapist whom you've grown to trust and depend on.

Although techniques differ, all competent mental health professionals should do the following:

- Make an effort to know you well enough to make sense of your symptoms and your personality
- Provide a secure, reliable environment where you can share intimate details of your life without feeling belittled or embarrassed
- Uphold your confidentiality. Bear in mind, however, that many therapists are legally or ethically bound to report cases of suspected or admitted child abuse, elder abuse, and a client's threats of violence toward him- or herself or others.

## PSYCHIATRIST

A psychiatrist is a medical doctor with specialized training in diagnosing and treating mental illness. Psychiatrists are also knowledgeable about other illnesses, can prescribe antidepressants and other types of medication, and can prescribe procedures such as electroconvulsive therapy (ECT).

Because psychiatrists may specialize in one particular type of therapy, such as psychoanalysis, you'll need to ask about this before making an appointment. Your primary-care physician may refer you to a psychiatrist if you have severe depression that interferes with daily functioning, if you have suicidal thoughts, or if the antidepressants or other drugs she's prescribed haven't improved your condition in several months.

## CLINICAL PSYCHOLOGIST

A clinical psychologist has a doctoral degree in psychology and several years of postgraduate training, including at least two years of clinical training with clients. Psychologists must be licensed by a state board in order to practice, which involves taking a lengthy examination. They also keep up with new developments by taking continuing education courses geared to clinical work. Psychologists aren't M.D.'s, so they can't prescribe medication. However, they can do biofeedback, hypnosis, and all types of talk therapy.

Of all the mental health professionals, clinical psychologists have typically taken the most course work in understanding behavior and intervening for behavioral change, making them the best trained professionals to treat depression with talk therapies.

## Clinical Social Worker

Clinical social workers usually have a master's degree in social work and are certified by the national Academy of Certified Social Workers. They're trained to provide intervention in crisis situations and are capable of offering psychotherapy to mild- to moderately-depressed patients. They may also use biofeedback, hypnotherapy, and other techniques. Their expertise depends on where they received their training, what their casework involved, and how many continuing education courses they've taken.

## Psychiatric Nurse

Psychiatric nurses are registered nurses who usually have a master's degree in psychiatric nursing. They can provide psychotherapy and may also counsel patients who are hospitalized for reasons other than mental illness, such as cancer, heart disease, or stroke. Psychiatric nurses often work with depressed elderly patients, developing long-term therapeutic relationships. They may work in hospitals or in outpatient settings, such as hospices or drug rehabilitation programs. In some states, psychiatric nurses are licensed and can set up a private practice.

## Marriage Therapist or Family Therapist

A marriage therapist or family therapist has a graduate degree in social work, psychology, or family therapy and is certified by the American Association for Marriage and Family Therapy. These practitioners work with families or couples when depression is rooted in or affecting family dynamics.

## PASTORAL COUNSELORS

Aside from the standard training involved in becoming a chaplain, pastor, or priest, some choose to take advanced training to become more effective counselors. A deep understanding of spiritual beliefs and how they affect health gives pastoral counselors an advantage over other types of counselors, especially when spiritual concerns are playing a role in someone's depression. While visits to pastoral counselors are generally not covered by health insurance, the Denver-based Sloans Lake health plan is an example of an innovative insurance plan that does cover these services through a spiritual care benefit for its members.

## PRIMARY-CARE PHYSICIAN

Besides treating your medical conditions, your primary-care physician or family doctor can diagnose depression and treat mild-to-moderate cases with medication, monitor drug effects, and also recommend self-help measures. Although a physician can offer support and encouragement, he or she isn't likely to have the time or training to counsel patients. Your physician can be a big help, though, by referring you to qualified therapists.

## SHOP AROUND

Once you've identified several potential therapists, do some comparison shopping. Call their offices and ask to speak to each therapist briefly, on the phone or in person. Here are some key questions to ask:

- Are you experienced in treating depression?
- How long have you been in practice?
- What is your training and where did you receive it?
- Do you have advanced training in any area?
- Do you use a particular approach to psychotherapy? Why?
- Do you work mostly with individuals, groups, families, or couples?
- What is your typical treatment plan for a depressed patient?
- Do you prescribe antidepressant drugs? For what percentage of patients?
- How long does therapy typically last?
- How often will we meet and how long will each session be?
- What are your office hours?
- Where are you located? Do you have any other offices?
- Are you affiliated with a hospital or teaching institution?
- Do you charge for the initial meeting?
- What is the cost of therapy per session?
- What insurance plans do you accept?

Asking these questions also gives you some idea of the therapist's listening skills, his level of empathy, and how well you interact with him or her. You may be working with this person for many months, so you need to find out if the two of you are compatible.

If you belong to an HMO or other health plan that only reimburses for treatment received from participating providers, ask them for a directory of approved providers for you to choose from. Ask your family doctor, friends, and family if they're familiar with any of the names on the list. Then contact them to see which one best suits you.

Making the decision to participate in therapy can be a difficult one. After functioning a certain way for many years, it's hard to learn new ways of thinking, modify your behavior, or change the way you act in important relationships. The emotions and feelings stirred up during psychotherapy are often difficult to deal with and may upset you for a while. But before long, you'll see that changing your way of thinking and responding to stress and other situations can make an enormous difference in your quality of life. Finding the right therapist to guide you through this process is half the battle.

# 7

## Antidepressants and Other Medical Interventions

Despite tremendous discoveries in the last two decades, scientists don't fully understand how imbalances in neurotransmitters cause the symptoms of depression. They also aren't sure whether changes in neurotransmitters are a cause of depression or a result. They do agree, however, that severe depression creates a vicious cycle that must be broken quickly with aggressive treatment.

Without treatment, serious depression can last up to a year or longer. Your gloom-and-doom mood will follow you around like a perpetual black cloud, siphoning off your energy, flattening your emotions and sensory perceptions, coloring your relationships, and draining all the joy out of life. Without treatment, you also boost the odds for another, perhaps even more serious, depressive episode down the road.

In this chapter we'll take a look at the various antidepressants available, learn how they work, understand how your doctor chooses the right one for you, and explain their possible side effects and interactions with other drugs. We'll also discuss other more aggressive medical options that are available in those cases of prolonged or intractable depression that do not respond to either conventional medical or CAM treatments.

## THE CHOICE IS YOURS

Antidepressant medications have revolutionized the treatment of depression by providing hope and fast, lasting relief to millions of depressed people. These medications may be used alone—or more often in combination with talk therapy and other nondrug interventions—to stop depression and prevent it from returning by restoring the natural balance and function of various neurotransmitters (usually serotonin, norepinephrine, and/or dopamine).

But antidepressants are not for everyone. As effective as they've been for many people, for others they're of little help, or carry a heavy price tag in the form of intolerable side effects.

While antidepressants seem like magic when they work, they are, at best, a hit-or-miss proposition. Each person's depression—and the factors leading up to it—represents a unique case. What worked for your sister or coworker or friend may or may not work for you. Even an antidepressant that worked wonders for you last year may prove useless or even counterproductive if depression returns.

Only a medical doctor—for example, your family physician or a psychiatrist—can prescribe antidepressants. Your physician will strongly recommend these drugs if you have moderate-to-severe depression that will probably worsen or linger without drugs, or if you appear to be at high risk for suicide. He or she will make the recommendation based on your symptoms, your laboratory test results, and perhaps the recommendation of your psychotherapist. Still, the choice is ultimately yours, so along with the likely benefits of such therapy, the doctor will discuss possible side effects and other issues to help you make an informed decision. He or she will probably also explain that years of clinical experience with millions of patients have proven that antidepressants are safe and nonaddictive. He or she will also reassure you that antidepressant medication isn't a sign of weakness or being "crazy," but rather a sign that you recognize that you have a treatable medical condition.

## Overcoming Objections

Some groups oppose the use of antidepressants for philosophical or religious reasons. To these groups, I would say that there are times when our biochemistry, genetics, or physiology gets in the way of self-help or faith-based approaches. When this occurs, medication is both rational and compassionate. Philosophy and religion should serve the best interests of suffering humanity and not vice versa.

To tell someone that they're having problems because they aren't trying hard enough or their faith isn't strong enough only causes guilt and greater depression. Sometimes we just can't pull ourselves up by our bootstraps. On the other hand, our national obsession for a "quick fix" or "magic pill" is also unrealistic and should be avoided in the treatment of any illness, including depression.

## HOW ANTIDEPRESSANTS WORK

We don't know exactly how antidepressants work, but that's true for many categories of drugs. What we do know is that antidepressants regulate the brain's mood centers, which are composed of brain cells or neurons. Neurotransmitters are chemicals that allow neurons to relay information to each other. The main neurotransmitters—serotonin, dopamine, and norepinephrine—tell the brain to do things like relax, get excited, and flee or fight. They exist in gaps called synapses, where nerve impulses jump from one neuron to another.

Sometimes, one or more of these chemicals is absorbed from within the synapses—a process called reuptake. Reuptake or breakdown of the neurotransmitters is normal and prevents overstimulation of the nerve cells. On the other hand, if the levels of neurotransmitters in the synapse are low (from low production or excessive breakdown), then communication between neurons in the brain's mood centers is impaired, and depression can be the result. Antidepressant medications bring the amount of neurotransmitters back up to healthy levels, either by inhibiting reuptake, boosting production, or preventing breakdown, thereby regulating mood and alleviating depression.

## FINDING THE RIGHT ANTIDEPRESSANT

Finding the appropriate drug to treat your depression can be easy or challenging for you and your doctor. In order for any antidepressant to help you, it has to bring *your* particular brain chemistry closer to a healthy balance. Every person's biochemistry is unique and every antidepressant on the market works slightly differently, with its own set of potential side effects and interactions with other drugs. Since doctors cannot analyze your brain directly, they rely on a combination of indirect laboratory tests, mental health assessments, educated guesses, and just plain luck to find the best drug for you. You may feel better with the first antidepressant you try, or you may have to try a number of medications, each for several weeks or months, before landing on something effective.

When choosing an antidepressant, you and your doctor will consider several factors, such as:

- The drug's potential side effects
- What side effects you say you're willing to tolerate
- What other prescription and over-the-counter drugs you're taking

- How you've reacted to various drugs in the past
- Your overall health and other medical problems

Be sure to tell the doctor if you've had an allergic reaction to a certain antidepressant in the past—he obviously won't prescribe that one again. Also tell him if you have heart problems, high blood pressure, or a history of stroke, so he won't prescribe monoamine oxidase inhibitors (MAOIs), which can aggravate these conditions. Antidepressants should be used cautiously with the following conditions: allergies to other drugs, impotence, chronic constipation, diarrhea, seizures, glaucoma, urinary retention or neurogenic bladder, overactive thyroid, dizziness or orthostatic hypotension (getting dizzy when you stand up due to a drop in blood pressure), bipolar disorder, heart arrhythmias, and liver disease.

Also inform the doctor if you have any of the following conditions, which may also be helped by antidepressants: migraine headaches; panic disorder, obsessive-compulsive disorder, and other anxiety disorders; bulimia; chronic pain; irritable bowel syndrome; fibromyalgia; and Parkinson's disease.

Reactions to antidepressants vary considerably, so try not to be discouraged if the first drug you take doesn't agree with you. Some people have few side effects; others have severe ones. If you don't get better on one drug or you have severe side effects, your doctor will try another or a combination of drugs until he finds one that works for you.

Although media attention has focused on newer drugs that have fewer side effects, the older tricyclic antidepressants and MAOIs are just as effective and are still useful weapons against depression, especially in people who don't improve on the newer medications.

## What to Ask Your Doctor

After your physician recommends an antidepressant, he or she will discuss side effects and other details with you. Be sure the doctor answers the following questions:

- What dose of the drug do I take and when do I take it?
- How long do I need to take the drug?
- Should I take it with food?
- What are the possible side effects? Will it affect my sleep? Will I have more or even less energy? Will it affect my sex life? Will it make me gain or lose weight? Will it make me drowsy?
- Is it okay to take other medicines or supplements along with this drug?
- Will this drug improve or worsen my other medical conditions?
- When should I start feeling better?
- What should I do if I don't feel any better?
- When is my next office visit?

Your pharmacist can answer any lingering questions when you get your prescription filled. Most pharmacies also provide detailed written instructions with each prescription. Of course, don't hesitate to call your doctor's office to ask questions or discuss problems.

# WHAT'S AVAILABLE IN ANTIDEPRESSANTS?

More than 20 effective antidepressants are now on the market. Each differs in how it works, what side effects it may produce, and how it may interact with other drugs. Although newer drugs like Prozac have been touted as "wonder drugs" and have received a great deal of publicity, research shows that *all* antidepressants on the market alleviate the symptoms of depression, although some have more side effects and risks than others. In all, 60 to 80 percent of people with moderate-to-severe depression improve after several months if they use the drug that's been prescribed as directed.

The four main classes of antidepressants are:

- Monoamine oxidase inhibitors (MAOIs)
- Tricyclic antidepressants (TCAs)
- Selective serotonin reuptake inhibitors (SSRIs)
- Atypical antidepressants

Each class of antidepressants has its own unique characteristics, side effects, and cautions.

## MONOAMINE OXIDASE INHIBITORS (MAOIS)

MAOIs were the first antidepressants developed by medical researchers in the 1950s. Initially, they were used in treating tuberculosis, but they proved to be much more useful for elevating patients' moods. MAOIs work by inhibiting the production of the enzyme monoamine oxidase, which breaks down serotonin, epinephrine, and norepinephrine in the synaptic space between neurons. This increases the amount of neurotransmitters at the synapses and alleviates depression.

Unfortunately, inhibiting monoamine oxidase can also cause life-threatening side effects. Why? Because the body needs this enzyme to metabolize tyramine, a substance found in many foods, and to metabolize sympathomimetic amines, substances found in many over-the-counter decongestants, cold remedies, allergy drugs, and appetite suppressants. When these substances go unmetabolized, blood pressure can rise to dangerously high levels, and severe headache, nausea and vomiting, irregular heartbeat, stroke, and even death may occur.

For this reason, people on MAOIs must not take medications containing sympathomimetic amines. In fact, they should check with their doctor before taking *any* other medications, because several drugs, including Novocain, Demerol, and other antidepressants also interact adversely with MAOIs.

They must also avoid the following:

- All cheese except cottage cheese and cream cheese
- Beer, red wine (especially Chianti), vermouth, whiskey, liqueurs, nonalcoholic beer and wine
- Soybeans, fava beans, bean curd
- Smoked, fermented, aged, or pickled fish
- Ginseng, St. John's wort, and 5-HTP
- Sauerkraut
- Shrimp paste

- Aged or processed meats, such as bologna, sausage, and salami; meat or protein extracts; soups containing these extracts
- Yeast extract or brewer's yeast (yeast used in baking is okay)

Foods that may be safely eaten only in small amounts include white wine and port, caffeine, chocolate, dairy products, nuts, raspberries, and spinach.

Because of these risks, MAOIs are seldom used today, except in people who've tried all the other classes of antidepressants without success. Even then, you must be highly motivated and extremely conscientious. Nardil (phenelzine), Parnate (tranylcypromine), and Marplan (isocarboxazid) are the most commonly prescribed drugs. They should never be given to patients with high blood pressure, heart disease, or a history of stroke. Other side effects include fainting, headache, muscle twitching, dizziness, tremors, confusion, memory impairment, weakness, anxiety, agitation, drowsiness, blurred vision, and heart palpitations.

## TRICYCLIC ANTIDEPRESSANTS (TCAs)

Also developed in the 1950s, tricyclic antidepressants were originally given to schizophrenics. Although the drugs failed to improve symptoms of that disease, they did improve the mood of depressed patients. TCAs also stimulate appetite, increase activity levels, and help people sleep. These drugs—which include Tofranil (imipramine), Norpramin (desipramine), Sinequan (doxepin), Pamelor (nortriptyline), and Elavil (amitriptyline)—inhibit the reuptake of neurotransmitters, keeping the levels of these chemicals higher than usual in the synapses and thus relieving depression.

At one time, TCAs were the treatment of choice for depression. But although they cause fewer problems than MAOIs, they can still be dangerous in certain patients. They aren't recommended for people with glaucoma and should be used cautiously by anyone with seizures, hyperthyroidism, or urinary retention. They can also cause abnormal heart rhythms, so they're not given to elderly patients or those with heart disease. Some patients may need an EKG before starting treatment. The drugs should be used with caution by people with liver and kidney disease because they are metabolized in the liver and excreted by the kidneys.

One major drawback of TCAs is that overdoses may be fatal. Because many depressed people are potentially suicidal, doctors are often hesitant to prescribe these drugs. Other potential side effects include dry mouth, nausea, drowsiness, vomiting, blurred vision, constipation, dizziness, anxiety, nervousness, restlessness, nightmares or sleepiness, headache, fatigue, irritability, confusion, constipation, hair loss, mood swings, impotence, difficulty urinating, and increased heart rate. Because TCAs affect the salivary glands and cause dry mouth, gum disease and dental problems can occur. The drugs may also reduce tearing in the eyes, causing problems for people who wear soft contact lenses. Consult your physician immediately if you are using TCAs and experience seizures, tremors, difficulty breathing, fever, loss of bladder control, elevated blood pressure, unusual muscle stiffness, fatigue, or weakness.

TCAs may cause fatal reactions (seizures and stroke) if taken with MAOIs. In addition, toxic blood levels of TCAs can occur if they're taken along with antiarrhythmic drugs like Rythmol, because these drugs decrease the liver's ability to break down TCAs. Many people complain of feeling "hung over" or overly sedated with the TCAs. The use of TCAs, and the resulting dizziness or orthostatic hypotension, is a common cause of falls and hip fractures in elderly patients.

## SELECTIVE SEROTONIN REUPTAKE INHIBITORS (SSRIs)

When SSRIs were introduced in the late 1980s, they revolutionized the treatment of depression. They act more specifically than other types of antidepressants, blocking the reuptake of the neurotransmitter serotonin by the adjacent nerve cells. Commonly prescribed SSRIs include Prozac (fluoxitene), Zoloft (sertraline), Celexa (citalopram), and Paxil (paroxetine).

SSRIs have become the preferred treatment for depression because they cause fewer and more tolerable side effects and are safer than MAOIs and TCAs. Nevertheless, the side effects do present significant problems for some people and can include nausea, headache, insomnia, tremor, sexual dysfunction, dry mouth, dizziness, constipation, drowsiness, nervousness, sweating, weakness, loss of appetite, and weight loss. Minor side effects like nausea or lightheadedness usually last only a few weeks.

One major side effect is sexual dysfunction. Forty to 50 percent of people taking SSRIs complain of sexual dysfunction, including the inability to reach orgasm, erection problems, loss of lubrication in women, and decreased libido. Sleep problems are also particularly bothersome. Patients feel tired because their sleep is constantly interrupted by "micro-awakenings" throughout the night. This can be dealt with by taking your medication early in the day. On the other hand, if these drugs make you drowsy, take them before bedtime.

SSRIs can be lethal if combined with MAOIs. SSRIs also shouldn't be taken with TCAs, antipsychotic drugs, or anticonvulsant drugs because they inhibit the liver's ability to metabolize these drugs, causing SSRIs to build up in the blood in toxic levels. If St. John's wort is combined with SSRIs, a dangerous condition called serotonin syndrome can develop.

## ATYPICAL ANTIDEPRESSANTS

Atypical antidepressants don't fit into any category. They work in a variety of different ways to inhibit the breakdown or reuptake of selective neurotransmitters and seem to act in a similar way to TCAs and SSRIs. Some of the best known drugs include Wellbutrin (buproprion), Serzone (nefazodone), Remeron (mirtazapine), Effexor (venlafaxine), and Desyrel (trazodone).

All of these drugs can produce a number of side effects, including drowsiness, dizziness, weight gain or weight loss, increased or decreased appetite, constipation, nausea, and dry mouth. Remeron and Serzone are preferred by some because they rarely cause sexual dysfunction or worsen sleep problems. A disadvantage of Desyrel and Serzone is the risk of priapism—an extremely painful, sustained erection. Remeron can raise cholesterol.

Wellbutrin can cause severe adverse reactions if taken with MAOIs; it can also cause seizures, especially when combined with alcohol. This drug can affect the results of certain diagnostic and lab tests. For example, it may cause abnormalities on an EKG and a drop in white blood cells on a blood test. Another form of this drug, called Zyban, is used to help people quit smoking.

## SOME WORDS OF CAUTION

When taking any antidepressant, keep these precautions in mind:

- Don't drink alcohol. It can worsen your depression, and antidepressants can increase alcohol's intoxicating effects. Some drugs may also cause seizures when combined with alcohol.
- Remember that most antidepressants can cause drowsiness or dizziness. Avoid driving, operating machinery, or doing anything that requires alertness until you know how the drug will affect you.

- Don't take any other prescription or over-the-counter drugs without first consulting your doctor. If you recently stopped taking St. John's wort or another herbal preparation, inform your doctor before you begin antidepressant therapy.

- Tell your doctor if you're pregnant, breast-feeding, or planning to become pregnant. Contact him immediately if you become pregnant while taking antidepressants.

- Stay out of the sun if you're taking a TCA. Wear a sunscreen and protective clothing to avoid a photosensitivity reaction (rash and skin blotches).

- Consult your doctor if you develop signs of an allergic reaction to the drug, such as hives, itching, a rash, or any other unusual symptoms.

- Keep in mind that antidepressants don't magically change your personality or your life. They only help you recover from depression.

- Elderly people may need lower doses of antidepressants because the drugs aren't cleared from their systems as easily. Older adults are also more prone to drug interactions because they often take many other drugs.

## Depressed and Expecting?

If you're pregnant, thinking about getting pregnant in the near future, or think you might become pregnant while you're on antidepressants, discuss this with your doctor as soon as possible. Using antidepressants during pregnancy can harm the fetus. In fact, it's wise to talk to your doctor before you take *any medication* during pregnancy, including herbal remedies, vitamins, and other dietary supplements.

Understandably, it may be very difficult for a woman with recurrent depression or bipolar disorder to go nine months without drug therapy. Even withholding medication for three months may be a problem. You and your doctor will decide whether the potential benefits to you justify the risk to the fetus. If your bipolar disorder is so acute that you might endanger your own life and, consequently, the life of your unborn baby, or if you're so depressed that you can't eat or if you begin to use alcohol or drugs, the best plan may be to continue your antidepressant therapy.

The safest treatments for depression during pregnancy are psychotherapy and acupuncture, ideally in conjunction with exercise, sound nutrition, stress reduction techniques, socialization, journaling, and other lifestyle strategies.

You should also realize that the postpartum period carries with it a higher than normal risk of depression, even for mothers with no previous history of depression. Be alert to symptoms that could signal the onset of a depression. Also keep in mind that most antidepressant drugs do appear in breastmilk, so breastfeeding isn't advised if you're taking antidepressants for postpartum depression.

# FINDING THE RIGHT DOSE

Once you and your doctor decide which antidepressant is probably best for you, he or she will prescribe a starting dosage. The goal is to give the smallest dose that will relieve your symptoms without causing side effects. Therefore, you may be started on a very low dose to avoid major side effects, then instructed to gradually increase the medication until you reach the target dose—the amount known to be most effective in easing depression.

Because some drugs work faster than others, your doctor will tell you approximately when you should expect to feel some relief. Usually, the first symptoms to improve are your sleeping and eating patterns (overeating or lack of appetite). Family members may notice your improved mood before you do. Most drugs don't reach their full effect for six weeks, but you should feel some improvement in two to three weeks. If you don't, contact your doctor because your dose may need adjustment. Never increase the dosage on your own—you can intensify the drug's side effects or even give yourself an overdose. Psychotherapy can also help "tide you over" until your antidepressant starts working.

Once you achieve a "complete clinical response" (you no longer feel depressed), the doctor may continue drug therapy for several more months. The duration of therapy depends on many factors. For example, if you respond well to drug therapy, don't have a prior or family history of depression, and the factors that triggered your depression have been addressed and resolved (usually through psychotherapy), then the doctor will probably wean you off antidepressants after four to six months.

You may need antidepressants for a year or two if you have recurrent major depression, ongoing stress, or a strong family history of depression. Your first episode of major depression leaves you with a 50 percent chance of becoming seriously depressed again in the next five years. After a second episode, you have a 70 percent chance of becoming depressed again within the same five-year period, and after a third episode you have a 90 percent chance. Patients with recurring depression may continue antidepressant therapy indefinitely.

When first-line antidepressants (usually SSRIs like Prozac) don't work, your doctor may try combining drugs or switching to another class of drugs, such as TCAs or, as a last resort, MAOIs. While these drugs can be effective, they also have significantly more side effects.

If you're changing medications, your doctor may have you go through a "washout" period first—a time when you take no antidepressants at all. For example, MAOIs cause dangerous interactions with other drugs, so if you stop taking them you may have to wait several weeks before starting another drug. The reverse also applies.

When you and your doctor agree that you no longer need medication, he or she will generally reduce the dosage gradually to prevent a discontinuation reaction. Common withdrawal effects can include dizziness, headaches, sleep disturbance, flu-like symptoms (such as nausea, vomiting, or diarrhea), and a recurrence of depression.

## Drugs That Treat Bipolar Disorder

If you have bipolar disorder, antidepressants will not be useful in treating the depressive cycle of your illness. In fact, they can make matters worse by causing a rapid shift into mania or by increasing the frequency of cycling between depression and mania. The treatment of choice for maintaining a stabilized mood is Lithobid (lithium), with antidepressants taken only during your depressive episodes.

Lithium is nonsedating, nonaddictive, and apparently can be taken indefinitely without harmful effects. But it can be a difficult drug to take. Early side effects include nausea, vomiting, diarrhea, stomachache, hand tremors, thirst, frequent urination, fatigue, muscle weakness, and a dazed feeling. Luckily, most of these side effects disappear. Although hand tremors, thirst, and increased urination may persist, they can be treated with other drugs or by adjusting the lithium dosage. Some patients also gain weight, and a few develop hypothyroidism (underactive thyroid) or short-term memory loss.

Blood lithium levels are monitored periodically while taking this medications. Too little lithium can be ineffective; slightly too much is toxic.

Drinking a lot of tea or coffee can lower lithium levels, and some medications, such as antibiotics and anti-inflammatory drugs like Advil and Motrin, can increase lithium levels. Anything that lowers the sodium level in your body can cause lithium to build up to toxic levels—for example, perspiring heavily from exercise or a fever or switching to a low-salt diet.

Signs of lithium toxicity include fatigue, sleepiness, confusion, muscle weakness, limb heaviness, slurred speech, worsening hand tremor, unsteady gait, jaw tremor, muscle twitches, upset stomach, and ringing in the ears.

Other drugs that are being tried for bipolar disorder include Tegretol and Depakote, which have been used for years to control epileptic seizures. They aren't good at alleviating depression, but they do a great job of preventing depression and mania from recurring. Initial side effects of Tegretol include dizziness, drowsiness, unsteady gait, confusion, headaches, double vision, nausea, diarrhea, and rash—but these usually disappear over time. A rare but more serious side effect is a reduction in the number of red and white blood cells. The drug also interferes with birth control pills, so women on Tegretol should use another method of contraception.

Depakote has fewer, milder side effects, including drowsiness, indigestion, nausea, and vomiting. Liver damage is rare, but possible.

## OTHER MEDICAL OPTIONS

If antidepressants, psychotherapy, and/or CAM approaches do not manage your depression effectively—or if your depression is so severe at the time of diagnosis that you pose a danger to yourself or others—your doctor may try some of the other medical treatments.

## HOSPITALIZATION

In most cases, even severely depressed patients can safely be treated at home with medication, ideally supplemented by psychotherapy. However, hospitalization may be recommended for certain individuals who:

- Attempt or threaten suicide
- Attempt or threaten to harm another person
- Show extreme apathy, to the point that they are unable to perform simple activities such as eating, washing, and getting dressed
- Show severe agitation or psychosis
- Need complicated antidepressant therapy that requires close monitoring
- Also have another medical condition, such as diabetes or heart disease, that requires medication or medical attention

Depressed patients may be admitted to a public or private psychiatric hospital or the psychiatric unit of a general hospital. On a typical unit, patients eat in a common dining room, and patients and staff dress in street clothes. Treatment varies, with some hospitals being more medically and others more psychotherapeutically oriented. Most hospitals, however, follow the same standard procedures.

The patient is examined by a psychiatrist, family doctor, or internist to rule out any medical problems that may affect personality. A psychologist administers tests to gain insight into the patient's personality and suggest physical illnesses that might affect personality. Several different types of psychotherapy are offered every day. These may include individual, group, recreational, educational, art, movement or dance, vocational, and family therapy. The patient sees a variety of therapists at several therapy sessions each day, usually three to five times a week. Just being in the psychiatric unit ("milieu therapy") can be therapeutic because patients can support each other by sharing their thoughts and feelings.

Most people hospitalized for depression stay in the hospital about two weeks. Unfortunately, because of managed care and third-party payments, many depressed patients are discharged before treatment is complete. Few people can afford to stay on to complete treatment when hospitals charge up to $1,000 or more per day. Check with your insurance carrier to see how much of inpatient care your policy covers.

## ELECTROCONVULSIVE THERAPY

Electroconvulsive therapy or ECT has been used for more than 50 years to treat serious, unresponsive depression. Today, "shock treatments" are usually a last resort for severely depressed and/or suicidal patients who need immediate intervention and can't risk waiting three weeks for antidepressants to start working. ECT also offers fairly quick relief for patients with acute mania or elderly patients who can't take or don't respond to antidepressants.

During ECT, an electrical current passed through the patient's head causes a brief seizure, changes the brain's chemistry, and temporarily alleviates symptoms of depression. Before the procedure, the patient is sedated and anesthetized to temporarily paralyze the muscles so he won't move during the seizure. (The seizure is detected on an EEG or by watching for faint neurological signs such as goose bumps on the skin.) Although thousands of studies have been done, experts still aren't sure exactly how ECT works. It may affect the same neurotransmitters as antidepressants do, or it may activate endorphins, opiate-like chemicals that elevate mood.

ECT is rapid and effective in about 80 percent of patients. The main side effect is short-term memory loss, which is almost always restricted to events immediately surrounding the ECT and is usually temporary. Less than one-half of one percent of patients suffer severe, permanent memory loss. Dry mouth, headache, muscle stiffness, and confusion also occur immediately after treatments but go away within an hour. Studies show that ECT doesn't cause anatomical damage to the brain; however, it's unclear whether brain cells and neurotransmitters, which control learning and memory, are damaged.

Most patients need six to 10 treatments, two or three times a week. Some patients never need more than the first course of treatment; others need a few maintenance treatments periodically to prevent depression from recurring. However, depression almost always comes back unless antidepressants are used concurrently. ECT is just as effective as lithium in treating acute mania, but patients need to take lithium afterward to avoid relapse.

Research on ECT is ongoing, but for the most part, the procedure remains frightening and controversial because of movies like *One Flew Over the Cuckoo's Nest*, which showed ECT being used as punishment, and because of other misinformation.

## CINGULOTOMY

Cingulotomy is a treatment of last resort for patients with severe, life-threatening depression who haven't responded to multiple medications, psychotherapy, or even ECT. It is a brain surgery that severs fibers deep in the frontal lobe between the cingulate gyrus and the limbic system, areas of the brain that control emotions and mood. The procedure is performed very rarely and only in a few research hospitals.

Although cingulotomy doesn't noticeably affect intellectual function, it may cause subtle personality changes, loss of motivation, and seizures in some people. There have also been reports of relapses with time, suggesting that the brain goes back to its "normal" state and resists change.

## NEW ON THE MEDICAL HORIZON

A number of diagnostic and medical treatments for depression are still in the developmental stages. Three of the most promising are described here.

## Repetitive Transcranial Magnetic Stimulation

Repetitive transcranial magnetic stimulation (rTMS) is being studied as an alternative to ECT for severely depressed patients. In this procedure, a figure-eight-shaped magnet is placed over the left frontal cortex, and high-intensity magnetic pulses generate an electrical charge that stimulates the brain only in the area beneath the magnet.

Although this therapy is similar in action to ECT, it doesn't have all risks and side effects. Patients stay awake and don't need general anesthesia. They also don't have seizures and subsequent memory loss.

Typically rTMS is given daily for at least a week. Preliminary tests show that 30 percent of patients show marked improvement in mood after several days of treatment. However, more research is needed to confirm the effectiveness of this technique and better understand how it works.

## Positron Emission Tomography

Also called a PET scan, positron emission tomography is a diagnostic tool that is helping researchers understand how depression causes changes in the brain. In this imaging technique, the patient is injected with radioactive glucose, oxygen, or drugs. These substances are then tracked to see where they go in the brain and what parts of the brain are activated when the patient performs a designated task. In this way, a

PET scan creates two-dimensional, color-coded images of the "working" brain.

A PET scan can help us understand the physiology of mood disorders by measuring chemical activity in the brain during depression and comparing it to changes after treatment. It shows that depression is a genuine illness with a chemical basis, and therefore is helpful in dispelling some of the stigma associated with the disorder.

## Vagus Nerve Stimulation

Researchers at Columbia University are testing a device that delivers electrical stimulation to the body for the treatment of depression. The device is surgically implanted under the patient's collarbone and automatically delivers electrical stimulation to the vagus nerve in the neck. This procedure has been found to be effective in some severe forms of epilepsy and researchers are hopeful that it will also be useful in treating depression.

## A QUESTION OF BENEFITS AND RISKS

While antidepressant medications and other conventional medical treatments can be extremely effective, they are not totally without risks. In cases of severe depression, the benefits of these interventions clearly outweigh the risks. In cases of mild to moderate depression, starting with less aggressive interventions is reasonable. If less aggressive measures fail to produce a satisfactory response within a reasonable time frame, then the use of more aggressive interventions is entirely appropriate.

# 8

## Eat Better, Feel Better

When you're faced with a difficult problem like depression, it can be hard to focus on nutritional needs. When you are feeling blue, ice cream and chocolate can seem more comforting than romaine lettuce and fresh fruit.

In this chapter and the one that follows we'll offer some specific advice on diet and supplements that can help you combat depression or prevent a recurrence. But before we get into specific nutritional and metabolic strategies, it's wise to remember that depressed or not, you still have to pay attention to your basic nutritional needs, just like everyone else. This is particularly important given the fact that depression often coexists with chronic illness or is one of the factors responsible for what becomes a long slide down to poor health.

## BUILDING A NEW YOU

Each day you are given the opportunity to reinvent yourself. With every breath you take, every meal you eat, every drink you swallow, you are literally building a new you. Day in and day out, you lose millions of cells from your body. And simultaneously, you take in new building materials to reconstruct yourself—new atoms, molecules, and compounds from the air you breathe and from the food and drink you consume.

Each day, as you recreate yourself, remember this: *You are an important person worthy of the best building materials!* Good nutrition is not just some nice little "extra" in life, like good table manners or nice penmanship. Good nutrition is *essential* to creating the healthy life you want and deserve. Every day, from this day forward, your future is in your own hands.

Eating a healthful, well-balanced diet of fresh, whole foods is the key to optimal health. Most nutritionists, registered dietitians, and other health care providers favor a whole-foods diet that emphasizes plant-based foods— vegetables, fruits, legumes (beans), and other whole grains. Other foods included in a whole-foods plan are moderate amounts of fish, poultry, and low-fat dairy products. The diet limits the intake of red meats, high-fat foods, sugar, sodium, and processed foods.

Eating a nutritious diet can strengthen your immune system, increase your stamina, enhance your sense of well-being, and help you cope with whatever life throws your way. Too many people, however, take the "Band-Aid" approach to nutrition. Given our busy lives, it's easy to understand why lots of folks look for quick fixes in the form of convenience foods bolstered by nutritional supplements and the occasional healthful meal.

The trouble is, quick fixes just don't work. If your breakfast, lunch, and dinner consist mostly of processed foods, you aren't going to combat your depression simply by eating an occasional cup of yogurt or popping a vitamin pill. When it comes to long-term health, there is absolutely no substitute for the positive impact of a diet composed of whole, nutrient-rich, real foods. Nutritional supplements can help make up for the "rough spots," but they won't erase the nutritional damage created by a diet of junk foods high in salt, fat, and sugar, or processed foods loaded with refined white flour, partially hydrogenated oils, preservatives, artificial flavorings, and dyes.

The bottom line is you must *eat better to feel better.*

## WHAT'S TO EAT?

No single magic menu fits every person at every stage of life. We each have a unique genetic and biochemical make-up, and each of us thrives on very different diets depending on our different circumstances. For example, adults with high blood triglycerides and low HDL levels may do better on a reduced-carbohydrate diet. Many children thrive on lots of complex carbohydrates and moderate protein. Some people feel their best when they follow Ayurvedic dietary guidelines; others prefer the traditional Chinese medical diet.

The basic principles of good eating are still the subject of much debate. It seems as if every time we turn around, yet another "expert" is recommending some newfangled way to eat right. Lately, there's been a lot of talk about working toward "optimal ratios" and percentages. We've been told, for example, to be sure that no more than 30 percent of our calories come from fats. We hear that we should consume about 30 grams of fiber daily. We've gotten so caught up in ratios and statistics that we've lost sight of the primary focus of optimal nutrition: the actual *foods* we eat. When you choose a diet based only on grams or percentages, you miss the point of good nutrition. A meal of butter, soda, and beef jerky can give you exactly the "right" ratios of fats, carbohydrates, and protein, but where does it leave you nutritionally?

Rather than micromanaging the numbers, it makes more sense to chose *whole, unprocessed, living foods*— the kind of foods humans thrived on for thousands of years before we invented food-processing factories, Wonder Bread, and solar-powered calculators to figure the ratios. Instead of crunching the numbers, we ought to be crunching real foods:

- Vegetables
- Fruits
- Whole grains
- Legumes (beans)

The most striking thing about this list of "power foods" is that they all come from plants. That doesn't mean you need to go entirely vegetarian, although it certainly wouldn't hurt. Contrary to popular myth, people who choose vegan diets (eliminating all animal products, including meat, fish, chicken, eggs, and dairy) can get all the protein and other nutrients they need from vegetables, grains, fruits, beans, nuts, and seeds.

But whatever you choose, the secret to smart eating is to select the freshest, most nutrient-rich foods available. The standard American diet is currently dominated by animal foods like meat, eggs, and chicken. As a result, we consume too much protein and fat, too little fiber, and not enough of the vital nutrients. The fastest, simplest way to improve your diet is to *gradually* increase your plant-based foods while decreasing the amount and frequency of animal foods.

### Basic Dietary Guidelines

These are the food recommendations established jointly by the U.S. Departments of Agriculture and Health and Human Services.

**Breads, Cereals, Rice, and Pasta**—Try to get 6 to 11 servings from this group daily. These foods supply complex carbohydrates, fiber, and minerals. One serving equals one slice of bread; half a cup cooked cereal, rice, or pasta; half a small bagel or muffin; or 1 ounce dry cereal. For maximum fiber, use

**Fruits**—Reach for 2 to 4 servings daily. Fruits provide vitamins A and C, potassium, and fiber. One serving equals one medium apple, banana, orange, or peach; half a cup chopped, cooked, or canned fruit; or three quarters of a cup of juice.

**Vegetables**—Go for 3 to 5 servings daily. Vegetables, especially the deep-yellow and deep-green varieties, are packed with vitamins, minerals, and fiber. One serving equals 1 cup raw leafy greens, half a cup of cooked vegetables, or three quarters of a cup of juice.

**Meat, Poultry, Fish, Dried Beans, Eggs, and Nuts**—Get 2 to 3 servings from this group daily. These foods are sources of protein, B vitamins, iron, and zinc. One serving equals 2 to 3oz of cooked lean meat, poultry, or fish (about the size of a deck of cards); 1 egg; or half a cup of cooked beans. To keep fat intake low, choose legumes, lean meats and fish, and skinless poultry breast meat.

**Milk, Yogurt, and Cheese**—Aim for 2 to 3 servings from this group. Dairy products are a source of protein, vitamins, and minerals—especially calcium and some B vitamins. One serving equals 1 cup (8 ounces) of milk or yogurt; 1½ ounces of a natural cheese, such as cheddar or Swiss; or 2 ounces of processed cheese, such as American. Use fat-free or reduced-fat products to keep your fat intake low.

**Fats, Oils, and Sweets**—Limit intake. This group includes butter, margarine, oils, candy, soda, cakes, cookies, and similar foods. One serving equals 1 teaspoon butter, margarine, or oil.

If you're serious about making improvements to your daily diet, there's more to know about the nutritional basics. We'll start with the macronutrients.

## MUNCHING THE MACRONUTRIENTS: PROTEINS, CARBOHYDRATES, AND FATS

You get your energy from eating macronutrients. "Macro" simply means large. Relatively speaking, your diet consists of large amounts of proteins, carbohydrates, and fats (which are measured in grams), compared to vitamins, minerals, and other micronutrients (which are measured in milligrams [mg], one thousandth of a gram).

Calories simply measure how much energy is contained in food. Think of the number of calories you are allowed to eat each day as an amount of money available to spend. There is no one perfect way to spend that money, just like there is no one perfect diet. But you do not want to blow your budget on "trinkets" and have nothing of lasting value to show for it in return. So try to spend those calories wisely by choosing a nutrient-dense diet.

To consume fewer calories without losing important nutrients, build your diet around nutrient-rich, unprocessed whole grains, fruits, and vegetables. Shun the nutrient-poor foods, such as soda, chips, candy, and cake. Collard greens, for example, have only 40 calories per $\frac{1}{2}$ cup and provide 3.6 grams of protein, 400 milligrams of potassium, 178 milligrams of calcium, 1 milligram of iron, and 6,500 International Units (IU) of vitamin A. Compare that with a 40-calorie serving of coffee cake (just *one* bite!), which provides less than 1 gram of protein, 1 gram of fat, no calcium, 10 milligrams of potassium, and 2 IUs of vitamin A.

This doesn't mean you can never eat coffee cake or other nutrient-deficient food. Just be aware of how you are spending your calories—your nutritional cash—so that by the end of the day, you've invested wisely.

## PROTEINS

In a plant-based diet *at least three-quarters* of the food on your plate should come from grains, fruits, and vegetables. Most Americans were raised on a diet that is just the opposite, with large servings of meat, fish, and chicken, and smaller portions of "side dishes." Building your diet around animal foods is counterproductive, because when you fill up on proteins, you have less room for the vitamin-rich foods that are your best sources of phytonutrients, antioxidants, and fiber. If you do eat animal protein, limit yourself to 2 or 3 ounces per meal—a serving size no larger than a deck of playing cards.

Rest assured, a plant-based diet is *not* a low-protein diet. The RDA for adults 50 years old and under is 0.8 grams of protein per kilogram (kg) of body weight, or about a half-gram for every pound you weigh. This means a woman who weighs 130 pounds (59 kilograms) needs only 47.2 grams of protein per day to meet the RDA.

Even vegetarians can get enough protein. Not long ago, vegetarians were advised to follow some pretty strict guidelines. That's because some nutritionists believed that certain amino acids had to be eaten together in specific combinations in order to provide "complete" proteins. The theory was that plant proteins were "incomplete" and needed to be combined with the "complementary proteins" found in beans, nuts, or grains to make a truly nutritious vegetarian meal. We now know this is untrue. Your body can use the amino acids consumed at breakfast and combine these with different amino acids consumed at lunch or dinner to make all the proteins it needs during the day.

When you opt for a plant-based diet, you can still get plenty of protein by replacing animal protein with vegetable protein found in legumes (for example, pinto beans, black beans, split peas, or black-eyed peas), grains, soy products, meat substitutes (soy hot dogs or veggie burgers), nuts, and seeds. Soy protein has been shown to lower cholesterol and may prevent cancer. If these foods are new to you, introduce them gradually, but steadily, into your diet. Be daring. Try split pea soup and a veggie burger for dinner tonight!

## CARBOHYDRATES

Nutritionists continue to argue over the optimal amount of carbohydrates in the diet, but experts tend to agree that most of your calories should come from carbohydrates. The body uses carbohydrates (or starches, as Grandma used to call them) to make blood sugar, which provides the fuel used by the brain and the muscles, including the heart.

The real benefit of carbohydrates for people with depression is their effect on the calming, feel-good neurotransmitter called serotonin. Serotonin is made from the amino acid tryptophan, which must cross over into the brain before serotonin can be made. The best way to get tryptophan to your brain is by eating carbohydrates. When you eat a lot of protein, all of the amino acids, not just the tryptophan, crowd around that crossing into the brain. But when you eat carbs, the tryptophan has no competition, so it can readily cross over. That's why carbohydrates are called nature's mood equalizers.

Because they break down into sugar slowly, complex carbohydrates—like corn, potatoes, whole wheat bread, oats, and legumes—are far better for you than the simple carbohydrates found in sugary cereals, pies, cakes, cookies, and other processed foods made from white sugar and/or white flour. Whole grain breads and cereals are the best sources of complex carbohydrates because they also provide iron, B vitamins, and fiber—contributing nicely to the 25 to 35 grams of fiber needed daily.

The USDA Food Guide Pyramid recommends 6 to 11 servings of grains per day. That sounds like an awful lot until you realize that one serving equals one slice of bread or one ounce of dry cereal. A big bagel represents 4 servings of grains! For best nutrition, choose one made with whole wheat flour and for goodness' sake, don't ruin it with a thick layer of butter or cream cheese. If you want a tasty topping, choose a fruit spread or some hummus (a Middle Eastern dish made from mashed chickpeas, sesame seed paste, and other healthful ingredients).

Make sure that at least half the grains you eat are whole grains, rather than white flour. When whole wheat flour is milled into white flour, 25 nutrients are lost, and only five nutrients are added back (to give you so-called enriched flour). Good whole grain choices include whole wheat pasta, whole wheat bread, oatmeal, and brown rice. Try a different grain each week. Whole grains like quinoa and millet are great tasting and easy to cook.

In addition to whole grains, fruits and vegetables are also excellent sources of complex carbohydrates. Scientific research continually supports the fact that diets high in nutrient-rich fruits and vegetables promote optimal health. Ever see a study saying broccoli is bad for you? One study showed that people who consumed lots of fruits and vegetables had the lowest heart attack rates and cut their risk of developing certain cancers by half.

The USDA Food Guide Pyramid recommends getting five to nine servings of fruits and vegetables per day. Yes, five to nine servings. "Five a day" is a great slogan, but research shows five is really not enough. Eating nine servings may look difficult, but if you start your day with a glass of juice and some fruit on your cereal, you've already packed in two right there with breakfast. Help yourself to a vegetable at lunch and two more at dinner. Snack on fresh fruit or cut-up raw vegetables. You'll find you've reached your goal in no time. An easy way to get enough vegetables is to double your portion size. If you eat a full cup of broccoli at dinner, you've eaten two servings instead of just one!

*Sugar*

While the complex carbohydrates found in whole grains and vegetables are good for you, the simple carbohydrates, a.k.a. sugar, should be strictly limited.

Sweets can be a real problem for people with depression. You feel like you're dragging, so you think a doughnut or a candy bar or a frozen dessert might help. It might, momentarily, because as soon as you eat it your blood sugar—and your energy level—starts to soar. Then just an hour or two later your "sugar high" passes, and you crash. You're left feeling more lethargic, more "down" than before.

It really is better to skip the sweets altogether. That said, having an *occasional* sweet at the end of a meal is not the end of the world, because when eaten along with other foods, it has less of an effect on your blood sugar and ultimately your mood.

## FATS: THE GOOD, THE BAD, AND THE UGLY

Not all fats are the same. While experts debate the merits and amounts of dietary fat, everyone seems to agree that saturated fat should be limited. Saturated fat is found in red meat and in solid shortening. Hydrogenated oil—liquid oil that is chemically treated with hydrogen to solidify it at room temperature—is found in many processed foods, including margarine, crackers, cookies, and chips. Hydrogenated fats create trans-fatty acids, which increase the risk of cancer and heart disease.

Eliminate as many saturated fats and hydrogenated oils from your diet as you possibly can. An excellent start is to reduce animal foods and processed foods like potato chips and commercially made cookies.

## WHY SOME FAT IS GOOD

The nerve cells in your brain (neurons) are coated with a protective layer of fat that works just like the colorful plastic insulation on a wire. Without that layer of fat, your nerves would short-circuit.

Current research indicates that the type of fats you eat can alter this protective insulation and thereby interfere with proper functioning of the brain and nervous system. Optimal nerve functioning is critical in people with depression. Diets high in saturated fats seem to stiffen the coating on the neurons and reduce their ability to receive chemical signals from the neurotransmitters. But don't make the mistake of eliminating every trace of fat from your diet. Diets too low in fat also seem to damage the insulation around nerve cells, reducing their ability to send messages.

Moderating fat intake is also important if you're on antidepressant medication. These medications may not be as effective if there's too much or too little saturated fat in your diet. If the neurons are in bad shape, then serotonin's chemical signal will fall on deaf ears. It is like shutting off the ringer on your phone. The message might be coming in, but you never know it.

When it comes to fats, monounsaturated fats (found in olives, olive oil, and canola oil), occasional servings of high-fat foods (such as nuts, nut butters, full-fat soy foods, and avocados), and omega-3 fatty acids (found in fatty fish such as salmon, flaxseed, and fish oil capsules) may be the best bets overall.

## FATS: THE FINAL WORD

So now that you know that fats are important for overall health, exactly what are you supposed to do? Here are some useful guidelines:

1. Keep the overall amount of fat in your diet to a reasonable level, approximately 20 to 30 percent of your total calorie intake. Do not strive for a fat-free diet.
2. Avoid saturated fats like those contained in beef, butter, full-fat cheeses, and processed foods that contain hydrogenated fats.
3. Make the most of the fat in your diet by choosing monounsaturated fats like those found in olive oil or canola oil. These good fats are also found in nuts, seeds, and avocados.
4. Increase the omega-3 fats in your diet by consuming flaxseed, fatty fish, or fish oil supplements.

# SPECIAL DIETARY ISSUES FOR PEOPLE WITH DEPRESSION

## CAFFEINE AND ALCOHOL

Like sugar, caffeine and alcohol have a play-now/pay-later effect for the person with depression. Each may appear to offer temporary respite from a low mood, but there's a price to pay. Caffeine, it's said, doesn't so much give you energy as borrow it. Payback time comes later in the day when your morning jolt of caffeine wears off and you reach for a sugary food or even an alcoholic beverage to get you through the next few hours.

Stop "robbing Peter to pay Paul" and eat and live in the moment. When you're in the mood for a snack, stop a moment and ask yourself, "What's the most nourishing thing I can offer my body?" It's likely the answer isn't coffee, wine, or a cruller—but some juicy melon, crisp fresh vegetables, or half a turkey breast sandwich on whole wheat bread.

## FOOD ALLERGIES AND SENSITIVITIES

A surprising link in the food-mood connection can be food allergies or food sensitivities. After doing some detective work (see *Dear Diary*), you may find a pattern indicating that certain foods seem to have a negative effect on your mood.

Food allergies occur when the body's immune system misreads a particular food or ingredient as a threat to the body and, as a result, produces antibodies to that food. Each time that food is eaten, the immune system reacts as if a virus or other disease-causing agent has invaded the body and it launches an attack. Not all physicians agree on the importance of food allergies/sensitivities in chronic illness.

Food allergies are different from respiratory allergies, and those who have them can express a wider range of symptoms. People with food allergies or sensitivities may experience nausea, diarrhea, itchy skin, rashes, hives, headaches, congestion, joint and muscle aches, watery eyes, and/or sore throat. Psychological symptoms are common and include mental fatigue, cognitive fog, mood swings, and insomnia.

Some people outgrow food allergies acquired in childhood, only to acquire new sensitivities as adults. Common causes of food allergies include: cow's milk, eggs, fish, shellfish, wheat, corn, peanuts, soybeans, and tree nuts. Altogether, more than 160 different foods are recognized allergens.

### Dear Diary

If you suspect you are allergic to any food or have problems with your digestive system, the best way to track down the culprits is to keep a food diary. Writing down everything you eat and any symptoms you experience can help you and your doctor sort out possible food sensitivities.

The operative word here is *everything*. Write down everything you eat and drink every day for a week. Break down mixed food into its components. If you feel poorly after eating stew, you need to know all of the ingredients to determine if it was the meat, carrots, or wheat flour that was the problem. A few visits to a registered dietitian who specializes in allergies can help you with this detective work.

If you suspect multiple allergies, or are just not sure what might be causing the problem, your health care professional may suggest a strict elimination diet to help with diagnosis. Start on a bland diet of mostly rice, apple juice, and turkey for a couple of days. Then slowly add foods to which you think you are not allergic, one at a time, recording any adverse reactions. Next, try a food which you suspect you may be allergic to, again recording any reactive symptoms. The key to surviving the elimination diet is to eat enough food. The first couple of days, you'll be eating a lot of turkey and rice. Hang in there; it won't last forever.

Once you discover which food or foods have a negative effect on your mood, you must eliminate them from your diet. Read labels carefully to avoid ingesting any allergen that is an ingredient in a prepared or processed food.

The next step is to focus on foods to add to your diet. If you need to avoid dairy, be sure to add nondairy sources of calcium like dark green, leafy vegetables and calcium-fortified orange juice. If you need to eliminate wheat, make up the deficit with other grains like quinoa, amaranth, and brown rice. For more information, contact the Food Allergy Network at *www.foodallergy.org* or call 800-929-4040.

## SPECIAL DIETARY RESTRICTIONS FOR PEOPLE ON MAO ANTIDEPRESSANTS

Monoamine oxidase inhibitors (MAOIs), medications that are sometimes prescribed for depression (such as Nardil and Parnate), work by inhibiting an enzyme called monoamine oxidase (MAO). MAO is a substance that breaks down monoamines (naturally occurring food substances that often result during fermentation) to form the amino acid tyramine. If you eat foods high in tyramine or dopamine while taking an MAO inhibitor, the monoamines can build up and cause your blood vessels to constrict. The result can be a dangerous spike in blood pressure.

For this reason, if you're taking an MAOI, certain foods are *completely off-limits:* sour cream, bananas, plums, avocado, figs, raisins, sauerkraut, aged game, liver sausage, salami and other cured meats, meats prepared with tenderizer, cheese, salted dried fish such as herring or cod, caviar, broad beans, eggplant, yeast concentrates, bouillon cubes (which contain yeast), tofu, and soy sauce. You also must avoid coffee and tea and alcoholic beverages including distilled spirits, wine, beer, and ale.

Since the MAO enzyme can interact with many herbs and supplements, I generally suggest avoiding the use of supplements and herbs when on MAOIs. St. John's wort, which is discussed in Chapter 11, should not be combined with MAOIs. Similarly, some of the supplements listed in Chapter 9 (tyrosine and 5-HTP, for instance), should definitely not be used in combination with MAOIs.

# 9

## Taming Depression with Dietary Supplements

Everything you eat and drink affects how good you feel. As you learned in Chapter 8, there's no single better way to boost your overall health than to consume wholesome, nutrition-rich foods and beverages every day.

That said, we know from USDA data that about half the people in this country routinely eat a poor diet, getting only about 60 percent of the Recommended Dietary Allowance (RDA) of several of the basic essential nutrients. That's the RDA, mind you—amounts we already know to be inadequate in terms of promoting optimal health. It's clear, then, that diet alone is only part of the answer when it comes to nutritional strategies for treating and preventing depression.

Another part of the therapeutic answer lies in dietary supplements. Supercharging your diet with vitamins, amino acids, and in some cases, hormones, can help you combat depression and bring you closer to optimal health. A number of these supplements can be used along with standard antidepressant remedies. Others cannot. In this chapter we'll take a closer look at all the possibilities—including what's available for those who are not helped by, or cannot tolerate, standard antidepressant therapies and/or for those who simply prefer a more natural approach.

Speaking of the natural approach, millions of people with mild to moderate depression have already discovered the mood-lifting benefits of the herb St. John's wort. Even though many people think of St. John's wort as a dietary supplement (because that's the way it's marketed in this country), we'll save our discussion of this herb for Chapter 11.

In this chapter our emphasis will be on vitamins and amino acid supplements, including the product S-adenosyl-L-methionine (SAMe), now being touted as the next big "natural therapy" breakthrough in the treatment of depression.

As always, no advice, no matter how wise or well-intentioned, works for all of the people all of the time. Consult your physician, dietitian or nutritionist, and other practitioners in your health care team before starting any new regimen of supplements, hormones, or herbs—*especially if you are currently using any prescription medications, are receiving chemotherapy, or are under treatment for any other serious illness in addition to depression.*

# MAXIMIZING YOUR MICRONUTRIENTS: VITAMINS AND MINERALS

Here's some sound advice you can use right now: regardless of your health or diet, you should take a daily multivitamin-mineral supplement.

Given the depleted condition of our farm soils and the rush and stress of modern life, no one gets all the nutrients they need from food alone. Daily supplementation can serve as your nutritional "insurance policy." Skeptics argue that eating a well balanced diet provides all the nutrition you need and that taking supplements just makes "expensive urine." While everyone should strive for a well balanced diet (and not take supplements to replace a healthy diet), research shows that we would have to eat huge amounts of certain foods to get enough vitamins and other nutrients to prevent disease and optimize health. While it's certainly possible to get carried away and spend too much money on supplements, a good multivitamin is an excellent investment in your overall health.

When you're considering taking supplements *in addition to* your multivitamin, check to see if you're already getting an adequate amount of that vitamin or mineral in your multi. You want to be sure your total daily dosage of any one nutrient does not exceed maximum recommended amounts.

When choosing your multivitamin, look for one that contains plenty of antioxidants: vitamin A (beta-carotene), C, and E, and the trace mineral selenium. With careful shopping, you can find one that also contains phytonutrients (bioflavonoids, carotenoids, and proanthocyanidins). Antioxidants are nutrients that are found in fruits and vegetables and are known to destroy or neutralize free radicals, the naturally occurring unstable molecules present throughout our bodies. Free radicals are implicated in the aging process and contribute to the onset of numerous diseases, including cancer and cardiovascular disease. Simply speaking, raising your intake of antioxidants boosts your immune system, slows down the aging process, and lowers your risk for heart disease, stroke, and cancer. This is a smart nutritional strategy for everyone, not just people with depression.

Women, in particular, will want to make sure their multivitamin includes plenty of calcium and vitamin D, two other vital nutrients that can, among other things, help prevent or delay the onset of osteoporosis.

Keeping all this in mind, in this chapter we're going to focus on the B vitamins since they play such a critical role in mood regulation.

## LOVE THOSE Bs

The B vitamins help us convert the food we eat into energy. They also are essential to the proper functioning of the chemicals in our brain, in particular, to the production of the neurotransmitter serotonin. Some cases of depression have even been linked to a simple B vitamin deficiency. For that reason, be sure your multivitamin contains a healthy measure of the B vitamins, particularly folate, vitamin $B_6$, and vitamin $B_{12}$. Your physician may even recommend that you take a separate high-potency B vitamin supplement. Your urine should turn neon yellow or fluorescent orange if you are absorbing your B vitamins. If you have a great deal of difficulty absorbing nutrients, intravenous or intramuscular B vitamin therapy may be helpful.

### Folate, $B_{12}$, and the Brain

Deficiencies of folate and vitamin $B_{12}$ may result in psychological problems, including depression and dementia. To better understand the relationship between vitamin $B_{12}$, folate, and depression, you need to understand the way folate functions in the brain.

Your body needs folate and vitamin $B_{12}$ to convert the amino acid homocysteine to another amino acid called methionine. Methionine is used to make the chemical S-adenosyl-L-methionine, called SAMe, discussed later in this chapter. High levels of homocysteine have negative health effects, including elevating your risk for heart disease. In the Framingham Heart Study, men who had high levels of homocysteine also did poorly on written tests of mental abilities. In fact, men with the highest levels of homocysteine actually did as poorly on those tests as people in the early stages of Alzheimer's disease.

## SUPPLEMENTING WITH AMINO ACIDS

Studies have established that when neurotransmitter activity is low, depression can result. Since the protein building blocks known as amino acids play a critical role in the formation of the neurotransmitters that help to regulate mood, they can provide particular benefits for some people with depression.

There are two ways that amino acids can be used in depression. One way is to do a blood test that measures fasting amino acid levels. If, for genetic/biochemical reasons, an individual has significant amino acid imbalances, a customized amino acid blend can be formulated to correct the imbalance. Although this type of individualized testing and supplementation can be helpful in depression, it can also be rather pricey. The second, more common way to use amino acids is to take specific amino acids that are known to raise the levels of certain neurotransmitters. In both cases I suggest doing this only under medical supervision, to monitor the effectiveness of what you are doing. The following are examples of specific amino acid supplements that have been, or currently are, available in health food stores.

### L-TRYPTOPHAN AND 5-HTP (5-HYDROXY-L-TRYPTOPHAN)

The amino acid L-tryptophan is the main component of serotonin, the brain chemical so important in regulating mood, behavior, sleep, and appetite. You might wonder if, in order to make more serotonin, you could simply just eat more foods containing tryptophan.

However, most people don't find it practical to consume vast quantities of bananas, beef, turkey, pasta, peanuts, processed cheese, pineapple, dates, and figs.

L-tryptophan used to be a popular over-the-counter supplement that was used to treat insomnia and depression. Some years ago, due to toxic contaminants, several people using L-tryptophan became very ill with a rare disorder called eosinophilia-myalgia syndrome (EMS), a condition marked by severe muscle aches and high levels of eosinophil (a type of white blood cells). Unfortunately, a number of patients died from this disorder, and the supplement was pulled off the market. It is now available again, only by prescription and only through compounding pharmacies. Naturally, the cost is much higher now that L-tryptophan is classified as a prescription drug. It does, nonetheless, appear to be a safe and effective intervention for depression.

Even though L-tryptophan is no longer available over the counter, there is a closely related amino acid derivative, 5-HTP, that may be even more effective in treating depression and is currently available in health food stores. In the process of making serotonin, the body converts tryptophan into a chemical called 5-hydroxy-L-tryptophan (5-HTP), one step closer to serotonin. Therefore, one way to boost serotonin production is to supplement with 5-HTP at a dosage of 100 to 300 milligrams three times daily. Research shows that 5-HTP easily crosses the blood-brain barrier, where it can effectively increase production of serotonin and other neurotransmitters. About

70 percent of the compound ends up in the bloodstream, an indication that it is well absorbed.

The supplement 5-HTP is a botanical chemical extracted from the seed of an African plant. It has been available as an over-the-counter treatment since 1995, and several double-blind studies have shown it to be as effective in lifting mood as antidepressant drugs. People who use 5-HTP at therapeutic levels say that, in addition to elevating mood, it helps control appetite, reduces anxiety, and decreases insomnia—and it's associated with fewer and milder side effects than standard antidepressants.

One study compared 5-HTP with one of the SSRI antidepressants, fluvoxamine (Luvox, a drug very similar to Prozac). Participants who received 5-HTP reported better, faster relief of depressive symptoms than those who were given the SSRI—and a higher percentage of them had a positive response.

CAUTION—Even though 5-HTP has been fairly well researched as a treatment for depression, it's wise to take it only under a physician's supervision. Few long-term studies have been done, so do not use it on a continuous basis (longer than three months). Do not take 5-HTP if you are also treating your depression with SSRI antidepressants or St. John's wort. This combination could lead to too much serotonin, a dangerous medical condition called serotonin syndrome. 5-HTP should also not be used with MAOIs as this could increase the risk of a hypertensive crisis.

Another reason for caution is that in 1998 researchers from the Mayo Clinic and the U.S. Food and

Drug Administration (FDA) reported finding potentially harmful impurities in several over-the-counter 5-HTP products. These chemicals were supposedly similar to the contaminants found in L-tryptophan supplements that appeared to cause the previously mentioned outbreak of EMS. The EMS outbreak, which occurred in 1989 in Japan, killed at least 30 people and sickened more than 1,500. The supplement industry has countered the report, maintaining that the link between contaminated L-tryptophan and the alleged contamination of 5-HTP remains unproven. Given the complex regulatory politics and substantial financial interests of the pharmaceutical manufacturers, I would not be too surprised if 5-HTP suffered a regulatory fate similar to that of L-tryptophan in the near future.

## DL-Phenylalanine (DLPA)

DL-phenylalanine (DLPA) is an essential amino acid found in protein-rich foods. Once ingested, your body converts it into another amino acid, tyrosine, which it uses to manufacture adrenal and thyroid hormones. We know that phenylalanine raises levels of endorphins, the body's natural painkillers and "feel-good" mood lifters. It does this by inhibiting the enzymes programmed to destroy the endorphins, allowing them to continue providing pain relief.

DLPA, isolated from the lupine plant, is a mixture of the essential amino acid L-phenylalanine and its mirror image D-phenylalanine. Therapeutically, DLPA has been shown to relieve acute and chronic pain, particularly headache pain. This effect is boosted when DLPA is taken along with small doses of over-the-counter painkillers such as acetaminophen, ibuprofen, or aspirin. DLPA also produces feelings of relaxation and calm and has positive effects on memory, concentration, and mental alertness.

Because DLPA increases synthesis of endorphins and other neurotransmitters, it can also be effective in the treatment of depression, particularly in those cases where neurotransmitter levels are low. Preliminary research reported that supplements of DLPA elevated mood for 31 out of 40 depressed people.

Some individuals find that taking just 75 to 200 milligrams of DLPA per day helps to improve mood. I generally recommend taking 500 to 1,000 milligrams of DLPA twice daily. Take DLPA 30 minutes before a meal or two hours after a meal to reduce competition from other amino acids for transport into the body's cells.

## TYROSINE

Tyrosine is an amino acid synthesized from phenylalanine in the body. Food sources include dairy products, lean meats, tofu, eggs, seafood and fish, green beans, peas, whole wheat bread, and oats. Like phenylalanine, tyrosine is converted into dopamine, norepinephrine, and epinephrine, the neurotransmitters that transfer nerve impulses and help regulate mood.

Studies suggest that L-tyrosine, the name under which the compound is marketed, can help people perform more effectively when under stress. It can also aid in treating depression and can reduce the irritability, fatigue, and depressed mood seen in women who suffer from premenstrual syndrome. Doses of 4 grams per day appear effective.

CAUTION—Do not take L-tyrosine if you are taking an MAO inhibitor, have high blood pressure, skin cancer, or suffer from migraine headaches.

## SAMe

SAMe (S-adenosyl-L-methionine) is a natural chemical compound found in all body tissues and fluids and seems to be needed to process and produce a broad range of chemicals that maintain normal cell function. As such, SAMe has a role in regulating more than 35 different bodily processes. It helps the body maintain cell membranes, removes toxic substances, and helps control the activity of various hormones and neurotransmitters, including serotonin, melatonin, dopamine, norepinephrine, epinephrine, and adrenaline. Depression has been linked to low levels of these neurotransmitters. SAMe may also aid in the repair of myelin—the protective fatty sheath that insulates nerve cells just like the colorful plastic insulation on a wire.

SAMe is relatively new to the U.S. over-the-counter supplement market, having been introduced in 1996 after being available by prescription in Europe for years. Physicians there have used it with great success to treat patients with depression, arthritis, chronic fatigue syndrome, and fibromyalgia. In Russia and China, it is often prescribed for the treatment of liver disease.

For people with depression, the most important fact about SAMe is that it makes brain cells more responsive to neurotransmitters. We know that neurotransmitters need a place to attach to brain cells before they can do their jobs. These attachment points, called receptors, float in the membrane of brain cells like a water lily floats on a pond. If the cell membrane gets thick and rigid (due to age, a diet high in saturated fats, or other problems), the receptors cannot pass along chemical signals. SAMe prevents the membrane from becoming gluey and therefore helps the receptors stay ready for action.

On the basis of this activity, SAMe appears to be a very effective antidepressant. Available only by prescription in 14 countries, doctors in those countries have used it to treat depression for over 20 years. Patients who get a good response note an increase in energy, alertness, and concentration, and experience an enhanced sense of well-being. Since the 1970s, the results of 40 clinical studies on SAMe involving roughly 1,400 patients have been published in the scientific literature. The findings are remarkably consistent and indicate that SAMe is safe and effective and works about as well against depression as standard tricyclic antidepressants—and it's clearly less toxic, meaning fewer side effects.

In one study, researchers at the University of California, Irvine Medical Center, gave 17 severely depressed patients either a four-week course of SAMe (1,600 milligrams daily) or the prescription antidepressant desipramine. Those who received SAMe had a significantly higher response rate (62 percent) than those on desipramine (50 percent).

Studies do suggest, however, that just like other antidepressants, SAMe may trigger manic episodes in people with bipolar disorder, so it is not a recommended treatment for that condition.

SAMe offers a secondary benefit as well: relief from symptoms of arthritis. Some of the first patients who tried SAMe for depression also suffered joint pain from osteoarthritis. SAMe provided relief from both conditions. It seems that when the body is done using a molecule of SAMe in the brain, it breaks it down into sulfur-containing compounds that move through the blood to the joints, where they help maintain joint cartilage. If you're considering treating your depression with SAMe, the recommended dose is 200 to 400 milligrams three to four times daily.

CAUTION—Other than nausea (and in a very small percentage of cases, dry mouth and/or insomnia), SAMe does not seem to cause adverse side effects, even at higher dosages. However, studies are still needed to determine long-term safety. One drawback to SAMe is its relatively high cost, close to a dollar per 200 milligram dose. As the use of this supplement becomes more popular, we can only hope that the economic laws of supply and demand will bring prices down to a more reasonable and affordable range.

# Dehydroepiandrosterone (DHEA)

Dehydroepiandrosterone (DHEA) is a hormone that is used as a building block for steroid hormones in the body, including sex hormones. This naturally occurring substance has been linked to a wide range of potential health benefits, including reversing the aging process, enhancing the immune system, preventing heart disease and cancer, and building muscle.

Chronic stress overworks your adrenal glands, the glands responsible for producing DHEA. In addition, production of the hormone drops off steadily as you age. The chronic use of steroid medications to treat allergies, asthma, autoimmune disease, or to prevent rejection of organ transplants, suppresses the adrenal glands and can also result in a dramatic drop-off in DHEA production.

If you're wondering whether DHEA level is a significant health issue for you, your health care provider can get a reading by testing your blood or saliva. Low DHEA levels have been linked to autoimmune disorders (often a side effect of the treatment), low sex drive, and exhaustion. If your blood level of DHEA-sulfate is low (DHEA levels can fluctuate quite a bit, but DHEA-sulfate levels remain relatively stable), I usually recommend supplementation. Women should start at a dose of 10 milligrams, taken each morning. For men I usually advise a starting dose of 20 to 25 milligrams in the mornings. A follow-up reading of DHEA-sulfate levels should be done six to eight weeks into treatment to see if the dosage needs to be adjusted. DHEA is a hormone and it needs to be administered carefully.

DHEA also appears to offer some relief from depression. A number of studies have pointed to low levels of DHEA in people suffering from postpartum depression, anorexia nervosa, and schizophrenia. In a study reported in 1999 in the *American Journal of Psychiatry,* 22 people with severe depression were given either DHEA or a placebo. After six weeks, none of the 11 who took the placebo experienced a significant improvement, but five of the 11 DHEA users showed a decrease of 50 percent or more in depressive symptoms.

Researchers are not sure how DHEA elevates mood, but they believe it may protect against the damaging effects of cortisol, a hormone associated with stress. It's also believed that DHEA directly increases serotonin levels.

The best known effect of DHEA is on the sex hormones estrogen and testosterone, which also have been linked to mood. While its effects on these two hormones can be beneficial, there is also a dark side. It is feared that DHEA could accelerate the growth of tumors of the prostate, breast, cervix, or uterus. Studies have shown higher levels of DHEA (and the estrogens made from it) in women with breast and endometrial cancer.

If you're considering supplementing with DHEA, read labels carefully and choose a reputable brand. Supplements that claim to contain DHEA vary widely in purity and percentage of active ingredient. A new version of DHEA, called 7-Keto DHEA, offers the potential benefits of DHEA with fewer risks. Once DHEA is converted to the 7-Keto form, it can no longer be used to make the sex hormones that figure in elevated cancer risk. One 28-day human safety trial on 7-Keto DHEA confirmed that it does not raise levels of sex hormones at doses of up to 200 milligrams per day.

Products manufactured from wild yam are sometimes sold as "natural sources" of DHEA, but they don't contain the compound in a form your body can readily use. Compounding pharmacies are a good resource for a quality product.

Your physician can give you more information about these special pharmacies, or to locate one in your area, call the International Academy of Compounding Pharmacists at 800-927-IACP or go to their Web site at *www.iacprx.org.*

CAUTION—Since DHEA is a powerful hormone, you should use it only under a doctor's supervision, particularly if you are in a high-risk category for any of the cancers mentioned here. Blood levels should be monitored on a regular basis. With DHEA, as with most supplements, too much of a good thing is as bad as not enough. Excessive DHEA use has been associated with acne, unwanted (male pattern) hair growth, hypertension, and liver damage. If you're having any of these side effects, or find you're chasing cars down the freeway in fits of rage, stop the DHEA and consult your physician.

## INOSITOL

According to several double-blind studies, inositol, a substance that enhances the ability of the body to utilize fatty acids, has been found to be helpful in relieving depression and obsessive-compulsive disorder. Doses of up to 12 grams per day appear to be safe. Inositol has been used in conjunction with lithium to reduce the side effects of lithium. Inositol should not be used during pregnancy.

## SOME FINAL WORDS

Clearly, the effects of these various supplements can be explained on a biochemical basis. For more biochemically based interventions, see Chapter 11 for a discussion of herbal products.

While the supplements discussed here can be both safe and effective, you should always work with a physician to monitor their effectiveness and the possible need for more aggressive interventions if supplementation is not having the desired effect. The same can be said about the use of virtually all complementary therapies. The integrative medicine philosophy calls for using less aggressive interventions first (assuming it is not an emergency), but also understands the importance of using more aggressive measures when the initial treatments aren't working.

The next chapter will give you a general overview of what complementary and alternative therapies have to offer within the context of a balanced, integrative framework.

# 10

# Getting the Most from Complementary and Alternative Medicine

Perhaps you're in the midst of working through a mild to moderate depression, and the standard antidepressants have either not been very helpful in lifting your mood or produced too many negative side effects. Maybe you're one of the many who've heard about the good results some people are experiencing with herbal therapies, homeopathy, acupuncture, massage, or mind-body approaches, and want to leave no stone unturned in your search for treatment. Or, then again, perhaps you're prone to periodic bouts of depression and are interested in what complementary and alternative medicine has to offer in the way of prevention strategies.

Whatever is at the root of your depression—and whatever is driving your interest in nontraditional medicine—you'll be glad to know that there are a number of "natural" therapies that can help restore your equilibrium and promote a positive outlook on life. CAM approaches emphasize harmony and balance in mind, body, and spirit. You will find complementary/alternative medicine less authoritarian and more empowering, giving you a greater sense of control. In addition, CAM therapies can, in many cases, offer quick symptom relief, even as their emphasis on lifestyle changes can help you manage—or perhaps prevent—a recurrence down the road.

As you begin to explore complementary approaches, whatever you do, don't turn your back on conventional medical treatment—especially if you're severely depressed. But keep in mind that with depression, as with many other disorders, there are usually multiple roads to effective relief.

### Want to Know More?

For background information on the various complementary/alternative modalities, general cautions, and explanation of the particular therapies most often used for the treatment of depression, see Chapters 11 through 15. For further information on these modalities, check the resource listings at the back of this book.

# THE GROWING DEMAND FOR COMPLEMENTARY/ALTERNATIVE MEDICINE

Ten years ago you had to search for tiny health food stores or obscure specialty shops to find a simple herbal tea. Today, extracts of St. John's wort, echinacea, and hundreds of other herbs and natural remedies line the shelves of Wal-Mart, Kmart, CVS, and many other big chain stores across America. Mainstream supermarkets now carry soy milk, herbal teas, and a good selection of organic products. Even 7-Eleven sells convenient one-shot bottles of ginseng and travel packs of homeopathic medicines.

Dissatisfied with conventional medicine's focus on illness rather than wellness, consumers have been voting with their pocketbooks. Mainstream businesses have responded to the shift in demand. For the most part, mainstream medicine has lagged behind and done its best to ignore the growing public interest in "alternative" health care. But now, as consumer demand continues to swell, even conservative medical institutions like the American Medical Association and the National Institutes of Health have had to respond to the changing tide.

Unlike conventional medicine, with its focus on diagnosing and treating disease and suppressing symptoms, complementary/alternative medicine (CAM) is more likely to look at the entire person—body, mind, and spirit. In addition to treating immediate physical symptoms (like a runny nose or an aching back), these therapies typically take a more "holistic" approach to health and healing. CAM practitioners consider the underlying functioning of complex body systems (like the immune system), as well as the larger context of the patient's beliefs, personal circumstances, lifestyle choices, and external environment.

Complementary/alternative practitioners usually rely on gentler, less invasive diagnostic and therapeutic interventions than those routinely implemented by conventional physicians—often with fewer side effects. And most important, CAM approaches may provide relief (and occasionally even cures) when Western medicine falls short.

But that doesn't mean that all alternative therapies are right for all people. Some carry significant risks. Anything that is effective also has the potential to be dangerous if used improperly. Anyone considering nontraditional approaches to help manage depression should take charge of their health, learning as much as possible about the available options before pursuing any treatment.

## WHERE IS IT ALL LEADING?

In 1992, the United States Congress set aside $2 million to establish the Office of Alternative Medicine (OAM) as part of the National Institutes of Health (NIH). Renamed the National Center for Complementary and Alternative Medicine (NCCAM), the center disperses its now $90 million annual budget to fund research at facilities around the country.

In 1993, Harvard University researcher Dr. David Eisenberg reported in the *New England Journal of Medicine* the results of a 1990 survey revealing that as many as one in three Americans was using at least one form of unconventional therapy. The following year a Gallup Poll determined that 17 percent of Americans were using herbal supplements, a jump of 14 percent from the previous year.

Dr. Eisenberg subsequently reported in a 1998 issue of the *Journal of the American Medical Association* the results of a 1997 follow-up survey that showed that seven years later, 42 percent of Americans were using some form of unconventional therapy—a 25 percent increase since the first survey. During that same seven-year period, the use of herbal supplements jumped a noteworthy 380 percent, making herbal products the fastest growing segment of the CAM industry.

The most interesting (and most frightening) finding of both surveys was that most patients who use CAM therapies don't tell their medical doctors about it, probably fearing confrontation or ridicule. In fact, based on Eisenberg's second survey, more than 15 million adults in the United States routinely put themselves at risk for potentially dangerous interactions between their prescription medications and their "secret" CAM supplements.

As public interest in alternative and complementary practices has grown, the bastions of conventional Western medicine—medical schools and mainstream health care organizations—have begun to incorporate complementary medicine into their own programs and services. At the end of the millennium, a significant majority of U.S. medical schools were offering electives in nontraditional therapies.

Big-city medical centers can no longer afford to ignore the trend and are scrambling to establish CAM clinics to meet the public's demand for access to qualified practitioners. At the Center for Integrative Medicine at Thomas Jefferson University Hospital in Philadelphia, board-certified physicians will not only check your heart and blood pressure, they'll also suggest treatment options that might include yoga, massage therapy, or acupuncture.

For the past two years, I've had the privilege of working with Catholic Health Initiatives (CHI), a national organization based in Denver, to help guide and support efforts to establish integrative medicine programs at interested facilities across the country.

Even the American Medical Association (AMA) and its affiliate state and local medical societies can no longer ignore the trend. While not specifically endorsing complementary medicine, these organizations are encouraging their members to become more familiar with CAM modalities in order to more effectively discuss the proper use of these approaches with their patients.


## DOES CAM REALLY WORK?

Although most complementary practitioners argue that Western medicine has its drawbacks—pointing, for example, to drug side effects or new antibiotic-resistant strains of infection—the vast majority readily concede that Western medicine is absolutely peerless when it comes to acute and emergency care. Emergency situations call for emergency interventions. If you have a broken leg, you don't want an herb; you need a cast.

Conventionally trained health care practitioners have not been quick to return the compliment. More often than not, physicians turn a deaf ear when alternative practitioners and their satisfied clients suggest that their CAM therapies may be as effective as, or even better than, conventional medicine for promoting wellness, relieving chronic pain, treating mild depression, and managing long-term illnesses.

It's not hard to understand why. Years of rigorous academic training makes skeptics out of the vast majority of conventional doctors and systematically instills in them an appetite for that "gold standard" of medical proof, the double-blind–placebo-controlled (DBPC) study.

The drawback in a strict adherence to the DBPC standard is that even Western medicine cannot meet it all the time. By most estimates, more than half of all conventional medical treatments have *not* been proven in DBPC research. Yet most conventional Western medicine doctors continue to insist that CAM therapies are worthless unless they pass this test. This is clearly a double standard. If, in fact, Western medicine were restricted to only those therapies *proven* effective in DBPC studies, we doctors would have much less to offer our patients. The truth is that some therapies are very difficult, if not impossible, to study within this methodology.

The fact that academicians struggle with this challenge does not negate the practical value of the therapies in question. In other words, *a lack of research does not mean a lack of results*. And that's what patients care about—*results*. Patients are inclined to accept what seems to work rather than worry about academic hair-splitting.

Complementary therapies that have proven their clinical effectiveness for hundreds, even thousands, of years may not fit the conventional research protocols. But a growing number of studies meet the most stringent scientific criteria and demonstrate conclusively the benefits of complementary or alternative interventions in well defined situations.

For example, a 1997 panel organized by the National Institutes of Health concluded, after reviewing the scientific literature, that acupuncture can quell the nausea and vomiting associated with surgery, chemotherapy, and postoperative dental pain. Acupuncture can also be effective in treating addiction, stroke, and asthma. The panel also identified a number of pain-related conditions for which acupuncture can work in combination with, or as an acceptable alternative to, standard treatments. These disorders include headache, menstrual cramps, tennis elbow, lower back pain, carpal tunnel syndrome, and fibromyalgia.

In 1998, the *Journal of the American Medical Association* presented the results of six scientific studies in its special issue on alternative medicine. Among the findings:

- Moxibustion (the burning of herbs to stimulate specific acupuncture points) is a safe, effective way to turn fetuses in a breech position.
- Chinese herbal medicine can be useful in treating irritable bowel syndrome.
- Yoga can help ease the pain of carpal tunnel syndrome.

Still missing in many of these studies is a theory or mechanism that explains the outcome in the scientific terms that conventionally trained physicians understand. That's why a certain percentage of physicians continue to categorize the whole field as irrelevant, believing that the public's interest in other healing systems will go the way of the pet rock.

But with over 40 percent of Americans now using complementary approaches, that may prove to be a shortsighted, even dangerous position. If your conventional medical doctor falls into this category, you may want to consider shopping around for a more open-minded physician.

Hopefully, the health care delivery system of the future will integrate the scientific and technological strengths of Western medicine with the centuries-old body-mind-spirit orientation of complementary practice to provide each of us, in sickness and in health, the best of both worlds.

# INTEGRATIVE MEDICINE: HOW TO MAKE IT WORK FOR YOU

Integrative medicine is the term most commonly used to describe the blending of conventional Western medicine with complementary therapies. However, without understanding why or how to do this you are left with what I call "disintegrative medicine"—a random and chaotic blend of diverse therapies that may actually conflict with each other.

The only valid reason for combining conventional and complementary therapies is to provide more personalized and comprehensive (mind, body, and spirit) care that improves health outcomes and reduces side effects. The only legitimate way of doing this is through multidisciplinary collaboration. Physicians or CAM practitioners who are unwilling or unable to collaborate due to differences in perspective or philosophy value their own biases more than the patient's health. On the other hand, while integrative medicine requires physicians and CAM practitioners to set aside our biases and be open minded, it is not in the best interest of patients that we be so open minded that our brains fall out.

All therapies need to be looked at in terms of potential risks and benefits. We should require evidence of safety, efficacy, and some plausible mechanism of action for inclusion of any therapy. What constitutes reasonable standards of scientific evidence is an area of ongoing debate and controversy.

In order to weave together the various therapies it is helpful to classify them according to how we think they work. Most classification schemes for complementary therapies exclude Western medicine. The problem with this divisive approach is that it makes it more difficult to understand how complementary therapies and Western medicine differ, how they are similar, and how they might be rationally combined. The classification scheme described in this book is based entirely on presumed mechanisms of action and has six broad categories: biochemical therapies, structural therapies, movement therapies, environmental therapies, mind-body therapies, and energy therapies.

The two primary tools of Western medicine are the use of drugs (pharmacology) and surgery. Pharmacology is clearly a biochemical intervention that impacts the chemistry of the body and surgery is clearly a structural intervention that impacts the anatomic structures of the body. If we were to create a hierarchy of biochemical therapies, pharmacology would be the most aggressive because the substances used are extremely purified, concentrated, and powerful. If we were to create a hierarchy of structural therapies surgery would obviously be the most aggressive in that category. Therefore, for every category (based on mechanism of action) we can create a ranked hierarchy from less aggressive to more aggressive, from less risky to more risky, from less costly to more costly, and so on. When as a patient you are evaluated (history, physical exam, blood tests, imaging studies, etc.) you are first and foremost "triaged" or risk stratified. In other words, the first and most important step is to determine if this is an acute, medically unstable, dangerous, urgent, or emergency situation. If so then the most aggressive interventions are warranted ASAP to prevent serious complications or even death. A patient with suicidal or psychotic depression is a classic example of this. On the other hand, if the process of evaluation and risk stratification has determined that your condition is more chronic and poses no immediate health threat (such as mild depression) then it is appropriate to first recommend less aggressive (often complementary) therapies. The effectiveness of these therapies needs to be monitored. If after a predetermined time frame your condition has not improved then stepping up to more aggressive therapies is justified. By following this risk-stratified, stepped-care model, conventional Western therapies and complementary therapies can be rationally and seamlessly interwoven to provide the most appropriate level of care. Aggressive therapies are not withheld from anyone that needs them nor are they inappropriately forced on anyone that doesn't need them. The philosophy and clinical strategy (the "why" and the "how") for integrative medicine are summarized on the conceptual template diagram on the next page.

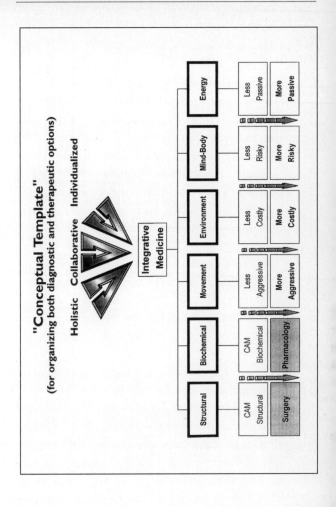

## SOME GENERAL CAVEATS

As you delve into the world of complementary and alternative medicine, keep in mind that a good deal of what we know about CAM "best practices" in the treatment of depression is based on observational or anecdotal evidence. That means many interventions have not yet been investigated or proven in rigorous scientific studies. The research data is often imperfect in terms of sample size, selection bias, investigator bias, duration of study, lack of blinding, or a failure to control for one or more variables. Also keep in mind that, in many cases, the long-term effects of various complementary therapies have not been determined.

While these caveats may hinder some physicians from recommending nontraditional approaches, growing numbers of men and women, less interested in academic debates, are finding the relief they're looking for by exploring and experiencing firsthand what CAM has to offer.

Complementary and alternative approaches focus on establishing harmony and balance in mind, body, and spirit. What could be more appropriate as you look for a way out of your depression? In addition, complementary therapies can, in many cases, offer immediate symptom relief, even as their emphasis on lifestyle changes can help prevent a recurrence and reduce your risk for a range of age-related illnesses including heart disease, certain cancers, osteoporosis, and diabetes.

As with traditional medicine, complementary therapy must be individualized for maximum benefit.

Rarely does a single therapy neutralize all symptoms of depression. For some people, one type of treatment may relieve one symptom or a cluster of symptoms; for most others, depression calls for a coordinated multitherapy approach. This generally means a mix of traditional Western medical interventions, psychotherapy, and one or more complementary/alternative therapies. Finding the therapies that are most effective for you may take some time, so go into the process with patience and with an open mind.

Once again, I remind you to discuss with your conventional physician what you're considering in the way of complementary therapies—particularly if you are also on standard antidepressant medication. Some therapies may be contraindicated for your condition—St. John's wort, for example, is known to be effective in cases of mild to moderate depression but is not recommended for those suffering from severe depression or bipolar disorder. Some over-the-counter "alternative" products may be off-limits for people taking certain synthetic drugs for other coexisting medical conditions.

# 11

## Biochemical Approaches

### HERBAL MEDICINE

If your depression is rooted not in external events but in biochemical abnormalities or hormonal imbalances, your search for effective treatment may lead you to a number of complementary/alternative approaches that can be explained, at least in part, in terms of the effects they have on the body's biochemistry. This same biochemical model provides the foundation for Western (allopathic) medicine and is used to explain the physiology of depression and help us understand the mechanisms behind standard antidepressant medications. In its simplest form, this model sees the body in terms of anatomic structures and systems that are sustained by biochemical processes.

The use of diet and supplements for depression are examples of biochemcal intervention. Nutritional approaches fit so comfortably within mainstream medicine and play such a major role in your general health and wellness that we've covered diet and supplementation in separate chapters. In this chapter, we'll take a close look at the practice of herbal medicine and, in particular, at St.

John's wort, an herbal remedy used successfully by millions around the world to treat depression.

## HERBS, PAST AND PRESENT

Herbs have been used in folk remedies around the world since ancient times. They were used in early Greek and Roman civilizations and were introduced to Europe during the Crusades. In the United States, herbal medicines (developed from plants, plant parts, and plant extracts) were for many years used to prevent illnesses and to treat minor complaints. Until the 1930s, in fact, herbs were the primary choice of many physicians in this country—for example, peppermint to soothe an upset stomach, garlic to prevent colds and flu.

As medical technology advanced and new pharmaceuticals were developed and marketed, the use of herbal remedies declined. Recently, however, there's been a renewed interest in natural botanicals, thanks in large part to the mounting expense of synthetic drugs and some of their serious side effects. Today, herbs are a booming business in the United States. In 1997, we spent an estimated $5.1 billion on natural plant remedies.

It's interesting to note that many common prescription and over-the-counter drugs were derived from herbs. Aspirin, for example, was originally developed from willow bark. Quinine, used to treat malaria, comes from the bark of an evergreen tree indigenous to South America and cultivated in hot climates. Taxol, a powerful drug used to combat breast cancer, comes from the Pacific yew tree. The painkiller morphine is derived from the opium poppy. Digitalis, a heart medication, is derived from foxglove.

It's usually safe to treat yourself with herbs for minor conditions. For colds, try some echinacea; for mild digestive complaints, sip a cup of peppermint tea. But even herbs that are generally safe need to be used with caution. By stimulating the immune system, echinacea can create problems for persons with autoimmune disease. Peppermint tea can bring discomfort to anyone suffering from heartburn/reflux. High doses of licorice root can raise your blood pressure. Chamomile can trigger a reaction if you're allergic to ragweed. And too much ginger can cause gas, nausea, and vomiting—although in smaller doses it can ease those very same symptoms.

## WHY SOME DOCTORS ARE SKEPTICAL ABOUT HERBS

Western-trained physicians are likely to be skeptical about claims made for herbal therapies. Many have ingrained doubts about the effectiveness of botanical remedies in general. Others admit they are simply not well enough informed to venture an opinion. A common complaint of physicians relates to multiherb formulas. Doctors contend that when several herbs are combined in a single product targeted to a broad range of symptoms, it's impossible to evaluate in any scientific way which ingredients are acting on which symptom. Doctors also point out that many of the research studies cited by the manufacturers of herbal remedies are still not being published in peer-reviewed journals.

Critics of herbal therapy also contend, with some justification, that because herbal preparations are not regulated by the Food and Drug Administration (FDA) as pharmaceuticals are, potency can vary from brand to brand, even from bottle to bottle from the same manufacturer. With poor regulation of this industry and lack of universal standardization, herbs may be contaminated, adulterated, or otherwise of unknown quality. It's best to stick with well known products from reputable companies.

## SAFETY GUIDELINES FOR HERBAL THERAPY

Before embarking on herbal therapy, it's a good idea to have your health problem diagnosed by a qualified medical practitioner. It's important to know exactly what you're treating so you can rule out a more serious condition that could require conventional drugs. Also, it's possible to mask the symptoms of a serious underlying condition with the use of natural remedies.

- It's always best to use herbs under the care of a health care practitioner who is familiar with herbal medicine. In the United States this might be a naturopath, a specialist in botanical medicine, an acupuncturist trained in Chinese herbalism, an Ayurvedic healer, or a trained medical or clinical herbalist.
- Herbal medicine is not a one-size-fits-all therapy. Your practitioner will devise a treatment strategy based on your condition and on your medical and family history. The type of preparation and the

dosage will depend on the strength of the herb, your age, and the results sought.

- Inform *all* your health care practitioners about *all* the medicines and herbal preparations you're taking. Some herbs can cause allergic reactions or don't mix well with conventional drugs.

- Learn as much as you can about an herb before you take it. Are there side effects or warnings? How much and how often should you take it? Does it work best as a tablet or capsule, a tincture or tea?

- Avoid taking potentially toxic herbs, including chaparral, comfrey (taken orally), ephedra (*ma huang*), germander, Indian snakeroot, lobelia, pennyroyal, wormwood, and yohimbe.

- Buy from reputable manufacturers. In the past, European botanicals have tended to be of higher quality. Recently, however, several U.S. companies have introduced more stringent standards and now produce top-of-the-line botanicals.

- The FDA now requires herbal preparations to be labeled with the herb's scientific name, the amount of active ingredient(s), and the plant parts used. Product labels should also include the company's address, batch and lot numbers, expiration date, and dosage guidelines.

- Start with the lowest possible dose, and do not exceed the recommended dose. The toxicity of herbal products is largely untested.

- Don't pick herbs yourself from chemically treated lawns or gardens.
- In general, it's best to avoid herbs if you're pregnant.
- Consult a physician before taking herbs if you have allergies, are sensitive to drugs, or are taking prescription medications for chronic illness.
- Stop using herbal medicines two to three weeks before any scheduled surgery. Some herbs may have dangerous interactions with medications used during anesthesia or may increase the risk of bleeding complications.
- Consult a physician before giving herbs to children under 12 or to adults over 65.
- Be patient; herbs take longer to work than synthetic drugs. It may take six to eight weeks before you notice any benefits. However, the good news is that herbs retain their therapeutic strength over several years, so you won't need to keep increasing the dosage.
- If you experience any side effects, such as diarrhea or headache, stop taking the herb immediately and call your doctor. You can also call the FDA hotline at 800-332-1088.

## What to Look For on the Label

The phrase *caveat emptor* is particularly appropriate when it comes to purchasing nutritional and herbal supplements. In a recent study reported in the *New England Journal of Medicine* (1998), up to 25 percent of Chinese herbal supplements contained either significant contaminants (sometimes toxic levels of lead or arsenic) or unlabeled adulterants (such as cortisone) that were added to boost the effect of the labeled ingredients. Studies done by consumer groups, using independent laboratory assays, have found huge variations in the amount or percentage of active ingredients in nutritional products made by different manufacturers.

The virtual lack of regulation within the nutritional supplement industry forces wise consumers to seek out companies that voluntarily regulate themselves to control quality and meet high standards of safety. To judge whether a product is made by a responsible manufacturer, look for these important clues on the packaging:

**Address and phone number**—A mailing address and/or e-mail address or Web site should be provided for contacting the manufacturer with questions or problems. A toll-free number is ideal.

**Expiration date**—Many supplements have a limited shelf life, and it's hard to know how long they've been sitting in a warehouse, store, or medicine cabinet before consumption. Discard supplements if past their expiration date.

**FDA registration of manufacturing facilities**—Some companies have gone to the trouble of having their facilities inspected and have submitted extensive documentation in order to secure FDA registration. This is good evidence that a manufacturer is not cutting corners.

**GMP compliance**—Voluntary adherence to Good Manufacturing Practices (GMP) is another sign that the company is behaving responsibly.

**Independent laboratory assays**—Anyone can make content claims on a label, but they should be able to prove these claims with objective, unbiased data. Independent laboratory verification of both the amount of active ingredients and the absence of contaminants or adulterants is important, but may not be documented on the packaging. Responsible manufacturers are able to readily provide this information on request. The Web site *www.consumerlab.com* provides independent laboratory analyses of a number of popular brands of herbs and supplements.

**Lot/Batch number**—Product tracking through lot and batch numbers is vital for quality control purposes.

**Milligrams of each ingredient per dose**—Avoid products that have a long list of ingredients but give only the total milligram dosage. It should be clear how many milligrams or units of each ingredient are in each dose (capsule, tablet, dropper, or teaspoon).

**Percentage of active ingredient**—In many cases research has shown a certain percentage of a specific active ingredient is needed for clinical efficacy. If this type of research is available, then the manufacturer should meet that standard.

**Recommended daily dose**—You run the risk of both overdosing and underdosing without explicit instructions on the bottle.**Return policy**—Reputable companies will refund your money if you're not satisfied with their product.

**Side effects/Precautions**—Responsible manufacturers warn consumers of contraindications to using their product, as well as potential interactions and side effects.

**Product-specific research**—Look for evidence of research done with that company's specific product and not something similar (you hope) made by a different manufacturer.

# HERBAL TREATMENTS
# FOR DEPRESSION

A review of various nonmedical books on complementary/ alternative medicine produces a short list of herbs claimed to be helpful in treating depression. These include wild oats, lemon balm, ginseng, wood betony, thyme, rosemary, borage, clove, basil, and St. John's wort. Only the last has been the subject of intense scientific investigation.

## ST. JOHN'S WORT

Over the last several years, St. John's wort *(Hypericum perforatum)* has received a great deal of attention for its therapeutic benefits in cases of mild to moderate depression. The herb is natural, inexpensive, and widely available over-the-counter in pill form—and for these reasons its popularity among U.S. consumers is soaring. Nevertheless, I want to stress that St. John's wort is an effective treatment only in cases of mild to moderate depression; it is not appropriate for severe clinical depression. If you suspect that your low mood is more than just a case of the "blues," or if you try St. John's wort and it doesn't provide relief within a reasonable time frame, seek medical attention without delay.

St. John's wort has long been used in Europe to treat mild depression. In Germany alone, almost 3 million prescriptions a year are written for the herb. In 1996 the *British Medical Journal* summarized 23 randomized controlled trials of St. John's wort. More than 1,750 people participated in these studies, and the findings showed that 50 to 80 percent of those who were mildly depressed responded positively to the herb. In these trials, the herb was found to be three times as effective in reducing depressive symptoms as a placebo. Eight studies found that St. John's wort was as effective as standard antidepressants. In addition, those on the herbal therapy had lower dropout rates and reported fewer negative side effects.

Among the many studies that even conventional physicians find impressive is one conducted in 1993 by a German physician by the name of K. D. Hansgen. In a four-week investigation, Dr. Hansgen and his colleagues compared the effects of St. John's wort and a placebo in treating 72 patients drawn from 11 different medical practices. The results of the study, published in the *Journal of Geriatric Psychiatry and Neurology*, showed that those treated with St. John's wort showed significant improvement over those taking the placebo. The improvement was measured on the basis of the HAM-D test, a systematic rating scale for depression. (The scale uses a combination of doctors' observations and patients' responses to questions to determine a number that indicates the severity of depression. The higher the number, the more serious the depression.) Those taking the herbal remedy showed a better than 50 percent drop in their scores, while those taking the placebo improved by only 26 percent.

Researchers speculate that St. John's wort works in the same manner as antidepressants, by changing the levels of serotonin, dopamine, and norepinephrine, but in a gentler way. Hypericin, one of the active ingredients, has been shown to increase theta waves in the brain, the waves that normally occur during sleep and are associated with deep meditation.

In the United States, St. John's wort is not a prescription medication; it can be bought over-the-counter in drugstores, supermarkets, and natural food stores. The usual dose is 300 milligrams three times a day, taken near mealtime. Look for a brand that is standardized to 0.3 percent hypericin. As we discussed earlier in this chapter, it's best to buy any herbal preparation, including St. John's wort, from a reputable company, since herbal remedies are not FDA-regulated.

Like most herbal therapies (and like most standard antidepressants as well), St. John's wort does not improve depressive symptoms immediately; it could take three to six weeks before you notice any significant effects.

Why has St. John's wort become so popular? In addition to the fact that studies have shown that it's safe and it works, many people simply prefer an herbal remedy over a synthetic one because they feel it's more in keeping with their "natural" or holistic philosophy. Patients who have a good response report that St. John's wort gradually and gently elevates their mood and raises their energy level, without causing the adverse side effects—especially loss of libido—associated with many prescription antidepressants. In addition, many people who take the herb find that it helps them stay alert, think more clearly, concentrate better, and cope with stress.

Though St. John's wort does not induce sleep per se, many people who use it also report that they enjoy a sounder and more restful sleep.

Natural does not mean ideal, however, and St. John's wort does not work for everyone. Some people report no improvement at all, while others maintain it makes them feel even more down in the dumps. So while it certainly is not a miracle cure, it is another tool to use in the fight against depression.

### St. John's Wort and Depression

If you're thinking about treating your depression with St. John's wort, keep the following in mind:

- Use St. John's wort only for mild to moderate depression.
- Do not take it with other antidepressants or with stimulants.
- Do not take with birth control pills, cyclosporine, or antiretroviral drugs.
- Watch for signs and symptoms of major depression such as withdrawal, insomnia, anorexia, and thoughts of suicide.
- Give the herb at least three weeks to reach a therapeutic level.
- Do not take it if you are pregnant or nursing.
- Avoid excessive sunlight.
- Do not take along with 5-HTP.
- Notify your primary care provider if major depressive symptoms occur or if depression persists three weeks after taking St. John's wort.

CAUTION—If you experience fatigue, nausea, restlessness, or dizziness, or if you develop a rash, stop taking the herb immediately. St. John's wort may also cause a sun-sensitive rash in fair-skinned people, particularly at higher dosages; if you're in this group, avoid bright sunlight. Recent research suggests that St. John's wort may increase the incidence of cataracts, probably through its photosensitizing effect. If you use St. John's wort, invest in a good pair of sunglasses to reduce the UV exposure to your eyes.

Do not take St. John's wort if you're already taking a prescription antidepressant. The herb may cause serious problems such as "serotonin syndrome" if used in conjunction with SSRI antidepressants (Prozac, Paxil, etc.), or hypertensive crisis if used with the MAOI antidepressants (Parnate, Nardil, etc.). Obviously, these combinations should either be avoided or monitored very closely by an adventurous physician with good liability insurance.

Another potentially serious drug interaction is that St. John's wort may reduce the effectiveness of certain chemotherapy drugs. One such drug is etoposide (VePesid), sometimes used to treat lung and breast cancer. You certainly don't want to compromise the effectiveness of chemotherapy treatment by using St. John's wort. St. John's wort also speeds up the liver metabolism of several drugs and reduces their effectiveness by lowering drug levels. Examples of drugs affected this way include birth control pills, cyclosporine, and antiretroviral drug.

## KAVA

Kava (sometimes called kava kava) is another herb that has received a great deal of media attention and is sold over the counter to millions worldwide. Many herbalists believe that kava can be helpful to people with depression, particularly if anxiety is a significant component of the problem.

The kava plant (*Piper methysticum*), a member of the pepper family, is indigenous to the Polynesian islands of the South Pacific. Polynesians have used kava for over 3,000 years, preparing it as a drink used for ceremonial purposes; to settle disagreements; to celebrate rites of passage such as births, weddings, and deaths; for social purposes; and as a sedative, muscle relaxant, diuretic, and remedy for anxiety and insomnia. Kava first came to the attention of Westerners when it was discovered by explorer Captain James Cook, who gave it the name of "intoxicating pepper." It was first mentioned in scientific records in 1886. Today native Polynesians prepare kava as a beverage and use it recreationally, much as they would use alcohol; the bonus is that kava is not addictive and does not result in hangovers.

Outside Polynesia, kava has been recommended as a safe, effective, natural sleep aid, as a muscle relaxant, and as an anti-anxiety remedy. Its active ingredients, *kavalactones,* produce physical and mental relaxation and feelings of well-being. Recent clinical studies have shown that in some situations the herb is as effective as prescription anti-anxiety medications that contain benzodiazepines, such as Valium. Unlike benzodiazepines, however, which can promote lethargy and mental impairment, kava has been reported to improve concentration, memory, and reaction time for people suffering from anxiety.

Like St. John's wort, kava is available over-the-counter in capsules or as a tincture. For anxiety, the typical dose of kava is 100 milligrams two to three times daily of a product standardized to contain 70 percent kavalactones. To promote sleep, try 200 milligrams 30 to 60 minutes before bedtime.

Kava has not been studied as extensively as St. John's wort, and because its effects last only several hours with each dose, it is not considered as viable an antidepressant therapy as St. John's wort or prescription medications.

CAUTION—Do not use kava if you are pregnant or nursing or if you are already taking a prescription antidepressant. Do not exceed the recommended dosage or use for longer than four to six months, as misuse can lead to muscle weakness, visual impairment, dizziness, and drying of the skin, as well as hypertension, reduced protein levels, blood cell abnormalities, or liver damage. If skin or visual problems develop, stop the kava and consult a physician.

Kava may enhance the effect and thus the toxicity of alcohol, barbiturates, or benzodiazepines (Valium, Xanax, etc.) and should not be used in combination with these agents. Coma has been reported in patients combining kava and Xanax. Avoid driving or any other activity that requires a quick reaction time.

## VALERIAN

Valerian is another herbal remedy that can be effective in treating some common depressive symptoms. It has a long history of use as an aid for insomnia and mild anxiety related to tension and stress. Valerian acts as a mild tranquilizer and depresses the central nervous system. However, unlike other anti-anxiety drugs (including Valium and Xanax), it does not appear to be addictive.

According to legend, the Pied Piper lured rats from the village of Hamelin with valerian. The ancient Greek physician Dioscorides prescribed valerian for digestive problems, nausea, liver problems, and urinary tract disorders, while another early physician, Galen (131–201 A.D.), recommended it to treat insomnia.

Researchers are still trying to determine exactly how valerian works but believe it has some effect on serotonin or gamma aminobutyric acid (GABA)—two neurotransmitters that help regulate mood, sleep, and states of relaxation.

Since valerian root has an unpleasant taste and smell, capsules are usually tolerated best. The usual dose for insomnia is 300 to 500 milligrams of a product standardized to contain 0.8 percent valeric acid, taken about an hour before bedtime. Those who use valerian report that they are able to get to sleep more easily and enjoy a deeper, more restful sleep, with fewer awakenings and no "morning after" grogginess—an effect frequently associated with drugs prescribed for insomnia.

Based on its effectiveness for insomnia, valerian is being examined more closely for its ability to reduce the symptoms of stress and mild anxiety. Early research indicates that valerian extracts may ease withdrawal symptoms for those being weaned from benzodiazepines (such as Valium and Xanax) and may be effective as a nonaddicting substitute. To treat anxiety, the recommended dose is 150 to 300 milligrams taken in the morning, in addition to the evening dose listed previously.

Use a product standardized to 0.8 percent valeric acid. If you experience unwanted sedation, reduce the dose.

Although valerian appears to be safer than prescription sedatives and can safely be used every night for a few weeks, it's best not to use it indefinitely, since there have been no long-term studies of the herb. If headaches and restlessness occur, discontinue use.

CAUTION—Do not take valerian with alcohol or barbiturates, or if you're already taking a prescription tranquilizer or sedative. Use caution when driving or performing tasks that require mental alertness until you know how valerian affects you. Do not give valerian to children under age 12.

## OTHER HERBAL REMEDIES YOU CAN TRY

### To Stabilize Mood

Some people find a cup of lemon balm tea is mildly stimulating because it helps to lift mood and counter feelings of lethargy and apathy. Drink 3 or 4 cups of tea every day, or take ½ to 1 teaspoon of tincture up to three times a day.

### To Promote Restful Sleep

Everyone experiences a bout of insomnia at one time or another. But for people with depression and/or anxiety, sleep disturbances can be a nightly event.

Chamomile has a calming effect and has been used medicinally around the world for many centuries. Drinking a couple of cups of chamomile tea in the evening may help you relax at bedtime. If you're allergic to ragweed, don't use chamomile, as it may trigger an allergic reaction.

Valerian has been used for more than a thousand years as a sleep aid and has the added benefit that it appears to be nonaddictive. You can buy valerian tea if you don't mind drinking something that smells and tastes like well aged, sweaty socks. If you're like most people, you'll prefer using the herb in capsule form.

There are a variety of "sleepytime" teas that combine chamomile, passionflower, hops, vervain, skullcap, or other calming or sedating ingredients. Enjoy a cup before turning in for the night.

### For Sexual Problems

For some people, one unwanted side effect of some prescription antidepressants is reduced sex drive. However, the use of standard drug therapy doesn't have to mean the loss of your sexual self. Ginkgo biloba, used in combination with libido-sapping SSRI medications, has been shown to restore sex drive in some patients.

A typical dose of gigko is 40 milligrams three times daily or 80 milligrams twice daily of a product standardized to contain 24 percent ginkgosides.

CAUTION—Because ginkgo biloba has a blood thinning effect and because of reports of bleeding complications when used in combination with aspirin, it should generally not be used in combination with medicines known to thin the blood (aspirin, Coumadin, Persantine, Ticlid, etc.). Also it's a good idea to stop taking ginkgo two to three weeks prior to any surgery to reduce the likelihood of bleeding complications. Some patients notice headaches after starting ginkgo; you may want to stop taking the herb in this case. Higher dosages may cause diarrhea, irritability, and restlessness.

# 12

## Energy Therapies

### TRADITIONAL CHINESE MEDICINE
Acupuncture
Acupressure
Chinese Herbal Medicine
Chinese Dietary Therapy

### AYURVEDIC HEALING

### HOMEOPATHY

### PHOTOTHERAPY

The alternative and complementary approaches grouped under the umbrella term "energy therapies," in my opinion, hold the most potential for the future of integrative medicine, and they are also the ones that most directly challenge the prevailing Western biochemical model. For conventional doctors, the energy therapies are the most intellectually, academically, and professionally risky because they cannot be explained by prevailing dogma.

In simple terms, conventional Western medicine is based on a model consisting of anatomic structures and systems that are sustained by biochemical processes. Traditional Chinese medicine (TCM) and Ayurvedic healing are grounded in a completely different model— one based on the flow of energy within the body (called *"chi"* in TCM, *"prana"* in Ayurveda). In these healing traditions, illness is attributed to energetic imbalances, and health is restored when the imbalances are corrected.

From a conventional medical standpoint, all this is nonsense. Conventional physicians point to an absence of consistent anatomic structures that correspond with acupuncture points and meridians (energy pathways) of TCM. They also are likely to explain the clinically demonstrated effects of acupuncture, for example, in terms of the biochemistry of endorphin release.

Those who have taken the time to investigate the energy therapies know, however, that several studies have documented that our bodies have areas of low electrical resistance and high electrical conductivity. This being the case, the concept of electrons (a current) following the paths of least resistance in the body becomes plausible, and the concepts of *"chi"* and *"prana"* seem less farfetched.

Therapeutic touch, which paradoxically often involves no touching at all, is another type of energy therapy that has been tossed aside by skeptics. In fact, there are scores of well designed scientific studies documenting physiologic changes as a result of therapeutic touch, including accelerated wound healing, increased hemoglobin and oxygen levels, and even in vitro altered enzyme activity. Unfortunately, to date such studies have usually been published mostly in the nursing literature or in CAM journals. Despite the impeccable scientific rigor of some of these studies, they have typically been excluded from publication in mainstream medical journals.

Clearly the Western biomedical model is inadequate to explain many of the well documented responses to energetic interventions. Because of this, these therapies have the greatest potential to challenge our thinking and expand our understanding of how the human body works.

In this chapter we'll be looking at four energy-based approaches that can offer some measure of help to people with depression. These include traditional Chinese medicine (acupuncture, acupressure, Chinese herbal medicine, and Chinese dietary therapy), Ayurveda, homeopathy, and phototherapy.

Keep in mind that TCM and Ayurveda straddle the energy-based category and the biochemical category, as medical professionals trained in the Western tradition often try to explain the effects of these healing systems in terms that are more familiar to conventional medicine.

## TRADITIONAL CHINESE MEDICINE

Traditional Chinese medicine (TCM) is one of the oldest healing systems in the world and has been practiced in China and Eastern Asia for nearly 5,000 years. In the Eastern tradition, TCM is thought of as an energy therapy; in the West, the conventional medical community likes to explain the effects of TCM in terms of the bio-chemical model they already understand.

Two concepts are central to TCM: balance and flow. The TCM practitioner helps the individual achieve internal balance *(yin and yang)*, as well as balance with the external environment. The second concept, flow, relates to the energy or life force *(chi)* circulating within each individual.

According to TCM, the nature of your illness depends on the particular imbalance between your *yin* and *yang*. Too much *yin,* for example, results in "cold" symptoms like chills; too much *yang* results in "hot" symptoms like fever. Different organs are characterized as *yin* or *yang;* the liver, for example, is *yin,* while the stomach is *yang*.

If the Eastern terminology *(chi, yin,* and *yang)* is intimidating or confusing to you, it may be easier to think in the Western, scientifically neutral terms of *charge, electrons, electricity,* and *current,* which are devoid of cultural or metaphysical interpretations.

*Chi* is thought to move through the body along 12 energy pathways called *meridians*. Whether you call it *"chi"* (Eastern) or "electrons" (Western), correcting energy imbalances can have profound effects on physiology. Research has shown repeatedly that the acupuncture points and meridians are actually low-resistance electrical pathways, much like an electric grid for the body. TCM holds that when chi is blocked or out of balance, illness results. Studies have also shown that pathology (whether a fracture, a tumor, a cut, a muscle spasm, etc.) is accompanied by abnormal electrical activity, and that correcting the abnormal electrical activity can often bring improvement.

*Chi* can become weak, stagnant, or misdirected. Weakened *chi* can result in loss of appetite, dizzy spells, and a weak pulse. Stagnant or blocked *chi* can lead to tightness of the chest, abdominal pain, and painful and/or irregular periods. Misdirected *chi*, in which the energy flows in the wrong direction, can cause asthma, coughs, vomiting, and fainting. Re-establishing the normal flow of *chi* and balancing *yin* and *yang* is thought to restore health and prevent illness.

In traditional Chinese medicine, treatment may involve a combination of Chinese herbal medicine, acupuncture, acupressure, Chinese medical massage *(tui na)*, exercise (such as *tai chi*), and dietary therapy. TCM differs from Western medicine in that it focuses on the entire body, not just the specific parts that are affected by disease or injury. When Western medicine finally embraces the inseparability of energy and physiology, we can expect to see dramatic changes in health care.

Attempts to translate TCM terminology into Western terms can sometimes be confusing. However, there are many studies documenting its clinical effectiveness for depression and for a wide variety of other conditions including arthritis, asthma, cerebral palsy, colitis, depression, diabetes, drug withdrawal, hay fever, herpes, impotence, infertility, insomnia, menopause, nausea (associated with chemotherapy, pregnancy, or surgery), premenstrual syndrome, sciatica, stroke, and chronic pain reduction.

Traditional Chinese medicine is like the Western model in recognizing two basic types of depression. The first type, known as exogenous depression, results from situational difficulties such as divorce, grief, or unemployment. The second type is a result of chemical imbalances in the brain and is called endogenous depression.

Traditional practitioners may further say that depression is caused by the stagnation of the liver *chi,* or "life energy."

## ACUPUNCTURE

Acupuncture is an ancient technique that originated in China at least 2,500 years ago. The painless insertion of very fine disposable needles in points along the body's meridians is intended to relieve symptoms by correcting energy imbalances and restoring the normal, healthy flow of energy. As mentioned earlier, the acupuncture points and meridians have repeatedly been shown to be low-resistance electrical pathways, and the use of acupuncture needles or acupressure changes the electron flow (current) along these pathways.

Many Western-trained physicians and researchers prefer a more scientific (biochemical) explanation and hold that acupuncture works by releasing the body's endorphins—peptides secreted in the brain that relieve pain and promote feelings of well-being.

Regardless of whether you believe in energetic or biochemical mechanisms, acupuncture has proven useful for a number of conditions, including stress reduction, fatigue, headaches, pain, insomnia, and depression.

Most acupuncturists working today use presterilized disposable needles that come packaged in sealed envelopes. The number of needles used, and their placement, varies from person to person, even from session to session, depending on the results being sought. Some practitioners swab the acupuncture point with alcohol before inserting the needles. Others may use a treatment called *moxibustion*. This consists of applying heat directly above acupuncture points by means of small bundles of smoldering herbs, usually mugwort leaves. Moxibustion frequently accompanies the insertion of needles, but it can be used alone.

Once the needles are inserted, you usually lie quietly for 30 to 60 minutes. At the end of the session, the acupuncturist will remove the needles and discard them. You may develop a slight bruise if the needle has hit a blood vessel, but that happens only rarely.

The number of treatments depends on your condition. In some cases, one or two visits can do the trick; in other circumstances, six to 12 treatments might be in order. And once you feel that you're back on track, you may want to schedule treatment on a regular basis; many people opt for monthly or quarterly sessions to stay in balance.

Choose an acupuncturist or a physician who is certified by the National Certification Commission for Acupuncture and Oriental Medicine (NCCAOM). This organization publishes an annual directory of board-certified practitioners. You can also contact the American Association of Oriental Medicine and request a list of qualified acupuncturists in your area. Both organizations are included in the resource listing at the back of this book.

Currently medical doctors (M.D.'s) and chiropractors can perform acupuncture in many states; some practitioners are excellent, some are not. To experience maximum benefit, it's important to seek out a qualified practitioner. In addition to good training, it takes years of ongoing practice to become a superior acupuncturist. You cannot expect this level of skill from someone who's taken a weekend course in acupuncture or who merely dabbles in it as a sideline. Be sure your practitioner has had substantial training and devotes a large share of his or her ongoing clinical practice to acupuncture.

CAUTION—If you have an infection or are prone to bleeding easily, check with your physician before undergoing acupuncture.

## Acupuncture and Depression

Acupuncture seems to be one of the most effective alternative treatments for depression. According to a report published in the well regarded journal *Psychological Science*, acupuncture may reduce or *even eliminate* depressive symptoms. The report focused on a team of researchers at the University of Arizona in Tucson who examined levels of self-reported depression in a group of 38 women receiving either acupuncture or no treatment for a period of eight weeks. The women in the acupuncture group received one of two types of therapy— the first specifically focused on treating depression, and the second focused on treating another condition, such as back pain. The authors reported that after the treatment specifically designed to address depression, 64 percent of the women were depression-free.

Of course, this was a very small study, and even the researchers cautioned that the results needed to be confirmed by larger, controlled studies. They also recommended an investigation into how acupuncture actually achieves its effects. Traditional acupuncturists say that the treatment corrects the imbalance of energy in the body that can lead not only to depression but to other diseases as well.

Another study suggested that electroacupuncture (in which electrical stimulators are attached to the acupuncture needles to move more current along the meridians) might be more effective than standard acupuncture in the treatment of depression.

If further studies support this initial research, acupuncture may well prove to be a valuable alternative therapy.

## For Headache Relief

Before recommending a treatment plan for headaches, a TCM practitioner will take a history and perform an examination which includes looking at the tongue and checking the pulse. Treatment plans often include acupuncture, Chinese herbs, exercise, diet, and lifestyle changes. The goal of TCM is to identify and correct the individual pattern of energetic imbalance. Therefore, the acupuncture points stimulated will vary from person to person. The points stimulated may or may not be near the actual area of pain. A typical course of treatment is once or twice a week for four to 10 weeks, with periodic follow-up.

Stomachache and backache also respond to acupuncture therapy.

### To Promote Sound Sleep

Traditional Chinese practitioners believe that insomnia is caused by a kidney disorder or imbalance, resulting in a vicious cycle of tension and fatigue. Acupuncture is used to unblock and rebalance the flow of energy, or *chi,* within this organ and along the related meridians. Acupoints corresponding to the kidney, brain, and heart are involved.

## ACUPRESSURE

Acupressure, like acupuncture, is based on the concept of energy (*chi*) circulating through the body's pathways (*meridians*). When *chi* is flowing freely, you remain healthy and in harmony; when *chi* is stagnant, overstimulated, or unbalanced, you become ill. One of the best known forms of acupressure is called *shiatsu,* a Japanese word meaning "finger pressure."

Acupressure uses many of the same acupoints as acupuncture, but the practitioner uses deep finger pressure instead of needles. The technique is particularly helpful for stress-related symptoms such as headaches, neck and back pain, depression, anxiety, and insomnia.

Acupressure can be self-administered. Consult a practitioner or pick up a self-help guide to learn about the different acupoints. When you have identified the point that coincides with your symptom, press it lightly with one finger. Increase the pressure gradually until you're pressing as firmly as you can. Hold this pressure steadily until you feel a faint, even pulse at the point; this should take between three to 10 minutes, perhaps longer. (You may feel some discomfort; if the pressure is really painful, ease up.) Release the pressure slowly.

When performing acupressure, concentrate on your breathing; deep breathing helps the pressure points release pain or tension and increases the flow of energy, blood, and lymphatic fluid throughout your body. For best results, wear comfortable clothing. Don't try acupressure just before or after a heavy meal, while bathing, or within four hours of taking any drugs or medication, including alcohol. You can perform the procedure every day, but limit your sessions to an hour.

In addition to its healing benefits, acupressure may help you stay well. The release of muscle tension increases the flow of blood and nutrients to the tissues, promoting physical and emotional relaxation.

Unlike acupuncturists, acupressure therapists are not licensed. To find a trained specialist, contact the American Association of Oriental Medicine.

CAUTION—If you have a chronic condition or illness, check with your physician before trying acupressure.

**Try Acupressure Yourself**

To reduce stress and balance the emotions, have a partner apply pressure to the points known as Vital Diaphragm (B38), located between the shoulder blades and the spine, at the level of the heart. To apply the pressure yourself, lie on your back, placing two tennis balls on the floor at the appropriate spots underneath your upper back between your shoulder blades. Then close your eyes and breathe deeply for several minutes.

## To Relieve Depression

A number of points on the head, neck, and torso have been identified as important to mood regulation, emotional balance, and tension release. A qualified acupressure practitioner can help you locate the correct spots, or consult a book on acupressure technique.

## To Promote Sound Sleep

An acupressure expert may apply pressure to points along the same energy pathways used by the acupuncturist, and to an extra point located between the eyebrows.

## For Headache Relief

Acupressure shares the same underlying theory as acupuncture. Once a qualified practitioner has identified your specific patterns of energy imbalance and which acupressure points work best for you, with some guidance and instruction it may be possible for you to stimulate these points yourself. In some cases a practitioner may actually tape small beads over the appropriate acupoints to guide you to the right points.

## Chinese Herbal Medicine

Chinese herbs have always played a central role in traditional Chinese medicine. TCM, in fact, recognizes more than 6,000 healing substances, grouped by four basic properties—hot, cold, warm, and cool. Herbalists choose plants that can help balance conditions that are caused by excessive heat or cold. A "hot" herb, such as cinnamon bark, may be prescribed for an "inner cold" condition, such as chronic diarrhea or cold hands and feet. A "cool" herb, such as chrysanthemum flower, can correct an "inner heat" condition, such as rapid onset inflammation involving headache and fever.

Herbs are also classified by the five flavors: pungent, sour, sweet, bitter, or salty. Each flavor influences a certain organ—pungent for the lungs, sour for the liver, sweet for the spleen or pancreas, bitter for the heart, and salty for the kidneys. In Chinese philosophy, the concept of organs is much broader than it is in the West. The Chinese "heart," for example, refers to the physical heart as well as clarity of mind.

Chinese herbs are generally prescribed in combinations of five to 10 at a time. They are usually prepared in a soup or a strong tea to be drunk at room temperature (never hot). Many herbs are also available in powder or pill form, as tinctures, and as pastes that can be applied to the skin. Be prepared to be patient. Like Western herbal remedies, Chinese herbal treatments take some time to work.

If you live in a city with a large Asian population, you should be able to find a TCM practitioner who was trained in China or Taiwan or at one of the programs accredited by the National Certification Commission for Acupuncture and Oriental Medicine (NCCAOM). If not, look for a medical doctor, osteopath, chiropractor, or licensed acupuncturist who has received at least 500 hours of training in Chinese herbalism and who routinely applies this knowledge in clinical practice. You want to avoid practitioners that have just taken a weekend course or who may have had good training but only dabble occasionally in this field. My recommendation is to find a practitioner who meets NCCAOM standards and who practices full-time in this field.

CAUTION—To avoid potentially serious interactions, make sure you tell *all* of your health care practitioners about *all* prescriptions and herbs you are taking. Some Chinese herbs can be poisonous in large doses. In Western medicine we are often reminded that the only difference between a medicine and a poison is the dose. This is also true with complementary therapies.

## To Relieve Depression

Traditional Chinese medical practitioners may prescribe a combination of Chinese herbs including Chinese angelica *(dong quai)*, peony, licorice, and thorowax (one such combination is called "Free and

Easy Wanderer"); these herbs are believed to move the chi and balance the liver.

CAUTION—Don't take Chinese angelica or licorice if you're pregnant. Don't take licorice if you have high blood pressure.

### To Promote Sound Sleep

A number of Chinese herbs are commonly prescribed, including akebia, Chinese cornbind, wild Chinese jujube, nutmeg, poria, and schisandra. Combination formulas are sometimes recommended, depending on what's causing the sleeplessness and whether it's accompanied by night sweats, heart palpitations, and worry.

## CHINESE DIETARY THERAPY

Chinese dietary therapy is considered a powerful tool and is used in conjunction with acupuncture and herbs to balance a condition. In fact, food and medicine are considered equally important. Foods are used to strengthen digestion, increase energy, and balance the body's energy.

For a long, healthy life, traditional Chinese dietary therapy recommends bland, unprocessed foods. Natural foods—homegrown and chemical-free—are considered the best choices. Meat is generally limited to two to three ounces per meal, with red meat limited to about six ounces a week.

Foods are classified as warm, neutral, or cold. A person diagnosed with a "warm" condition works toward balance by eating "cooling" foods.

## AYURVEDIC HEALING

Ayurveda—a Sanskrit word meaning "longevity knowledge"—is an ancient system of healing from India. Ayurvedic treatments all strive to create internal harmony and balance with diet, exercise, meditation, herbal therapy, and other therapies. Ayurvedic medicine has become increasingly popular in the United States in recent years, thanks to the best-selling books and television appearances of physician Deepak Chopra. Dr. Chopra was born and raised in India, studied and practiced Western medicine in the United States, and then managed to integrate powerful Ayurvedic therapies into his conventional medical practice.

At the root of Ayurvedic medicine is the holistic philosophy that each person has a vital energy, known as *prana,* found in various internal energy centers, called *chakras.* An imbalance of *prana* is thought to cause illness. This balance can be restored through a variety of interventions involving diet, yoga, lifestyle modifications, nutritional supplements, herbs, stress reduction techniques, meditation, and individualized therapies.

The Ayurvedic practitioner develops a personalized treatment plan for each patient by analyzing his or her constitutional makeup. According to Ayurvedic philosophy, each person contains a particular proportion of the universe's five elements—earth, air, fire, water, and ether (or space)—which combine to express the three *doshas* or basic constitutional types: *vata, pitta,* and *kapha.*

*Vata,* or wind, combines air and space. It is said to influence the movement of cells and fluid through the body and thoughts through the mind. People who are strongly influenced by *vata,* say Ayurvedic healers, are active and often restless.

*Pitta,* or bile, is made up of fire and regulates the body's metabolic activities. Those who are influenced by *pitta* may be competitive and aggressive.

The third *dosha, kapha,* or phlegm, is made up of earth and water and accounts for the body's physical strength, stability, and recuperative powers. A person whose makeup is predominantly *kapha* typically has a heavy, muscular body and a serene personality.

A person's natural makeup, called his *prakriti,* is a balance of the three *doshas.* Every *prakriti* contains elements of all the *doshas,* but only one predominates. Ayurvedic healers believe that if you live the life your *prakriti* dictates, you will remain in balance, in harmony, and in good health.

An Ayurvedic practitioner will closely examine your pulse, tongue, nails, eyes, face, and posture, and ask you detailed questions about your life. He or she will design an individualized health plan for you based on your physical examination and medical history, and will recommend a combination of herbs, nutrition, massage, yoga postures, breathing exercises, and meditation.

By taking into account the uniqueness of each individual and the mind, body, spirit, and energy factors that affect health, Ayurvedic medicine aims to treat the whole person. This approach can be quite helpful for people with stress-related conditions or chronic disorders.

Ayurvedic practitioners say that depression differs according to the various *doshas*. The basic theory is that *vata* from the colon, *pitta* from the intestine, or *kapha* from the stomach moves into the circulatory system and gets "stuck" in the nervous system. This interferes with how the mind functions on a normal basis and results in depression. *Vata* depression is associated with fear and anxiety; *pitta* depression with fear of failure, losing control, or making mistakes; and *kapha* depression with fatigue and weight gain. *Pitta* types are said to be most prone to seasonal affective disorder. The first step, say practitioners, is to adjust your diet to rebalance the *doshas* (see the following section on the Ayurvedic diet).

*For vata depression, these home remedies may be helpful:*

- Try sipping ginger tea or gotu kola tea during the day (available in teabag form in natural food stores).
- Put 3 to 5 drops of warm sesame oil in each nostril every morning and evening on an empty stomach.
- Rub the top of your head and the soles of your feet with sesame oil, which will soothe *vata* and help ease *vata* depression. Massaging oils into the

feet and the head works to bring the whole body together as one.

- *Vata* depression is frequently associated with loneliness, so try to spend more time with family and friends.

*For* pitta *depression:*

- Massage your scalp and soles of your feet with coconut or sunflower oil at bedtime.
- Sip gotu kola or ginkgo teas throughout the day (available in teabag form in natural food stores).
- Perform yoga meditation daily.
- Use *brahmi ghee* nose drops in each nostril, twice a day on an empty stomach.
- Mix equal amounts of the herbs *brahmi, jatamamsi,* and *shatavari,* and use ½ to 1 teaspoon of the mixture to make a tea. Drink two or three times daily.

*For* kapha *depression:*

- Increase your exercise.
- Fast for 3 or 4 days on apple juice, which will lighten the heaviness associated with *kapha* depression. When you do begin eating again, stick to light meals until your depression has lifted.
- Drink ginger tea twice a day.
- Practice daily yoga meditations.

Ayurvedic products are available at many health food stores and at Indian pharmacies. If you're not feeling better after a few days of these remedies, see your doctor.

## To Promote Restful Sleep

Ayurvedic philosophy considers insomnia a *vata* problem, and in order to bring on sound, restful sleep, the overactive *vata* must be rebalanced. The practitioner may suggest one of the following remedies for sleeplessness:

- Drink a cup of warm milk before going to bed. If you don't like plain milk, add a pinch of nutmeg, some blanched or crushed almonds, along with a pinch of cardamom (the nuts can be prepared in a nut grinder or coffee grinder); or try garlic milk, prepared with 1 cup milk, ¼ cup water, and 1 clove of fresh chopped garlic, boiled gently until 1 cup of liquid remains.

- Drink a cup of tomato juice mixed with 2 teaspoons natural sugar and 2 pinches of nutmeg, between 4 P.M. and 5 P.M., followed by dinner between 6 P.M. and 7 P.M.

- Take a warm bath or shower just before turning in for the night.

- Try an herbal formula composed of 1 part tagar, 1 part valerian root powder, and 1 part chamomile. Take ¼ teaspoon of this powdered mix with a little warm water before going to bed.

- Snack on cherries during the day. Tart cherries can help ease pain and, therefore, relieve the stress and mental fatigue that can keep you from resting comfortably.

- Drink a cup of chamomile tea, long used as a sleep aid in folk remedies around the world.

- Treat yourself to a soothing warm oil massage before going to bed. Use slightly warmed sesame oil, *brahmi* oil, or *jatamamsi* oil, and massage it into the scalp and the soles of the feet.
- Yoga meditation is also effective.

## THE AYURVEDIC DIET

Dietary recommendations are based on the seasons and on the particular elements of your *dosha*. Foods are classified on the basis of whether they increase (stimulate) or decrease (pacify) each *dosha*.

| To pacify | Eat | Avoid |
|---|---|---|
| *Vata* | Spices; heavy, warm, oily, moist foods; eat at regular mealtimes | Raw, dry, cold, or frozen foods; leafy vegetables |
| *Pitta* | Salads, cooling herbs and spices | Alcohol; meat; sour, salty, spicy, and fried foods |
| *Kapha* | Plenty of vegetables, salads, dry, light foods; spices | Sweet and salty foods; dairy; fried foods; frozen foods |

The qualities of any given food change with different preparation techniques, so you would include or exclude particular foods depending on how they're prepared. For example, if you were following a *vata*-pacifying diet, you would avoid dry oatmeal (served cold and dry as granola) but could eat cooked oatmeal, which is warm and moist. You would avoid cold fruit juice but could drink it warmed.

Other dietary rules apply to all of the *doshas* and concern food combinations. Cooked and raw foods are not eaten at the same meal. Fruits are eaten separately from other foods. Milk is not taken with yogurt. Milk and yogurt are not mixed with citrus, fish, meat, or eggs. Vegetarian diets are generally encouraged, usually a lacto-vegetarian diet (milk and cheese are permitted, but not meat, fish, chicken, or eggs).

The *doshas* are influenced by the environment, so your dietary prescription will change with the seasons of the year. It's important to consult a qualified practitioner for guidelines.

CAUTION—Ayurvedic healers are not currently required to be licensed or certified in the United States. If you're already taking prescription medicine, talk to your doctor before using any Ayurvedic herbs or medicines. Some may contain dangerous substances such as lead, mercury, and arsenic; avoid any that contain even the smallest amounts of these ingredients.

# HOMEOPATHY

Homeopathy, developed in Germany over 250 years ago, uses highly diluted substances from plants, animals, and minerals as medicine. This healing system is based on the precept that "like cures like." While a conventional physician would tend to recommend a standard pharmaceutical remedy (such as acetaminophen) to reduce fever, a homeopathic practitioner would recommend a highly diluted remedy derived from a substance that actually causes fever in a healthy person. The diluted remedy is thought to stimulate the body's own protective healing response, somewhat like an immunization does.

Some homeopathic remedies are so diluted that if you tried to measure the concentration of active ingredient, you wouldn't find any! Thus many physicians reject homeopathy because it cannot be conventionally explained on a biochemical basis. Skeptical physicians attribute any benefit to the placebo response. In other words, they say, "It works because you expect it to work."

However, a number of double-blind–placebo-controlled studies have documented statistically significant responses to certain homeopathic remedies that cannot be explained by the placebo response. When confronted with this evidence, skeptical physicians still say, "I wouldn't believe it, even if it were true!"

At this time we can only speculate about the mechanism of action at work in homeopathy, but it probably can be classified as one of the therapies that cause energy changes in the body. One clue supporting this theory is that the effect of homeopathic remedies can be neutralized by strong magnetic fields. In light of this, it's best not to use homeopathic remedies along with acupuncture or magnetic therapy.

Another tenet of homeopathy is that the patient is not his or her disease. In other words, not every treatment works on every patient, and each patient must be seen as an individual, not as an illness. This holistic philosophy is one of the pillars of alternative medicine.

## USING HOMEOPATHIC REMEDIES

Homeopathic remedies should not be used as the only treatment for acute illness or medical emergencies. They are most effective when used to treat chronic conditions such as allergies, chronic fatigue syndrome, skin problems, headaches, premenstrual syndrome, colds and flu, and stress-related disorders. They are safe, however, to use with any medication you are taking, and can be taken by children, the elderly, and even pets.

There are about 200 to 300 commonly used homeopathic remedies, each designed to target specific patterns of symptoms. Preparations in tablet, powder, wafer, and liquid forms may be prescribed by a homeopathic physician or bought over the counter in health food stores, pharmacies, and grocery stores. Certain over-the-counter remedies are targeted to common ailments such as insomnia, colds, flu, sore throat, and headaches. For relatively minor problems, you can use these preparations to treat yourself.

If you're using homeopathic remedies on your own, look for products with a potency in the range of 6c to

12c. The number preceding "c" indicates how many hundred times the remedy has been diluted. The most diluted forms are paradoxically thought to be the most potent. A professional homeopath may use products with potencies of 30c or higher, but it's best to start out on the lower end if you're doing it yourself.

If you're using a homeopathic remedy in tablet form, be careful not to touch the pills. Pour the tablets into the bottle cap, then tip them directly onto or under your tongue. If you spill any, throw them away. Don't take anything by mouth for 15 minutes before or after taking the tablets, especially mint, mint-flavored toothpaste, coffee, or tea.

Keep homeopathic remedies in their original container, away from heat, sunlight, and strong aromas, such as perfumes, camphor, and eucalyptus, which may cause contamination.

For chronic conditions, it's best to check with a professional homeopath who will take an extensive medical history and discuss your physical and psychological symptoms before prescribing a remedy tailored to your individual needs. Response times vary from minutes to months, and the remedies can work in conjunction with most other conventional and/or complementary therapies.

Licensing requirements for homeopathic practitioners can vary from state to state. Many homeopaths have professional training, such as a degree in medicine, osteopathy, or naturopathy.

CAUTION—Homeopathy is incompatible with other energy therapies and thus should not be used simultaneously. Consult a homeopathic practitioner before taking any of these medications on your own to treat a chronic disorder.

## HOMEOPATHY AND DEPRESSION

More than 200 different homeopathic medicines have been used to treat depression in the past 150 years, but results have been reported mainly as case histories, and rigorous scientific research has been scarce. Since treatment is highly individualized, the practitioner will look for a homeopathic remedy that works with your particular complaints, state of mind, and body traits. If you've lost your appetite for life, for example, you may be helped by *Aurum metallicum*. Other homeopathic medicines used for mood and sleep troubles may include combinations of any of the following ingredients: *Ignatia amara, Phosphoricum acidum, Sepia, Pulsatilla nigricans, Lachesis mutans, Apis mellifica, Gelsemium sempervirens, Natrum sulphuricum, Natrum muriaticum, Chamomilla, Sulphur,* and *Nux vomica.* The usual potency for these preparations is between 6c and 30c.

Different homeopathic medicines are prescribed for different types of depression. *Ignatia,* for example, is used for the depression that accompanies grief; it can help improve mood, sleeping difficulties, and stomachaches, in addition to relieving itchy skin or hives caused by anxiety. For those who are depressed because of overwork or too many responsibilities, *Sepia* may be recommended; while *Pulsatilla* might be prescribed for people whose depression is characterized by mood swings or crying jags. See a homeopathic practitioner for an individual assessment and treatment plan.

CAUTION—Homeopathy may be appropriate in cases of adjustment disorder, for example, a depressed mood brought on by losing your job or ending a relationship. If your symptoms don't improve after a few weeks or if you're having suicidal thoughts, consult your doctor, who may want to prescribe conventional antidepressants and/or psychotherapy.

## PHOTOTHERAPY (LIGHT THERAPY)

Phototherapy, also known as light therapy, is the use of natural or artificial light to promote healing. There are several different forms of light therapy, differing primarily in the type of light involved. Full-spectrum light therapy consists of regular exposure to controlled amounts of either natural sunlight or artificial light that contains all wavelengths, from infrared to ultraviolet. Bright light therapy involves exposure to nonultraviolet white light in levels that are equivalent to the amount of natural sunlight found outdoors shortly after sunrise or before sunset. Cold laser therapy involves the use of small beams of low-intensity laser light applied directly to the skin, while colored light therapy makes use of different colored lights focused on the skin.

Researchers have found that everyone needs adequate exposure to a full, balanced spectrum of light. Adequate light is necessary for the regulation of circadian rhythms, the body's natural clock that governs such functions as hormone (melatonin) production and waking and sleeping routines. These rhythms run in regular cycles, reset by the light of the morning sun. If the rhythms are upset, health problems can result. While the effect of phototherapy on melatonin provides us with a plausible biochemical mechanism of action, in some cases light therapy may have an energetic or a direct mind-body mood-altering effect.

Light therapy has been used since the ancient Greek physician Hippocrates prescribed sunlight for certain disorders. In the Middle Ages, red light was used to treat smallpox—patients would be wrapped in red sheets, and red curtains hung from the windows.

Bright light therapy has been used to treat the late fall and winter depression known as seasonal affective disorder (SAD) since the 1980s, after researchers found that those who suffered from SAD and traveled south for winter vacations generally felt better for several weeks even after they returned home.

Scientists believe that SAD is triggered by winter's shorter daylight hours. They suggest that SAD is more common in northern countries because the winter day is shorter the farther north you go. According to the Mood Disorders Clinic at the Vancouver Hospital and Health Sciences Center in British Columbia, fewer than 1 percent of people in Florida suffer from SAD, while up to 10 percent of those living in Alaska experience winter depression.

After it was observed that people with winter blues felt better after a trip to the sunny South, home devices were developed to simulate bright daylight. Such devices do not include ultraviolet light, so exposure to this light will not cause sunburn or increase your risk of skin cancer. If you're affected by SAD, you can sit in front of a bright-light appliance in the morning, and by the time you've finished breakfast or read the newspaper, you've received your dose of sunlight for the day.

Most people begin to feel better about a week after the start of phototherapy. The effects do not last long, however, so treatment must be continued on a daily basis, usually from October through April.

In the mid-1990s, researchers discovered that some people who suffer from SAD could be effectively treated with a device that simulates dawn. These dawn simulators are night lights that are timed to turn on at 4 A.M. Over the next two or three hours, the light brightens— just as natural daybreak does—until you awaken. In one early study of dawn simulation, six of eight SAD sufferers reported feeling significantly better after two weeks of treatment. Other studies confirmed those results.

Why does light therapy work? No one really knows, but researchers believe that light has a biological effect on the hormones of the brain and how they function. One theory maintains that the biological clock of people with SAD is off-kilter and runs more slowly in the winter. Phototherapy, then, helps to "reset" the clock and get things back on track. Another theory postulates that the brain chemicals known as neurotransmitters are disturbed in patients with SAD, and that light therapy can correct these imbalances. Still another theory holds that people with SAD have less sensitivity to retinal light in the winter and that light therapy can correct this condition.

In addition to keeping the body's biological rhythms on track, people who are helped report that light therapy reduces stress and promotes relaxation.

The effects of phototherapy have been so encouraging that it's being studied for possible use in cases of nonseasonal depression. At the University of California at San Diego, 50 men with severe depression were divided into two groups. One group spent seven consecutive evenings in a room illuminated with 1,600 watts of bright light. The other group spent their time in a room with the lights turned low. Those who sat in the brightly lit room showed an 18 percent improvement in symptoms.

Bright-light boxes and dawn simulators can be ordered through specialty catalogs such as Sharper Image and Hammacher Schlemmer. But before spending the money, you may want to try these self-help measures:

- *Get more natural sunlight.* Keep your blinds and curtains open. Use bright colors inside your home.
- *Sit near windows whenever you can.* Do this at school, at work, at home.
- *Take a walk.* Spend more time outdoors. Even a daily one-hour walk in the midday winter sun can brighten your mood.
- *Take a winter vacation.* When winter sets in, head for the sunny South. It may be just what the doctor ordered.

# 13

## Mind-Body Therapies

RELAXATION THERAPY

MEDITATION

GUIDED IMAGERY

BIOFEEDBACK

HYPNOTHERAPY

EDMR

AROMATHERAPY

CONNECTEDNESS

In studies conducted at Yale and Rutgers Universities and reported in 1990 in the *American Journal of Epidemiology,* researchers found that mood, attitude, and beliefs can have an effect on almost every chronic illness. The mind-body connection is incredibly powerful. Relaxing your body will relax your mind, and vice versa. This is definitely a two-way street. Negative feelings can have a detrimental effect on health, whereas positive feelings can have a beneficial effect. The scientists found that how well a person *thinks* he is may, in fact, be a strong indication of how well he *will be* in the future.

The connection between mind and body is beginning to be taken seriously enough in the medical establishment that programs in mind-body medicine have sprung up at such prestigious institutions as Harvard University, the University of Massachusetts, Stanford University, the University of Miami, and the University of California at San Francisco. We're just starting to grasp how powerfully our thoughts affect our physiology, and we can expect this growing awareness to lead to more widespread use of these therapies.

Some of the best known mind-body therapies include the various psychotherapy interventions—including cognitive therapy, behavioral therapy, individual and group therapy, and family therapy—all discussed in detail in Chapter 6. But mind-body medicine is a broad field, encompassing various mental techniques or therapies that have been shown to alter physiology. For anyone suffering from depression, a number of these complementary interventions—including biofeedback, meditation, visualization or guided imagery, and hypnosis—are relevant treatment strategies.

Stress reduction is a primary goal of these interventions. This can be helpful in coping with the emotional challenges of depression and anxiety, both of which can be exacerbated by stress. The mind-body therapies typically produce measurable physical responses that include elevated endorphins, reduced levels of cortisol and adrenaline (stress hormones that lower immunity and alter circulation), reduced blood pressure, reduced blood clotting, reduced muscle tension, and improved circulation.

There's a great deal of research that supports the effectiveness of mind-body therapies in treating a variety of conditions. In addition to depression, the list includes allergies, angina, anxiety, asthma, back pain, headaches, hypertension, irritable bowel syndrome, post-traumatic stress disorder (PTSD), and Raynaud's disease.

In fact, eight of the initial 30 studies funded by the National Center for Complementary and Alternative Medicine (NCCAM) deal with mind-body medicine, including the use of biofeedback in treating low-back pain and in reducing the dosage of insulin required in Type I insulin-dependent diabetes; the benefits of guided imagery for patients with asthma, cancer, and AIDS; and the use of hypnosis in patients with broken bones, low-back pain, and cancer.

Keeping our focus on depression, we'll first take a brief look at deep breathing as a mode of relaxation. Many people use this technique to step back from stress and as a prelude to meditation and visualization.

## RELAXATION THERAPY

The term relaxation therapy covers several techniques aimed at reducing physical and mental tension. Preliminary studies indicate that relaxation therapies can help ease anxiety, lift mood, and enhance feelings of well-being in people with depression. In one British study involving 154 women who felt depressed while they were being treated for breast cancer, researchers found that relaxation therapy, progressive relaxation technique, and visualization therapy all improved mood significantly, when compared to a control group.

## DEEP ABDOMINAL BREATHING

Deep abdominal breathing is one of the stress-reduction techniques that can help you learn to relax. This can, in turn, reduce anxiety and promote more restful sleep.

When you learn to control your breathing, you can decrease the release of stress hormones in your body and slow your heart rate. Often people who are under stress will hyperventilate, taking quick, shallow breaths that move the upper chest more than the abdomen. This type of breathing is not only inefficient, it is also counterproductive and leads to even more physical and mental stress. Deep abdominal breathing can cause your body to release endorphins, those natural body chemicals that promote a sense of well-being.

To practice deep breathing, lie on your back in a quiet room with no distractions. Place your hands on your abdomen and breathe in slowly and deeply through your nostrils. If you are breathing correctly, your hands will rise as your abdomen expands. Inhale to a count of five, hold your breath for three seconds, then exhale to a count of five. Note the coolness of the air as it enters your nostrils and the warmth of the air as you exhale. Do this exercise 10 times at first, increasing to 25 times, twice a day.

When you get the hang of deep breathing, you can combine it with progressive muscle relaxation. This technique involves contracting and relaxing all the muscle groups in the body, one at a time.

Find a quiet place where you won't be disturbed. Sit comfortably with your feet flat on the floor, your back straight, and your hands resting on your thighs. Do not cross your feet, legs, arms, or hands. Close your eyes, and as soon as you are comfortable, begin to focus on your breathing. Take a few deep breaths, allowing your chest and abdomen to expand with each breath.

Now begin to focus on relaxing each part of your body, beginning with your feet, moving upward to your calves, your thighs, then to your fingers, hands, wrists, forearms, and upper arms. Allow each part of your body to go limp and heavy, as if you were going to melt into the chair and floor. Next, relax your stomach muscles, then your chest. Move on to your lower back, upper back, and shoulders. Finally relax the back of your neck, your face, your throat, and the muscles of your jaw.

Once you're completely relaxed, you're ready to meditate.

## MEDITATION

Meditation can help relax your body and mind. While the practice is used as a pathway to spiritual enlightenment in Eastern cultures, in the West meditation is used in a nonreligious context to promote peace of mind and ease stress-related symptoms such as chronic pain, high blood pressure, panic disorders, headaches, respiratory problems, insomnia, and premenstrual syndrome.

Practicing meditation every day can provide a respite from the stresses of everyday living. Meditation can move you into a calmer, more relaxed state by slowing your heart rate and breathing, lowering your blood pressure, relaxing your muscles, and clearing your mind. Slow, deep breathing accompanies each technique.

Many meditation techniques practiced today come from ancient Eastern traditions. One of the more widely recognized forms of meditation in the West is transcendental meditation (TM), introduced to the United States by Maharishi Mahesh Yogi in the 1960s.

People who practice TM sit quietly, focusing on their breathing, and repeating a single word or sound (often referred to as a *mantra)* over and over. A *mantra* may be selected for you by a meditation instructor, or guru. The traditional Sanskrit word used in meditation is *ohm,* but you can choose any word or phrase you like. With practice, you learn to focus on the word or the sound itself and not on any conscious thoughts. If other thoughts do intrude, don't get distracted, frustrated, or upset, simply acknowledge them and refocus on your chosen sound, word, or phrase.

Another way to meditate is to concentrate on a mental image such as a candle or flower. Gaze at the object for two minutes, then close your eyes while you continue to see the image in your mind's eye.

Scientists at the Medical College of Georgia who've studied transcendental meditation have found that the technique decreases blood pressure by reducing constriction of the blood vessels.

You can learn to meditate on your own by using self-help books, audiotapes, or videotapes, but a trained instructor can help you develop your skills more quickly. Each meditation session should last about 20 minutes, and you should aim for two sessions daily.

There are no national licensing requirements for instructors of meditation. Many hospitals, wellness centers, and continuing education programs offer classes and workshops.

## GUIDED IMAGERY

Guided imagery, also called visualization, can help you control how you feel through the use of vivid mental pictures of relaxing situations, such as a beach, a waterfall, or a sunset. Guided imagery, when used along with slow, deep breathing, can reduce anxiety levels and lower your heart rate and blood pressure.

The technique has been shown to enhance the immune system in cancer patients, improve circulation in people with Raynaud's disease, speed postoperative recovery, and reduce stress in patients with irritable bowel syndrome, tension headaches, and so on. Some cancer patients, for example, feel empowered by using guided imagery during chemotherapy to imagine their white blood cells swallowing up tumor cells like Pac-Man.

The technique is easy and you can do it anywhere. To get started, simply make yourself comfortable, close your eyes, take several slow, deep breaths, and imagine a tranquil setting. Take whatever time is needed to construct an elaborate image of the place, full of physical and sensory detail. Now put yourself into the picture and experience the setting with all your senses. The more real your image, the more your body can convince itself that it's actually "there." What do you see? How does the air feel against your skin? What sounds and smells make the setting distinctive?

Next construct a visual metaphor that symbolizes the release of tension. If you're picturing a beach, for example, imagine yourself sitting at the water's edge, the waves coming into shore and rolling gently around your shoulders. As the waves recede, feel them pulling the tension out of your body and carrying it out to sea. Or imagine that you're a feather floating gently to the ground, the tension leaving your body as you drift downward. When you finally reach the ground, picture yourself as totally relaxed.

You will notice that as you transport yourself to another place, your areas of physical discomfort begin to drift away. Continue to breathe deeply. When you're ready to return to the present moment, stretch your fingers and toes, even your entire body, and then open your eyes.

### See Yourself in a New Light

For mild depression, you may want to try an imagery exercise known as the Trapeze of Hope. Visualize yourself as a trapeze artist swinging in from the left on a trapeze bar. Imagine another trapeze swinging toward you from the right. Keep swinging. When you're ready, let go of the old bar and reach out and grab onto the new one. See yourself swing up and land safely on the far platform. Now grab a golden rope and use it to lower yourself to the ground. Tie the golden rope around yourself and someone you love, and then see the two of you standing in a golden light.

Try this visualization exercise first thing in the morning, and then twice more during the day if needed. Do it for three weeks in a row, and then stop for a week. If necessary, begin again after the week is up.

Another exercise that may be helpful to you is to visualize yourself being carried away by jet streams, those strong winds that can blow up to 400 miles an hour in the upper atmosphere. See the winds blowing away your depression and leaving you surrounded by a clean, white light. Then imagine yourself breathing in this pure light, which replaces all the darkness you've been feeling.

A professional therapist or commercial audiotapes can guide your visualizations and help open your mind to the power of subconscious healing.

Guided imagery is often used in conjunction with other mind-body therapies such as hypnotherapy or biofeedback.

# BIOFEEDBACK

Biofeedback uses a variety of devices to measure physical changes that signal the body's state of stress or relaxation. Normally, these internal processes—including heart rate, skin temperature, galvanic skin response (a measure of electrical conductivity), blood pressure, and even brain waves—go unnoticed, but when we are made aware of them through the aid of specialized equipment, we can learn various techniques to consciously control them. Using biofeedback, you can literally retrain your blood vessels to dilate when necessary, to increase circulation to a specific body part.

A common type of biofeedback used in medical settings is electromyographic (EMG) biofeedback, which measures electrical activity in the muscles. The procedure is painless, and people quickly get the hang of it. Electrodes can be attached to several sites on your body to monitor blood pressure, skin temperature, and other biological functions and/or neuromuscular activity. The responses are then interpreted, and the practitioner teaches you how to alter your mental and emotional states for healthier, less stressful functioning.

After some practice with biofeedback, you learn to be aware of your various body processes without the aid of equipment. Then you can use imagery, breathing, and progressive muscle relaxation techniques to reduce anxiety and keep your body in a more relaxed state while dealing with the demands and stresses of daily life.

Since the 1960s researchers have accumulated an impressive body of research confirming the therapeutic value of biofeedback. It has been used successfully to treat a number of stress-related conditions such as high blood pressure, anxiety, insomnia, tension headaches, migraines, irritable bowel syndrome, chronic back pain, and Raynaud's disease.

Biofeedback can be used to restore normal function to the diaphragm, which will improve breathing and reduce stress on the muscles of the neck and upper chest. Through biofeedback, you can also learn which activities cause you to "overdo," enabling you to modify those behaviors. Once you learn your body's natural patterns, you can work to adjust them for better relaxation and sounder sleep.

Anecdotal evidence indicates that biofeedback is effective in reducing the severity of all kinds of depression. The number of training sessions depends on the severity of your depression; for mild depression, you may need an average of 20 sessions, for more severe cases, 30 to 60 sessions.

As biofeedback becomes more mainstream, it's proving to be a very useful therapeutic tool.

### Try This at Home!

Thermal biofeedback is one technique you can do at home, without machines. All you need is a thermometer, your hands, and about 15 minutes.

Developed at the Menninger Clinic in Topeka, Kansas, thermal biofeedback is based on the idea that when a person is under stress, the body restricts blood flow to the hands and feet, so that they become colder than the rest of the body. If you warm your hands, the blood flow will increase, stress hormones will decrease, muscles will relax, and you'll feel less tense.

To try it, sit in a comfortable chair and wrap your hands around a thermometer so that your fingertips are touching. Rest your hands in your lap and focus your mind on whatever sensation you are feeling in your fingers. If you feel a tingling or pulsing sensation, that's a signal that your hands are warming up. Occasionally look at the thermometer but don't do anything in particular to warm your hands. The goal is to raise your finger temperature to 97 degrees Fahrenheit and keep it there for 10 minutes. As you become accustomed to this exercise, you should be able to raise the temperature of your hands without using the thermometer.

Once, when lecturing to a class of college students on the topic of biofeedback, I did a demonstration involving a sheet of temperature-sensitive material. When you placed your hand on this material, its color would change in response to your skin temperature. Much to my surprise my hand temperature was down in the low 80s—the coldest hands in the classroom! I guess I felt stressed that particular night when speaking to the students, and the resulting high levels of adrenaline reduced my peripheral circulation (without me even being aware of it). A simple relaxation exercise that combined deep breathing, progressive muscle relaxation, and visualizing my hands near a fireplace brought my hand temperature back up to 97 degrees before the end of the class. The students and I both learned a great deal from that totally unplanned and unexpected demonstration.

# HYPNOTHERAPY

Hypnotherapy, or hypnosis, was recognized by the American Medical Association as a valid and effective medical therapy in 1957. Under hypnosis, you achieve a state of focused attention or altered consciousness, a state between sleeping and waking in which you're completely relaxed yet able to concentrate intently.

Under hypnosis you're more open to the power of suggestion, so some people use it as a way to cope with fears and phobias, manage stress, and ease pain. It can also be used as a relaxation technique. Some psychotherapists treating patients with depression believe that hypnosis can be a useful aid to cognitive therapy by helping patients restructure negative thought patterns.

Hypnosis has been shown to be helpful for patients with fibromyalgia, irritable bowel syndrome, migraine headaches, and other painful disorders; warts or other skin conditions; asthma; and nausea.

There's no reason to be leery of hypnosis performed by an ethical practitioner. When you are in a hypnotic state, you can have as much or as little control as you want; you will be aware of everything that is going on around you, can speak as you wish, and can even stop the session if you begin to feel uncomfortable. An ethical therapist won't try to make you do anything you wouldn't otherwise do. The technique simply helps you focus your mental energy on banishing negative thoughts and harnessing it for health and healing. If, for whatever reason, you can't find a hypnotherapist you are comfortable with, you can still gain the benefits of hypnosis by using self-hypnosis techniques.

Under hypnosis, you may be more able to remember past events that may be causing current physical, mental, and emotional problems. The hypnotherapist can help you confront these memories and work through them so that they will no longer affect you. Hypnosis can also be used to control fear and anxiety. Once a patient is guided into a hypnotic state, the practitioner can help him use his imagination to re-experience the stressful situation, but in a more positive way.

A qualified hypnotherapist will begin a session by using a visualization technique that will suggest a feeling of drifting or floating. Your eyes and limbs will begin to feel heavy as you enter the hypnotic state. The mind is most receptive to suggestion when the body is in a relaxed state. You will be aware of everything around you, but will feel detached from it. While you are hypnotized, the therapist will make suggestions designed to bring about a change in your behavior or thought processes. When he is finished, he will bring you out of the hypnotic state with a simple suggestion or word.

Hypnotherapy cannot cure illness, but it can complement conventional medical interventions. The technique is being used more and more in standard health care settings, especially to overcome negative habits such as smoking or overeating. There are even reports in the medical literature of hypnosis being used effectively to treat recurrent warts that had not responded to the usual treatments of chemicals, freezing, burning, and cutting.

Warts are caused by a virus. When case reports document that the warts have literally melted away following hypnosis, we are seeing evidence of a dramatic change in the immune response, which now rejects the virus that had previously been ignored or allowed to coexist. This is a great example of psychoneuroimmunology at work. Psychoneuroimmunology, sometimes referred to as PNI, is a fifty-dollar word that simply means *our thoughts affect our immune system*.

Most people can be hypnotized and some can even learn to hypnotize themselves, although it generally takes weeks or even months to learn to do it effectively. Many conventional physicians are trained in hypnotherapy, as are many dentists, psychotherapists, and nurses.

Like many mind-body therapies, you can learn to use hypnosis on your own. To practice self-hypnosis, lie or sit in a comfortable spot where you won't be disturbed. Release any tension in your body by taking several deep breaths and then relaxing each part of your body, from the top of your head to the tips of your toes. To induce a focused state of mind, imagine yourself walking down a long path or descending a staircase; count from 10 to zero. Repeat to yourself statements that describe how you want to feel, such as "I enjoy my family," or "I am a person who can accomplish important things." You can also use a previously recorded audiotape that has your messages on it. After 20 to 30 minutes, bring yourself out of the hypnotic state by reversing the image you used—for example, climb back up the stairs, this time counting from zero to 10.

# Eye Movement Desensitization and Reprocessing

Eye movement desensitization and reprocessing (EMDR) is a medical treatment used to decrease depression, anxiety, guilt, anger, and post-traumatic reactions. It's also effective in increasing self-esteem and self-confidence. During a session, the client relates a painful or troubling emotion or memory while he follows the therapist's rapidly moving fingers with his eyes. This back-and-forth eye movement is similar to what happens when you dream and appears to hasten the emotional healing process.

EMDR allows you to confront painful memories in a safe environment. You decide how much to tell the therapist and when to stop talking. The therapist helps you stay focused and supports you if you're having trouble. Afterward, the unpleasant memory seems to retreat and lose its significance. However, you may continue to have insights, powerful feelings, and vivid dreams for several days or weeks, as you work through your problems.

EMDR must be performed by a therapist trained in the technique; otherwise it won't be effective and may even be harmful. To find an EMDR-certified therapist in your area, call or write the EMDR International Association.

# AROMATHERAPY

Aromatic oils, herbs, flowers, and other natural substances have been used since ancient Egyptian times for medicinal, cosmetic, and religious purposes. The modern scientific use of essential oils was discovered by French chemist René-Maurice Gattefossé, who worked in a perfume factory in the 1920s and coined the term aromatherapy.

The modality involves the therapeutic use of essential oils that are inhaled or applied to the skin. While absorption of essential oils into the body may cause a biochemical effect, the mind-body effect is usually more powerful. The mind-body effect is mediated through the olfactory nerve, triggering a strong emotional response via the limbic system—that part of our central nervous system that deals with strong emotions such as fear, joy, anger, and sexual desire. The limbic system, in turn, affects other parts of the brain which regulate such important functions as breathing, heart rate, and body temperature.

The essential oils used in aromatherapy may be helpful for such conditions as anxiety, headaches, insomnia, and depression. There is currently no licensing process for aromatherapy practitioners in the United States.

The oils are sold in tiny, dark-tinted bottles in health food shops, holistic pharmacies, and through the mail. Buy from a reputable merchant and make sure the bottle is well sealed and labeled "essential oil." Store in a cool place, away from the light.

Oils can be used by themselves or in combination, and can be inhaled from a cotton ball or handkerchief; misted into the air with a diffuser, humidifier, or vaporizer; massaged into the skin; added to the bath; or added to a sachet to scent a drawer or closet.

Essential oils are intensely concentrated and highly potent. For inhalations, sprinkle 4 or 5 drops on a hand-kerchief, tissue, or cotton ball, hold to your nose, and take several deep breaths. You can also add a few drops to a bowl of steaming water, cover your head with a towel, lean over the bowl with your eyes closed, and inhale for up to 10 minutes. Do not inhale oils directly from the bottle.

To use oils in a vaporizer, place 2 or 3 drops in a bowl with a small amount of water and place over a lighted candle. You can also mist the room with a diffuser (sold where you buy your oils) or with a humidifier to which you've added several drops of oil.

For an aromatherapy bath, add 6 to 8 drops of essential oil to a warm bath, and soak for at least 10 minutes.

CAUTION—Never use essential oils as a substitute for necessary medical care. Never use essential oils internally, near the eyes, or inhaled directly from the bottle. Essential oils should not be applied directly to the skin or mucous membranes full-strength, but should be diluted in a carrier oil such as apricot kernel oil, sunflower oil, or sweet almond oil. The customary formula is 10 drops of essential oil per 20 milliliters of carrier oil. If you have sensitive skin or if you are pregnant, use 5 drops per 20 milliliters. Make sure you're not allergic to the oil before using it. Test yourself by applying a drop of diluted oil inside your elbow and waiting 24 hours. If a rash develops, discontinue use. Keep all essential oils out of the reach of children. If you have asthma, check with your physician before using essential oils.

## RELAXATION HAS NEVER SMELLED SO NICE!

### To Ease Depression

Clary sage and rose oils can lift your mood. Some people respond well to the citrus oils: orange, grapefruit, lime, and mandarin. Geranium, lavender, and melissa are also worth a try. Use these in a bath or inhale them from a handkerchief or cotton ball. You can also mist them into the air from a humidifier, vaporizer, or diffuser.

CAUTION—Do not use clary sage if you're pregnant.

### To Promote Restful Sleep

To help you sleep better, add neroli, lavender, and chamomile oils to a warm pre-bedtime bath; all have sedative qualities and can promote sleep.

The essential oils of marjoram, sandalwood, juniper, and ylang-ylang are also good for relaxation. Try putting a couple of drops of one of these oils on your pillowcase.

### For General Relaxation

Try a warm (not hot) scented bath to which you've added 6 to 8 drops of essential oils of juniper, lavender, or rosemary (or 2 drops of each). Relax in the tub for at least 15 minutes.

## To Relieve Headaches

Lavender and peppermint oils, used alone or together, work well on headaches. Inhale from a handkerchief or cotton ball, prepare a cool herbal compress, or blend a few drops of the lavender oil with a carrier oil and rub on your temples, forehead, or back of your neck.

# CONNECTEDNESS: THE IMPORTANCE OF RELATIONSHIPS

While all of the interventions previously discussed in this chapter can help you be more connected with yourself, research has shown repeatedly that establishing and nurturing relationships with others (family/social network, spiritual activity, and even pets) can reduce the frequency, duration, and severity of both physical and mental illness (including depression). We touched on this topic in Chapter 5, in discussing how socialization promotes healing.

To paraphrase the famous line by poet John Donne, *No man, or woman, is an island.* Existing in emotional, social, and spiritual isolation (isn't that the American way?) exacts an unhealthy toll on us all.

I've had the privilege of attending two of the "Spirituality in Healing" conferences organized by Dr. Herbert Benson, a cardiologist, researcher, and well known author from Harvard. In these conferences, which have been attended by thousands of physicians over the past few years, the somewhat sticky and controversial topics of religion and spirituality are discussed candidly in terms of how they affect health. The conferences deal with both hard data documenting the health benefits of spiritual activity and with the softer heart of medicine, which recognizes the value of honoring patients' belief systems and relationships.

A number of studies published in medical journals have documented a variety of health benefits that come from engaging in prayer and religious activities. Whether these favorable outcomes are the result of mind-body physiology, the benefits of socialization, divine intervention, or some other unidentified factor remains a subject of ongoing debate.

Even talking about the distinction between religion and spirituality can sometimes be enough to get people upset. It is a real challenge to talk about the benefits of belief systems without seeming to imply superiority of one belief system over another. Data is the great equalizer that allows people of all faiths (or lack thereof) to sit at the same table for a long overdue discussion of the role of belief in the healing process.

Many physicians, Dr. Benson included, are most comfortable explaining the health effects of spirituality in terms of the mind-body connection—thereby skirting the more controversial topic of whether or not any particular belief system has advantages over others. The natural extension of this logic would be to call religion "the placebo of the masses," to steal a notion from Karl Marx and add a psychoneuroimmunologic twist.

Personally, I feel there is more to the story than mere mind-body physiology. But the important thing is that from a clinical perspective, it doesn't matter which camp you're in—whether you believe that religious beliefs manifest their clinical effects entirely through mind-body physiology, socialization, or divine intervention, when the data suggest that kneeling does in fact affect healing.

Spirituality means many different things to different people, and yet there is a commonality to all spiritual beliefs—a "highest common denominator," if you will. That common denominator is a need for connectedness. It is through our connections to other people that we find meaning in life. Isolation breeds torment, fear, and all manner of horrific acts. When we are connected, joy is multiplied and sorrow divided. The most meaningful, inspirational, and heroic acts are relationship-affirming acts of connectedness.

There is now an abundance of research demonstrating the health benefits of marriage, a rich social network, and spiritual beliefs. From the cradle to the grave we cry out for connectedness, especially when we feel ill or vulnerable. Without connectedness, infants fail to thrive and widows or widowers lose the will to live. We know that those who are isolated from others tend to suffer greater and more frequent health problems. We also know that healing occurs more easily in the context of connectedness and relationships. When we say that "there are no atheists in foxholes," we are recognizing the human cry for connectedness during difficult times.

As beneficial as it is to reconnect with yourself (using relaxation techniques, meditation, biofeedback, and so on), never underestimate the benefits that derive from having meaningful relationships with others. Gaining some insight into yourself through psychotherapy will take you a long way, as will using St. John's wort (or Prozac, for that matter), or acupuncture. But none of these interventions will ever take the place of connectedness.

Remember, when you "reach out and touch someone," they touch you back. So get connected!

# 14

## Movement Therapies

EXERCISE

YOGA

*TAI CHI*

*QIGONG*

DANCE THERAPY

One of the things all physicians and CAM practitioners agree on is that a program of regular, moderate exercise benefits everyone—and particularly those with depression—in a number of ways critical to short-term and long-term health. Exercise, quite simply, alleviates depression and is one step on the path to healthier living.

In this chapter, we'll look at the benefits of conventional exercise—the standard aerobic flexibility-strengthening routine—and introduce a number of exercise and movement activities that you may be less familiar with. The advantage of some of these other approaches is that they are particularly gentle on the body and are designed to address the whole person—

body and mind—in a relaxing, restorative program of physical and mental conditioning.

We'll also look at dance therapy, a structured treatment program aimed at encouraging you to express yourself in movement and thereby enhance your well-being.

## THE REWARDS OF EXERCISE

You may not feel like exercising when you're depressed, but it's one of the best things you can do for yourself. Physical exercise—whether leisure-time or work-related—just makes you feel better, a statement borne out by hundreds and hundreds of studies. A comprehensive analysis of 80 of these studies revealed that, overall, depression scores decreased *by approximately half* in the exercise groups. This finding applied across all age and gender lines, and the longer participants stayed with a program of regular exercise, the better they felt.

Even moderate physical activity improves blood flow to the brain, elevates the mood by triggering the release of the brain's "feel good" chemicals, known as endorphins, and relieves stress. Another benefit of exercise is that it lets you focus on something other than your depression and can also give you a feeling of control, a sense of accomplishment, and improved self-esteem.

### How Exercise Benefits You

- Brings more oxygen to your cells, which improves blood circulation, creates energy, and reduces fatigue
- Improves cardiovascular function, greatly reducing your risk of heart disease
- Burns calories, speeds up your metabolism, diminishes appetite, and therefore helps control weight
- Stimulates digestion and increases the absorption of nutrients
- Strengthens bones and stimulates new bone formation, helping reduce your risk for osteoporosis and resulting fractures
- Heightens your sense of well-being and wards off depression and anxiety
- Improves body image and self-esteem
- Improves your ability to handle stress
- Lowers the incidence of cancers of the breast, colon, and reproductive system
- Improves lung function and endurance
- Improves flexibility, loosens stiff joints, and reduces arthritic symptoms and low-back pain
- Helps prevent adult-onset diabetes
- Promotes sound sleep
- Improves muscle strength
- Enhances coordination and balance
- Helps prevent constipation

Researchers have reported that jogging for 30 minutes, three times a week, can be just as effective as psychotherapy in treating depression. You don't have to jog, though; any exercise you enjoy will work. Exercise does not have to be demanding to be effective either, and if you've been sedentary a long time, adding just 30 minutes of daily activity (such as walking, gardening, or housecleaning) to your routine will be beneficial. In fact, if you're in the midst of crippling depression, the simpler the exercise, the better. You don't want to set unreasonable goals for yourself, because you may feel even more depressed if you don't meet them.

Once you've incorporated some kind of daily exercise into your routine, you may want to start thinking about a long-term fitness regimen that includes these four components:

- Cardiorespiratory endurance
- Muscular strength
- Muscular endurance
- Flexibility

What does all this mean? *Cardiorespiratory (or cardiovascular or aerobic) exercise* moves your body's large muscles (arms and legs) in a rhythmic (or repetitive) motion for a sustained period, generally at least 10 minutes and up to 60 minutes. The goal is to get your heart pumping. This will release those endorphins we keep hearing about. In addition, aerobic exercise will make your heart stronger and more efficient. Not only will your heart stay in tip top condition, so will your lungs, arteries, and veins. And you'll enjoy the added bonus of burning calories.

*Muscular strength* is built up as your muscles work against resistance through activities such as lifting weights, swimming, or even carrying your groceries. When you perform strength-training exercises, you isolate specific muscles in the body, which tones and strengthens them.

The more you exercise your muscles, the more *muscular endurance* you'll have. This means you'll be better able to resist injury and less likely to lose muscle mass as you get older. You'll both feel better *and* look better.

The last component of your physical fitness program is *flexibility*. When your body is flexible, you can move your muscles, joints, and tendons through their paces without any stress, injury, or pain. Stretching regularly will keep your muscles long and supple, and keep you moving through your day without being stiff or tight.

## PUTTING IT ALL TOGETHER

A well rounded program starts with some warm-up exercises to raise body temperature and increase the heart rate, followed by a period of continuous, fast-paced aerobic conditioning. A cool-down set should finish your aerobic workout. Build in a flexibility routine that stretches muscles and puts joints through their full range of motion. Two or three times a week, add some muscle-strengthening activities.

Building and maintaining adequate muscle tone will help you burn more calories even while you are not exercising. In addition, good muscle tone will reduce the risk of falls and protect your joints from the stresses that tend to promote wear and tear and ultimately osteoarthritis.

A 5- to 10-minute warm-up prepares your muscles for exertion. Aerobic conditioning is essential for cardio-vascular health and weight control. Aim for 20 to 30 minutes of continuous exercise that works the large muscles of the body and elevates your breathing rate and your heart rate. Jogging or fast walking is ideal. Most people, even those with moderate osteoarthritis, are still able to walk at a good pace.

You may prefer a group activity—for example, an exercise class that incorporates music. The key is to give your muscles a good workout and get your heart pumping. How intensely you exercise is a function of your heart rate. As you increase the intensity of your workout, the muscles demand more oxygen and your heart beats faster. You want to get your heart rate up to 60 to 75 percent of its maximum capacity (220 minus your age) for 20 to 45 minutes, then cool down gradually.

The best time to work on flexibility is when the muscles are warmed up, after your aerobic workout. Stretching the muscles helps you maintain flexibility, balance, coordination, and agility. Allow about 10 minutes for stretching. Over time, stretching actually lengthens the muscles and strengthens tendons and ligaments, which helps prevent sports-related injuries.

To strengthen bones and to prevent or postpone osteoporosis, you'll want to add weight-bearing exercises to your training program. Walking and bicycling are excellent weight-bearing exercises, but strength training is even better. Strength training can help you build bone density in the hips and spine and also increases muscle mass. Aim for two or three sessions a week. The goal is not to become muscle-bound; you only need to do two sets (eight to 10 repetitions) of six to 10 exercises, working both the upper and lower body.

Fitness clubs offer instruction and an array of free weights and weight machines. But if joining a fitness club is not an option for you, it's easy to get the same benefits at home, working out with videos and three- to eight-pound dumbbells. To get the most out of your weight training program, be sure to take the time to learn the proper technique and form.

## How Long, How Often?

Start with three 30-minute exercise sessions per week (if you have been sedentary for quite some time, you may need to start with even shorter intervals). But to see real improvement, work up to four or five sessions as soon as possible. Daily 30-minute sessions of moderate intensity are ideal. This isn't as hard as it might seem; your 30 minutes of activity can be accumulated throughout the day and can include routine activities like walking up stairs, gardening, and vigorous housecleaning. Try not to get discouraged if you don't see immediate results; anything worth working for takes time.

It's often said that if you want an activity to become a habit, practice it for at least three weeks without fail. Apply that principle and you'll be on the right course. And don't get discouraged and give up if you miss a few days. Just pick up where you stopped and get back in the game.

## A Few Cautions Before You Start

If you have any doubts about whether you're fit enough to start an exercise program, see your doctor for a physical checkup.

Make fitness fun, not work, and you'll maintain a positive attitude. Countless people have embarked on a program of exercise (especially as a New Year's resolution), only to abandon it shortly afterward. Health club memberships and attendance usually surge after the New Year holiday, but the effect is not sustained. Studies show that many exercise dropouts had chosen an activity they didn't enjoy. If you don't like running, don't run. Don't swim if you hate it, and avoid aerobics classes if you think they're undignified and silly.

Consider asking a family member or friend to exercise with you. When you exercise with a partner, you're more likely to continue. You can motivate each other, and it's tougher to break a commitment than it is to skip a solo workout.

Outfit yourself with the proper shoes or equipment, but don't buy expensive equipment until you're sure you like the exercise. How can you be sure you'll like a stairclimber or a stationary bike before you buy it? Most reputable stores will allow you to test equipment. Visit the store in exercise clothes, prepared for a workout. If the thought of exercising in a store embarrasses you, visit a gym or ask a friend if you can try her equipment. Don't fall into the trap of furnishing your basement and garage with unused exercise machines.

By all means, set reasonable goals for yourself, and go at your own pace. Some discomfort and soreness is normal when you're getting back into shape; pain isn't normal. Don't overdo, or you'll be an early dropout.

## EVERY BREATH YOU TAKE

Proper breathing is beneficial during all types of exercise. Because breathing is automatic, few of us ever think about how to breathe properly. Unfortunately, many of us develop bad habits; but with practice, they can be overcome.

During exercise, you want to increase your air intake. Proper inhaling first fills the abdomen, then the middle chest, and finally, the upper chest. This is in sharp contrast to our image of correct posture: stomach in, chest out. Instead, we should relax our abdominal muscles, allowing our diaphragm to move freely and promote in a deeper, more healthful exchange of air.

Pay attention to your breathing while you exercise; try to prevent it from becoming quick and shallow. Practice proper breathing at rest, later incorporating it into your exercise routine. In general, you should breathe in through your nose and out through your mouth while exercising.

## YOGA

Yoga, a Sanskrit word meaning "union," originated in India more than 5,000 years ago. The practice of yoga is designed to quiet the mind by teaching you how to pay attention to your breathing and to the movement—or stillness—of your body. It was developed by spiritual students who wanted to strengthen and energize their bodies to better withstand the rigors of lengthy meditation. Although yoga is often practiced by followers of the Hindu religion, it is not itself a religion and can be practiced by people of all religions and philosophies.

The most popular form of yoga in Western culture is Hatha yoga, which focuses on the mind-body balance and uses physical postures (known as *asanas*), breathing techniques, and meditation.

Yoga postures re-establish structural integrity by stretching and strengthening muscles in your back, shoulder, abdomen, hips, and legs to expand your natural range of motion, massage internal organs, relax nerves, and increase blood circulation. Depending on which poses you use, yoga can work on every muscle, nerve, and gland in your body.

By helping establish the proper alignment of energy within the body, yoga promotes general good health in the individuals who practice it. Many people find the breathing exercises and meditation that accompany yoga movements beneficial when it comes to promoting relaxation and relieving fatigue. And because it focuses and calms the mind, yoga can help ease feelings of anxiety, fatigue, anger, and depression, preventing or alleviating many stress-related conditions. Yoga is also invigorating; if you do yoga exercises in the morning, you will have more energy to get through your day.

In general, yoga experts recommend that you perform the yoga postures at least 30 minutes each day, preferably in the morning or late evening, on an empty stomach. For people with depression, a good daily routine would consist of 30 minutes of meditation and at least 20 minutes of poses.

Wear loose clothing. Start with several minutes of deep breathing to calm your mind and increase the flow of oxygen within your body. Follow with several warm-up exercises, and then move on to the postures you have chosen for that day. Perform each pose slowly and gently; the *asanas* should not cause pain. End each session with the Corpse pose (see the description on page 343).

Yoga is undergoing a huge burst of popularity among baby boomers who are seeking gentler forms of exercise after years of bone-jarring aerobics and jogging. Layered with a swimming and walking program, yoga can provide all the targeted exercise you need for flexibility, heart health, and strong bones.

Classes are taught at health clubs, colleges, hospitals, and community centers. There are also a number of self-help books and videos that can teach you the basics. If you don't already have experience with yoga, enroll in a yoga class or seek help from a qualified instructor rather than simply trying these techniques on your own. This will help avoid potential problems and also ensure that you gain maximum benefit from your efforts.

Yoga instructors are not licensed. Some organizations do offer certification, but the requirements differ from group to group.

---

### Doing It Yourself

Experts say the following yoga *asanas,* or postures, can help ease depression and anxiety: Corpse, Mountain, Plow, Shoulder Stand, Sun Salutation, and Yoga Mudra. Several *asanas* specifically recommended for depression include Dancer, Windmill, Lion, and Knee Squeeze. The following instructions for several of these poses will give you a chance to try yoga for yourself. But to really get the full benefit of the activity, it's important to get professional instruction, if not in person, then at least by carefully following along with an exercise video.

---

## CORPSE POSE

Lie on your back on the floor or on a mat, your arms at your sides, palms facing up. Your legs are straight, with your feet in a relaxed position. Close your eyes and release the tension from your muscles. Breathe deeply, scanning your body for any areas of tension. If you feel tense in one area, concentrate on relaxing those muscles. Remain in this position for at least 30 seconds, but up to several minutes, until all your muscles are completely relaxed.

## MOUNTAIN POSE

The Mountain pose teaches correct posture and is the basis for all other standing poses. Stand with your feet together so your big toes are touching and your heels are slightly apart. Let your arms hang freely at your sides. Spread and lengthen your toes. Lift your kneecaps so they are facing forward. Keep your pelvis balanced on your legs. Lengthen your spine by stretching your inner legs upward from the inner heels to the groin. Continue to lengthen upward, opening your chest. Drop your shoulders and lengthen the back of your neck. Relax your face, your throat, and your eyes. Hold this pose for up to one minute.

## DANCER POSE

Stand straight, with your arms at your sides. Concentrate on a point across the room to establish your balance. Then bend your left leg up behind you and grab your left foot with your right hand. Raise your left arm, pointing your fingers toward the ceiling. Maintaining your balance, slowly raise your left leg back and away from your body, keeping your hand on your foot. When you reach a point that is comfortable for you, relax your abdominal muscles and breathe deeply from your stomach. Hold this pose for several seconds, then relax. Repeat with the right leg. (This pose is not recommended for people with lower back or disk problems.)

## WINDMILL POSE

Standing with your feet shoulder-width apart, toes pointing slightly inward, place your hands on your back at waist level, spreading your fingers on each side of your spine to support your lower back. As you inhale slowly, twist your torso slowly to the right, keeping your feet in place. As you begin to exhale, bend forward at the waist, bringing your forehead as close as you can to your right knee, then in a slow, continuous movement, to your left knee. Finish exhaling as your head reaches your left knee. Begin inhaling as you raise your torso to the left. Finish inhaling as you reach a full standing position. Hold your breath as you twist again to the right. Repeat three times in each direction. (Use caution if you have lower back pain.)

## LION POSE

Sit on the floor or on a mat with your knees bent and your feet under your buttocks. Keep your back straight and place your hands on your knees. Close your eyes and take a complete breath. Open your eyes, lean forward slightly, and exhale while making a growling sound. As you growl, open your mouth and stick out your tongue as far as possible. Spread your fingers wide. Repeat several times.

## KNEE SQUEEZE

Lie on your back on the floor or on a mat. Your hands should be at your sides, and your toes slightly pointed. Inhale slowly and deeply as you raise your right knee to your chest. Grab your right knee with both arms and hold it to your chest for a few seconds. Begin to exhale as you straighten your knee and lower it slowly to the floor. Repeat with the left leg. Do this a total of three times, alternating legs. Next, breathe in completely, then lift both knees to your chest at the same time. Wrap your arms around both legs and hold for a few seconds, then breathe out and lower your legs.

### To Relieve Headaches

For headache relief, ask an experienced yoga instructor to guide you in eye and neck exercises. Once you are familiar with yoga, the following poses can be effective: Corpse, Plow, and Shoulder Roll.

### To Promote Restful Sleep

Meditating in the Corpse position can promote deep relaxation as a prelude to sleep. First, go into a progressive relaxation exercise. Begin at the bottom of your feet and move upward, releasing tension from one muscle group at a time, ending at the shoulders, neck, head, and jaw. Once your body is thoroughly relaxed, focus on slow, deep breathing. Finally, repeat a phrase—such as one, ohm, or hum—and let the repetition of this single sound banish all conscious thought from your mind. You may actually fall asleep during this exercise.

Once you are adept at yoga, there are additional poses known to have a calming effect. These include the Cobra, Locust, Mountain, Posterior Stretch, and Shoulder Stand. You might consider a nightly program of three or four poses to relax your mind and body prior to bedtime.

## *TAI CHI*

For thousands of years, people in China have practiced *tai chi,* which combines physical and mental exercises in an effort to restore the energy and vitality of both your body and mind. The exercises consist of a series of slow, flowing, rhythmic movements accompanied by deep breathing and can be performed by virtually anyone, regardless of age or physical condition. Millions of Chinese and Taiwanese people begin their day with a *tai chi* session performed en masse in local parks.

When performing *tai chi,* you move your arms through a series of slow, controlled, and continuous circles while shifting your weight from one foot to the other. The movements and positions are known as forms and have names such as Salutation to the Buddha, Grasp Bird's Tail, White Crane Spreads Its Wings, and Embracing Tiger.

*Tai chi* has been shown to reduce stress—as well as improve breathing, posture, and balance—by emphasizing complete relaxation. A 1992 study published in the British *Journal of Psychosomatic Research* showed that *tai chi* reduces symptoms of stress. A 1998 study at the Johns Hopkins School of Medicine reported that *tai chi* exercises lowered blood pressure in older adults just as well as moderate aerobic exercise did.

*Tai chi* is recommended by the Arthritis Foundation for arthritis sufferers, because it emphasizes total relaxation and passive concentration with no risk of injury. Those who find exercise painful may find that *tai chi* enables them to slowly move their body through a full range of motion.

Although you can perform *tai chi* alone once you've mastered the exercises, you will need to find a good teacher to get started. To locate an instructor in your area, contact the American Oriental Bodywork Therapy Association at 609-782-1616 or look in the telephone book under *"tai chi,"* "martial arts," "self-defense," "health services," "holistic centers and/or practitioners."

## QIGONG

*Qigong* exercises involve gentle, rhythmic swinging postures, stretching movements, meditation, and deep-relaxation breathing, with the objective of increasing the body's vital energy and calming the emotions and the mind. The slow-paced exercises stretch ligaments and tendons and flex muscles. A technique that involves remaining still for an extended period—from several minutes to an hour—is designed to teach concentration and enhance sensitivity to the flow of your energy. The regular practice of *qigong* can result in improved circulation, balance, flexibility, and increased range of motion. The exercises also improve overall relaxation.

To find a qualified *qigong* instructor, contact the American Oriental Bodywork Therapy Association at 609-782-1616, or look in the telephone book under *"qigong," "chigong," "chi kung,"* or *"qi gung."* Holistic and wellness centers may also offer classes.

## DANCE THERAPY

Professional dance and movement therapists are experts in how the body and mind interact in health and illness. The discipline combines the dancer's special understanding of the body and the expressive spirit with the healing possibilities of psychotherapy and emotional/social/cognitive/physical rehabilitation.

Dance/movement therapy can be an effective treatment for people with developmental, medical, social, physical, and psychological impairments. Those who've been helped include autistic children, the mentally ill, and people with spinal cord injuries, as well as senior citizens, people with depression and low self-esteem, and people who simply feel ill-at-ease with their bodies. The intervention has been shown to be clinically effective in:

- Developing body image, improving self-concept, and enhancing self-esteem
- Relieving depression and reducing fears and anxieties
- Facilitating attention
- Expressing anger

- Reducing isolation, enhancing communication skills, and promoting solidarity
- Lowering body tension and reducing chronic pain
- Improving circulatory and respiratory function
- Promoting feelings of well-being

Ancient cultures have always appreciated the power of music and dance to lift the spirits and help people express their innermost feelings. In this country, dance therapy emerged as a distinct profession in 1942, and in the mid-1960s dance therapists from around the country formed the American Dance Therapy Association (ADTA), now 1,100 members strong, which maintains standards for professional practice, education, and training.

In the course of investigating complementary approaches, you may come across a dance therapy program offered through a local hospital, mental health clinic, rehabilitation center, day care center, skilled nursing center, community center, or educational institution. Individual and group formats are available, typically in weekly sessions lasting 30 to 40 minutes. Look for a program offered by a masters-level ADTA-registered therapist.

# 15

## Structural Therapies

CHIROPRACTIC

OSTEOPATHY

MASSAGE

REFLEXOLOGY

CRANIOSACRAL THERAPY

HYDROTHERAPY

If your experience with depression is accompanied by frequent backaches, muscle aches, tension headaches, or arthritis-like symptoms, you may want to seek relief from one or more of the complementary/alternative practitioners who specialize in musculoskeletal treatments, the so-called structural therapies. The effect of these interventions can be understood chiefly in terms of what they do to the anatomic structures of the body—the bones, muscles, organs, ligaments, and joints.

CAM practitioners working in this category include chiropractors, osteopaths, naturopaths, massage therapists, and hydrotherapists. These last two, along with physical therapists, fit very comfortably in the conventional medical framework as well, although some individual practitioners take a more holistic approach to treatment.

Reflexologists are sometimes grouped in this category because, to untrained Western eyes, reflexology seems to be nothing more than foot or hand massage. Practitioners of the art would disagree, maintaining that the goal of treatment is to increase energy flow and restore energy balance.

It need hardly be said that none of these interventions constitute primary care in terms of treating the underlying depression. But while you're making nutritional and lifestyle changes, or in psychotherapy or on antidepressant medications, it makes sense to support the healing process in every way you can. If persistent aches and pains are making your life miserable, and if you're already prone to depression, you may want to ask a chiropractor or osteopath what you can do to keep your neuromusculoskeletal system in tip top shape. You might even decide to make the investment in a weekly therapeutic massage. Sound nice? Read on.

## CHIROPRACTIC

Chiropractic is a century-old healing art form that emphasizes the prevention of chronic disease through the maintenance of a healthy neuromusculoskeletal system. The specialty dates back to 1895 when Dr. Daniel David Palmer apparently was able to cure a patient's deafness by pushing a vertebra in the man's back into proper alignment. Palmer took this as proof that spinal misalignment could lead to health problems and that spinal realignment could restore the flow of nerve impulses throughout the body.

Chiropractors may use medical diagnostic procedures, including, but not limited to, x-rays of the spine, to assess dysfunction. They then use a combination of spinal manipulation and exercise to adjust the spinal column, correct structural imbalances, and restore range of motion. Some chiropractors also incorporate nutritional therapy, acupuncture, and other techniques into their practice.

Chiropractic care can offer pain relief without the use of drugs or surgery. Many patients find it an effective way to manage lower back pain, tension and migraine headaches, and neck problems. It also can complement traditional medical treatment for such long-term disorders as asthma, ringing in the ears, dizziness, and chronic fatigue syndrome.

During an office visit, a chiropractor will take your medical history, ask you about your lifestyle and symptoms, and evaluate your posture and walk. During the examination, he will feel your vertebrae and joints and may perform a reflex test to check for nerve function. He will ask you to bend forward, backward, and sideways to check your range of motion. He may order x-rays to determine if there are any underlying joint problems that could be made worse by treatment.

Once a diagnosis is made, the chiropractor will adjust your joints by means of a controlled push that moves the joint beyond its restricted range of motion. Treatments are usually painless, and many people see results in nine to 12 sessions.

Today there are more than 50,000 chiropractors in the United States. More than 20 million people a year visit a chiropractor, making this the most popular form of nontraditional therapy (after the use of herbal and nutritional supplements).

Many physicians, however, continue to be skeptical of chiropractic care for any condition other than back pain and minor muscle and joint pain. These doubters maintain that chiropractors don't have the training to diagnose or treat any other conditions and could misdiagnose or prevent a patient from getting necessary medical treatment as quickly as possible. A competent chiropractor will, however, will refer a patient to a medical doctor if symptoms warrant.

As college undergraduates, chiropractors follow a premed course of study for at least two years, followed by four years at an accredited chiropractic college. The curriculum is similar to the medical school curriculum, with additional emphasis on anatomy, nutrition, physiology, and rehabilitation. Chiropractors are licensed to practice in all 50 states and in the District of Columbia. To be licensed, they must be graduates of an accredited chiropractic college and must pass a rigorous exam. Chiropractors maintain their licenses by taking continuing education courses.

CAUTION—Chiropractic manipulation can cause severe damage in cases involving an underlying, unidentified fracture or a tumor. If you have atherosclerosis of the carotid arteries, you should avoid vigorous manipulation of the neck as there is a small but distinct chance of dislodging some plaque and causing a stroke.

## OSTEOPATHY

Osteopathy, or osteopathic medicine, dates back to the 1870s, to frontier doctor Andrew Taylor Still who believed that a person's bones, muscles, ligaments, and connective tissues—the musculoskeletal system—was the basis for good health. Based on this belief, Dr. Still created a system of healing that employed touch and gentle manipulation of muscles and joints to trigger the body's own ability to heal itself, often without drugs or surgery.

Osteopathic physicians gear their treatment toward three objectives: relieving tension so that muscles, ligaments, and joints are properly aligned; improving blood circulation and stimulating the nervous system; and correcting posture and other body mechanics to prevent health problems.

In addition to performing a complete physical exam with standard lab tests, an osteopath will conduct a structural exam to evaluate your posture, spine, and balance. He or she will press on your muscles, tendons, and ligaments to see if you feel tenderness, tension, or weakness, and will evaluate your joints to assess your range of motion.

If a structural problem is found, the osteopath may use osteopathic manipulative therapy (OMT) that can involve massage, stretching, muscle pressure, and joint alignment. OMT is designed to relieve tension in affected muscles and ligaments, improve posture and movement, and promote better circulation to stimulate the body's own natural healing ability. It has been shown to work well for people with chronic pain (including low back pain, headaches, and migraines), menstrual pain, and knee and neck problems.

While many chiropractors limit their treatment to the spine, the minority of osteopaths who choose to incorporate OMT into their clinical practices may be more inclined to also work on the arms, legs, and skull in an effort to improve blood circulation, which is essential to healing. Some osteopaths who use OMT and have a holistic/integrative practice style may also recommend a regimen of treatment that would include acupuncture, massage therapy, or homeopathy, based on your individual symptoms. For acute illnesses and for those not caused by a structural abnormality, most osteopathic physicians will generally rely on conventional medical techniques, including drugs and surgery.

Doctors of osteopathy (D.O.'s) are licensed as physicians in all 50 states and can prescribe medication. They undergo the same training as M.D.'s in terms of basic and clinical sciences. They must be graduates of a four-year accredited college of osteopathy and must complete a one-year internship in primary care. Many osteopaths also complete a residency in one of 120 medical specialties.

Medical boards make no distinction between D.O.'s and M.D.'s when it comes to standards of medical practice. The main difference is that osteopathic doctors have additional training in musculoskeletal diagnosis and manipulation. Not all D.O.'s incorporate OMT into their practice, but those who do often have a more holistic approach to treating patients.

## MASSAGE

You know how good a massage feels. But do you know the health benefits it delivers? Massage, the manipulation of soft tissues, may not cure what ails you, but it can go a long way toward relieving certain symptoms, particularly those caused by stress. A good massage helps you relax. It can also be effective in the treatment of sports-related injuries, muscle and joint problems, headaches, and chronic pain—even sinus problems and digestive difficulties. A therapeutic massage changes your physiology in ways that facilitate the normal healing process.

Massage can stretch tissues, increase your range of motion, help lower blood pressure and heart rate, and improve breathing and circulation. It can also aid digestion and promote relaxation by loosening muscles and eliminating the buildup of lactic acid in the muscles.

Massage can help relieve the symptoms of depression by stimulating the release of endorphins, the chemicals that act as the body's natural painkillers, and promoting a feeling of comfort and well-being. The general sense of well-being produced by a massage can reduce the levels of stress hormones—such as cortisol and norepinephrine—which circulate throughout your body. Touch can convey caring and concern, and some massage therapists believe that touch itself can help release blocked emotions. In one study done at the University of Miami Medical School, women hospitalized for serious postpartum depression were given a 20-minute Swedish massage twice a week. They reported improved mood, and their blood levels of stress hormones declined.

The most gentle massage technique is stroking, or *effleurage,* which aids circulation and relaxes tense muscles. A massage therapist will move her hands smoothly over your skin, alternating hands, or using a slow circular motion. Other more vigorous forms of massage can also be beneficial. These include kneading, or *petrissage,* which stretches and relaxes muscles; friction, or *frottage,* which is deep, direct pressure applied to the muscles around the spine and shoulders; and thumping, or *tapotement,* a brisk percussive motion on the fleshy, muscular areas.

Your first few sessions may leave you exhausted as waste products in your body are released into your bloodstream. Since your kidneys and liver will be working overtime to rid your body of these waste products, help them along by drinking lots of pure water, avoiding alcohol and cigarette smoke—even secondhand smoke—and eating light, nutritious meals.

Your body may be sore the day after a massage, but the discomfort should disappear quickly, usually by the following day. If not, tell the therapist to be gentler the next time.

CAUTION—While massage is generally safe for most people, consult your health care practitioner if you have heart disease, circulatory problems, cancer, an infectious illness, or a skin condition. Massage enhances lymphatic and blood flow, and even though there is no research documenting problems, there is a theoretic concern that it may facilitate bleeding and the spread of infection or localized tumor cells. If there is a localized problem area, it's best to avoid massage in that part of the body.

## HEALING HANDS

### To Relieve Headaches

A regular schedule of professional massages may help prevent chronic tension headaches. You can also try self-massaging your scalp, face, neck, shoulders, and back.

### To Promote Restful Sleep

Massage encourages relaxation and can be a relaxing transition to a night of restful sleep. If you're on your own, try massaging a warm scented oil into your scalp and on the soles of your feet before bedtime. Or ask your partner to lightly massage your neck and shoulders for about 10 minutes. If your muscles are stiff and sore from work or exercise, a full-body massage by a trained therapist can be just the ticket.

## Other Structural Therapies Worth Investigating

There are many other structural interventions and techniques that we can't do justice to in the limited space of this book. Examples include Rolfing (also known as structural integration), soft tissue release (STR), neuromuscular technique (NMT), and *tui na* (Chinese medical massage). For tips on finding more information about these approaches, see the resource section at the end of this book.

# REFLEXOLOGY

Reflexology, sometimes referred to as "zone therapy," has been practiced in one way or another for centuries. Reflexology is based on the idea that reflex points on the feet, hands, and ears correspond to activity elsewhere in the body. Manipulating specific reflex points is believed to stimulate the natural healing response in the corresponding parts of the body.

Your toes, for example, correspond to your head and neck. Your heel corresponds to your pelvic area, and so on. Pressure on corresponding points may cause soreness or tenderness. The more tenderness you feel, say reflexologists, the greater the need to balance your energy in that area. While most Westerners characterize this modality as a form of massage, reflexologists feel it is an energy-based intervention that promotes overall health by helping correct energy imbalances.

Practitioners say the treatment improves blood circulation, balances overactive or underactive glands, and relieves stress. The technique is also used to treat a number of ailments including insomnia, headaches, premenstrual syndrome, sinusitis, and constipation. Daily treatment is thought to balance the body's energy, help you stay healthy, and enhance relaxation. In fact, a reflexology session performed by a qualified practitioner can be one of the most relaxing experiences you'll ever have.

You can try reflexology yourself or with a partner. Learn which points to work on by visiting a trained practitioner or by consulting self-help books.

The basic technique is called "thumb walking" and involves using the inside edge of the thumb pad or the index finger in a slow, forward movement, bending the first joint of the thumb or finger slightly as it moves ahead. Hold your foot with one hand—the sole flat and the toes straight—and work on it with the other hand. To work on the hands, use the thumb of one hand on the palm of the other, or the index finger on the areas between the fingers. Feel for tension or gritty spots beneath the skin, known as "crystals." These are believed to be signs of the blockage causing your individual symptoms.

Reflexologists are not licensed, but many are certified by the International Institute of Reflexology.

### To Reduce Stress

For soothing stress, concentrate on your hands by "walking" your fingers up and down the outer edge of your thumb, from below the nail to your wrist.

## To Relieve Headaches

For headaches, work on the points that correspond to your head, eyes, and ears. These points are found on your fingers and fingertips.

## To Promote Restful Sleep

A skilled reflexologist will often tackle your insomnia problem by concentrating on those points on your hands and feet that relate to the adrenal glands, diaphragm, parathyroid, pituitary, reproductive system, and spine.

## CRANIOSACRAL THERAPY

Developed by osteopath John Upledger at Michigan State University in the late 1970s, craniosacral therapy (sometimes called craniosacral release, or CSR) is a gentle, noninvasive method of evaluating and enhancing the function of the craniosacral system. It is thought that imbalances in this system—consisting of the membranes and fluids that run along the spinal cord from the cranium (skull) to the sacrum (tailbone)—can impede the normal flow of cerebrospinal fluid that carries nutrients throughout the central nervous system. Osteopaths, chiropractors, and massage therapists who use this technique lightly palpate these structures, detect the imbalances, and subtly adjust the bones. In doing so, they attempt to remove energy blockages and re-establish healthy flow, thus relieving the negative effects of stress and encouraging the body's natural healing mechanisms.

Craniosacral therapy has been used successfully to treat a variety of conditions, including chronic pain, recurrent ear infections, head and neck injuries, eye difficulties, motor coordination impairments, headaches, hyperactivity, and emotional trauma.

## HYDROTHERAPY

Hydrotherapy—the use of water to relieve symptoms of health problems—can be traced to many ancient cultures, among them the Romans, Egyptians, and Hebrews. Native Americans used sweat lodges for cleansing and for ceremonial purposes. For many centuries, Scandinavians have used saunas to detoxify the blood after long winters without fresh food.

Water has been used internally and externally in a variety of treatment applications, including whirlpool baths, ice packs, saunas, douches, colonic irrigation, sitz baths, compresses, wraps, and mineral drinking waters.

A warm (not hot) bath or shower just before bedtime can help relax, a prelude to an easy slumber. Hot water treatments can relax muscles, ease pain, and increase joint mobility. If a hot shower or a hot soak in a tub or whirlpool brings relief, keep the water no hotter than 110 degrees Fahrenheit (40 degrees Celsius) and don't stay in for more than 15 minutes. If hot baths seem to help, hot packs and heating pads may also provide relief.

Cold water (or ice) treatments can be effective for pain relief and for reducing inflammation. If using ice, wrap it in a plastic bag and apply to the affected area in a 20-minutes-on, 20-minutes-off pattern. Applications should not exceed 20 minutes, as extended exposure to extreme cold can damage the skin.

Alternating hot and cold treatments (called "contrast therapy") can increase blood circulation through the elimination organs (the kidneys, liver, and skin), thereby detoxifying the system and improving the quality of the blood. The heat relaxes; the cold stimulates. The contrast between the two improves your circulation, carrying more nutrients to your cells and ridding them more quickly of waste material. Applying heat to one part of the body while applying cold to another moves blood from the cold area to the hot, and often helps ease pain in the cold region.

When alternating between hot and cold, don't use hot water for more than five or 10 minutes at a time; keep the cold water to just a few minutes. Always end with the cold.

# 16

## Singing in the Rain

Scandal, injustice, tragedy, and disaster are all too common parts of our daily lives. If we were to judge by the newspaper headlines and the evening news, they would seem to be the sum total of our apparently miserable existence. Fortunately, our lives are filled with an infinitely greater abundance of blessings and opportunities—the sunlight above the storm clouds.

Our reality is in large part shaped by our perception. The tone and tenor of our lives is a function of what we choose to focus on. If we focus (as the headlines tend to do) on the dark and negative aspects, life becomes a troublesome, hopeless attempt to find the path of least despair. This is the fate of those trapped in the biochemical, mental, emotional, spiritual jail cell we call depression.

The purpose of this book is to let you know that there is a way out of solitary confinement. Depression does not have to be a life sentence. You can once again seek joy. You can once again sing, even in the rain.

The way out is different for everyone. Our bio-chemical, mental, emotional, and spiritual uniqueness requires an individualized approach for the treatment of depression. Integrative medicine by virtue of its expanded, holistic perspective and its collaborative philosophy can offer you a much more individualized path to recovery. With integrative medicine, you can draw on the best of both Western medicine and complementary therapies to help heal your brain (biochemistry) and your mind (thoughts).

The following case histories (names changed) are examples of the unique paths to healing experienced by some of the patients in my practice.

## ANNE

Anne was a 62-year-old who initially came to see me for chronic fatigue and fibromyalgia. She had been experiencing symptoms on and off for approximately seven years, following an automobile accident. When I saw Anne, she was restrained in her mannerisms, and her emotions and facial expression were flat. She seemed to take no joy in life and was plagued by general fatigue, chronic pain, and a litany of physical symptoms so debilitating that often she was unable to perform simple household chores. Her family was not particularly sympathetic, given that the medical community had said all her tests were normal and that there was nothing wrong with her.

Anne had seen multiple specialists and tried multiple medications (including several antidepressants) without relief. In fact, most of the medicines made her feel worse, due to intolerable side effects or allergic reactions.

After examining her and running some lab tests we found that her TSH (thyroid stimulating hormone) was normal but her Free T3 was low. Also, her DHEA-sulfate level was low. After supplementing with 10 milligrams of DHEA-sulfate in the mornings and using prescription Cytomel (T3), 5 micrograms twice daily, her follow-up lab tests were normal. She felt more energy and less pain but still found no joy in life. When stressed by the task of preparing Thanksgiving dinner for the family or by hosting guests, she would decompensate and return to her previous level of exhaustion and incapacity. On these occasions we were successfully able to restore her energy (temporarily) with a "Meyer's cocktail" (vitamin B complex, calcium, magnesium, and vitamin C) given intravenously over 10–15 minutes. However, the physical gains did little to improve her outlook on life.

On probing further I found out that since childhood Anne had assumed, without complaining, all responsibilities that had been thrust upon her. She viewed her acceptance by others as performance-based—contingent on her accomplishing the near impossible. Up to now, through a combination of competence, perseverance, and faith, she had always managed to get the job done. Over a period of several years when her husband suffered from alcoholism, she was able to keep the family business running, send the kids off to college, and pay the mortgage—

even though she felt like it was killing her. Her husband never openly acknowledged this or thanked her for all those years of tireless loyalty and superhuman effort.

When Anne's health deteriorated as a result of the accident, her husband tried to pick up the slack but eventually he became tired and resentful of her inability to do "her share." Anne couldn't discuss this with him or even with her pastor. She felt, in fact, there was no one she could talk to about her situation.

As I listened to Anne tell her story, it became apparent that she felt guilty that she couldn't perform up to her usual standards. She also felt guilty about feeling bitter and resentful toward her husband and other family members who expected so much of her and were unsympathetic to her plight. And she couldn't forgive herself for what she saw as her physical and spiritual inadequacies. Since she based her self-acceptance on her performance, she could no longer accept herself. On discussing her religious belief system, she admitted to me that she knew she had been forgiven by God.

At this point, I swallowed hard, took a big risk, and switched from listening to guiding. I asked Anne, *If God could forgive her, why could she not forgive herself? Did she have higher standards than God?*

This conversation was a turning point for Anne. She smiled warmly and gave me a big hug. For the first time in years, someone had listened to her. A simple observation had helped her see her situation in a new light. The new Anne was able to forgive herself and accept herself. She's doing much better these days and has once again found joy in life, even when the sun is hidden behind the clouds.

## BILL

Bill was a 47-year-old former tennis instructor whose zest for life could not be contained. His life was turned upside down when he was dragged under a car 15 years ago. He had tried to put his life back together and had made several unsuccessful attempts to restart his tennis career. But the changes in his physical and mental state had led to diminished self-confidence and ultimately a malignant insecurity. This insecurity affected every aspect of his life, including his ability to keep a job and sustain personal relationships.

Bill had seen several psychiatrists and counselors and had been diagnosed with a manic-depressive disorder. Over the years, he had taken a variety of prescription medications, including lithium and Depakote. Lithium was helpful but the side effects, at the prescribed therapeutic doses, were unacceptable. His manic episodes were characterized mostly by rapid thoughts, restlessness, and anxiety. His depressed episodes were black holes of despair from which escape seemed impossible.

Bill came to me looking for help with his mood swings. When he shared the tragedies and sorrows he had had to deal with, I fought back the tears and did my best to simply listen supportively.

Since lithium had been helpful but not tolerated at the "therapeutic doses" (900–1,800 milligrams daily is typical), I prescribed a low dose of lithium—300 milligrams once or twice daily as needed. Subsequent blood tests, following twice daily dosing for one month, revealed that his blood lithium level was in the "subtherapeutic" range. On this dose of lithium Bill felt much better, although not completely back to normal. To treat his occasional anxiety spells he uses kava, 100 milligrams twice daily, with good results. Bill is now holding down a job and his relationships are on the mend.

Even though the textbooks and medical experts have identified a "therapeutic range" for blood lithium levels, the range was toxic for Bill. As it turns out, there is research showing a significant correlation between patterns of behavior and the lithium content in the drinking water of different counties (at ranges that are all "subtherapeutic").

Clearly, one-size-fits-all medicine (in this case, one-range-fits-all medicine) flies in the face of what we know about biochemical individuality. In order to match the treatment to the patient (and not vice versa), it takes a practitioner who is willing to listen and pay more attention to what the patient says than to prevailing medical dogma.

Even though I am not a covered provider on his health insurance plan, Bill continues to check in with me periodically, to let me know how things are going. These days, when he shares the events in his life, I have to hold back my enthusiasm rather than my tears. The new Bill looks and acts differently. You can almost see his self-confidence growing!

# CAROL

Carol was a 32-year-old pharmacist who has had bouts of mild depression on and off over the years. Her depression had recently been aggravated by family stressors. Even though she dispenses medicines on a daily basis, she would rather not take prescription antidepressants. However, she welcomed my suggestion to use St. John's wort (300 milligrams three times daily of a product standardized to 0.3 percent hypericin). She also began psychotherapy to help her deal better with some of her family issues.

Unfortunately, despite these measures, her condition deteriorated over the next few weeks to the point where she was deeply depressed, agitated, and on the verge of being suicidal. I was concerned that something needed to be done immediately to improve the situation, perhaps even hospitalization. A respected acupuncturist working in the office was able to see Carol right away and performed acupuncture to correct her energetic imbalance (based on a traditional Chinese medicine diagnosis). Carol walked out of the office an hour and a half later calm and slightly blue, but definitely hopeful.

Based on her favorable response to acupuncture and her apparent short-term lack of response to St. John's wort and psychotherapy, I suggested an integrative approach—the antidepressant Paxil at a dose of 20 milligrams daily, along with follow-up acupuncture sessions twice weekly over the next three weeks.

Over the next month I talked with Carol every few days to be sure that she wasn't sliding back into dangerous territory. She took the Paxil faithfully but felt she was doing fine with only one session of acupuncture per week. Acupuncture may well have done the job for Carol, but the family budget was tight and though Paxil was covered by her health insurance, acupuncture was not. In light of both the severity of Carol's depression and her budgetary concerns, I proposed a reasonable compromise: the short-term use of acupuncture to keep her out of the hospital until the Paxil took effect.

This proved to be an effective strategy. Her mood stabilized and with counseling she was able to resume a fairly normal life. Her only complaint was a decrease in libido—a common side effect of the SSRI medications. Her sexual drive improved by supplementing the Paxil with 80 milligrams of ginkgo biloba, twice daily.

The new Carol was once again able to enjoy her family and her work. Where there had been despair, there was now hope.

## DAVID

David was a 26-year-old who had been a party animal in college. Now he found himself feeling tired, withdrawn, and bored with life. He wasn't looking forward—only back—and nothing in his present activities seemed particularly enjoyable or exciting to him. In addition, he was having a hard time concentrating and coping with the demands of his office job—particularly in the afternoons, after lunch. Lunch for David usually consisted of a peanut butter and jelly sandwich. He had noticed over the years that foods seemed to affect his mood, but he denied experiencing any of the classic symptoms usually thought of as "allergic" (rash, nasal congestion, sneezing, shortness of breath, wheezing, or itchy eyes) with food consumption.

A blood food allergy panel, which checks levels of antibodies to different foods, revealed that he had very high antibody levels to peanuts. Once he started eating something other than peanut butter sandwiches for lunch, his afternoon concentration and job performance improved.

Nonetheless, David continued to be relatively uninterested in recreational or social activities, so we decided to have him try St. John's wort, 300 milligrams in the morning and 600 milligrams in the evening. After six weeks David's mild depression had cleared and he was once again leading an active social life—with no side effects from the suggested interventions. The new David was the old David—happy, optimistic, making plans for the future, feeling on top of things—minus the wild college parties.

## LET IT RAIN

The four case histories cited here show different degrees and types of depression and give you a taste of how individual the paths to healing can be. The stressors and storms these people face have not changed. The grim nightly headlines have not changed. The only thing that has changed for these individuals is their internal balance—a combination of biochemical, mental, emotional, and spiritual healing. Correcting or rebalancing these factors allowed Anne, Bill, Carol, and David to perceive and relate to the world in a different way.

If you or a loved one is struggling with depression, rest assured that there is hope. For each of us, there is a unique path to healing. If you can't find the path on your own, ask for help from someone who will listen and who recognizes you as the unique and precious person that you are. The human spirit is indomitable, but sometimes each of us needs a little help through the storm. Ultimately the rain will pass.

# For More Information, Help, and Support

**ON DEPRESSION:**
American Psychological
  Association
750 East 1st Street, NE
Washington, DC 20002-4242
202-336-5000
*www.apa.org*

Center for Cognitive Therapy
33 South 36th Street,
  Room 602
Philadelphia, PA 19104
215-898-4100 (select option
  "5" for a referral to a cognitive therapist in your area)
*www.med.upenn.edu/psycct*

National Depressive and
  Manic-Depressive Association
730 North Franklin Street
  Suite 501
Chicago, Illinois 60610-3526
800-826-3632
*www.ndmda.org*

National Mental Health
  Association
1021 Prince Street
Alexandria, VA 22314-2971
703-684-7722
*www.nmha.org*

**SUICIDE HOTLINE:**
Dial "911" and ask the emergency operator to direct you
to the suicide hotline in your
area.

**WEB RESOURCES:**
Depression.com
  *www.depression.com*

Depression after Delivery
  *www.behavenet.com/dadinc*

Light in the Darkness
  Support Group
  *www.lightdarkness.com*

Manic-Depressive Web Ring
  *www.geocities.com/
  SunsetStrip/Lounge/1640/
  themanic.htm*

Mental Health Net
  *www.mentalhelp.net*

## COMPLEMENTARY AND ALTERNATIVE CONTACTS:

### ACUPRESSURE
American Association of Oriental Medicine
433 Front Street
Chatasauqua, PA 18032
888-500-7999
*www.aaom.org*

### ACUPUNCTURE
Acupuncture.com:
*www.acupuncture.com*

American Academy of Medical Acupuncture
5820 Wilshire Boulevard
Suite 500
Los Angeles, CA 90036
323-937-5514
*www.MedicalAcupuncture.org*

National Acupuncture and Oriental Medicine Alliance
14637 Starr Road, SE
Olalla, WA 98359
253-851-6896
*www.acuall.org*

National Certification Commission for Acupuncture and Oriental Medicine
Canal Center Plaza, Suite 300
Alexandria, VA 22314
703-548-9004
*www.nccaom.org*

### ALEXANDER TECHNIQUE
American Society for the Alexander Technique
3010 Hennepin Ave. South
Suite 10
Minneapolis, MN 55408
800-473-0620
*www.alexandertech.com*

### AROMATHERAPY
American Alliance of Aromatherpy
Post Office Box 309
Depoe Bay, OR 97341
800-809-9850
*http://205.180.229.2/aaoa*

National Association for Holistic Aromatherapy
Post Office Box 17622
Boulder, CO 80308
888-ASK-NAHA
*www.naha.org*

### ASTON-PATTERNING
Aston Training Center
Post Office Box 3568
Indian Village, NV 89450
702-831-8228
*http://members.aol.com/ SVUmassage/Aston.htmlf*

### AYURVEDIC MEDICINE
The Ayurvedic Institute
11311 Menaul NE, Suite A
Albuquerque, NM 87112
505-291-9698
*www.ayurveda.com*

**BIOFEEDBACK**
Association for Applied
  Psychophysiology and
  Biofeedback
10200 West 44th Avenue
  Suite 304
Wheat Ridge, CO 80033-2840
800-477-8892
*www.aapb.org*

**BIOMAGNETISM**
Biomagnetic Database
*www.biomagnetic.com*

**"BOGUS" THERAPIES**
Museum of Questionable
  Medical Devices
*www.mtn.org/quack/index.htm*

National Council Against
  Health Fraud
*www.ncahf.org*

Quackwatch
*www.quackwatch.com*

**BRAINGYM (EDUCATIONAL
KINESIOLOGY)**
Educational Kinesiology
  Foundation
1691 Spinnaker Drive
  Suite 105B
Ventura, CA 93001
800-356-2109
*www.braingym.org*

**CHIROPRACTIC**
American Chiropractic
  Association
1701 Clarendon Boulevard
Arlington, VA 22209
800-986-4636
*www.amerchiro.org*

International Chiropractors
  Association
1110 North Glebe Road
  Suite 1000
Arlington, VA 22201
800-423-4690
*www.chiropractic.org*

**COMPOUNDING PHARMACIES**
International Academy of
  Compounding Pharmacies
Post Office Box 1365
Sugar Land, TX 77487
800-927-IACP
*www.iacprx.org*

**CRANIOSACRAL THERAPY**
Upledger Institute
11211 Prosperity Farms Road
  D-325
Palm Beach Gardens, FL
  33410-3449
800-233-5880
*E-mail: upledger@upledger.com*

**DANCE THERAPY**
American Dance Therapy
  Association
2000 Century Place, Suite 108
10632 Little Patuxent Parkway
Columbia, MD 21044
410-997-4040
*www.adta.org*

EYE MOVEMENT DESENSITIZATION
REPROGRAMMING
EMDR Institute
Post Office Box 51038
Pacific Grove, CA 93950
831-372-3900
*www.emdr.com*

FELDENKRAIS
Feldenkrais Guild of North
  America
3611 SW Hood Avenue
  Suite 100
Portland, OR 97201
800-775-2118
*www.feldenkrais.com*

HERBAL THERAPY
American Botanical Council
Post Office Box 144345
Austin, TX 78714-4345
512-926-4900
*www.herbalgram.org*

American Herbalists' Guild
Post Office Box 70
Roosevelt, UT 84066
435-722-8434
*www.healthy.net/herbalists*

HELLERWORK INTERNATIONAL
Hellerwork International
406 Berry Street
Mount Shasta, CA 96067
800-392-3900
*www.hellerwork.com*

HOLISTIC MEDICAL DOCTORS
American Holistic Medical
  Association
6728 Old McLean Village Drive
McLean, VA 22101
703-556-9245
*www.holisticmedicine.org*

HOLISTIC DENTISTS
Holistic Dental Association
Post Office Box 5007
Durango, CO 81301
*www.holisticdental.org*

HOLISTIC NURSES
American Holistic Nurses
  Association
Post Office Box 2130
Flagstaff, AZ 86003-2130
800-278-AHNA
*www.ahna.org*

HOMEOPATHY
The National Center for
  Homeopathy
801 North Fairfax Street
  Suite 306
Alexandria, VA 22314
703-548-7790
*www.homeopathic.org*

### HYDROTHERAPY

To view abstracts of over 900 studies on the health benefits of this modality, use the National Center for Complementary and Alternative Medicine's search engine at: *www.nccam.nih.gov/nccam/ resources/cam-ci/search.cgi* Enter *Hydrotherapy* for "Term" and *All* for "Search Categories."

### HYPNOTHERAPY

American Board of
  Hypnotherapy
16842 Von Karman Avenue
  Suite 475
Irvine, CA 92714
714-261-6400
*www.hypnosis.com/abh*

### LABORATORIES

Great Smokies Diagnostic
  Laboratory
63 Zillicoa Street
Asheville, NC 28801
800-522-4762
*www.gsdl.com*

Meridian Valley Clinical
  Laboratory
515 West Harrison Street
  Suite 9
Kent, WA 98032
253-859-8700
*www.meridianvalleylab.com*

MetaMetrix Clinical
  Laboratory
5000 Peachtree Ind. Boulevard
Norcross, GA 30071
800-221-4640
*www.metametrix.com*

### MEDITATION

Insight Meditation Society
1030 Pleasant Street
Barre, MA 01005
978-355-4378
*www.dharma.org/ims.htm*

### MASSAGE

American Massage Therapy
  Association
820 Davis Street, Suite 100
Evanston, IL 60201-4444
847-864-0123
*www.amtamassage.org*

American Oriental Bodywork
  Therapy Association
Laurel Oak Corporate Center
  Suite 408
1010 Haddenfield-Berlin Road
Voorhees, NJ 08043
609-782-1616
*www.healthy.net/aobta*

Associated Bodywork and
  Massage Professionals
28677 Buffalo Park Road
Evergreen, CO 80439-7347
800-458-ABMP
*www.abmp.com*

**NATUROPATHY**
American Association of
  Naturopathic Physicians
601 Valley Street, Suite 105
Seattle, WA 98109
206-298-0126
*www.naturopathic.org*

American Naturopathic
  Medical Association
*www.anma.com*

Bastyr University
1307 North 45th Street,
  Suite 200
Seattle, WA 98103
206-632-0354
*www.bastyr.edu*

National College of
  Naturopathic Medicine
49 SW Porter
Portland, OR 97201
503-499-4343
*www.ncnm.edu*

Southwest College of
  Naturopathic and Health
  Sciences
2140 East Broadway Road
Tempe, AZ 85282
480-858-9100
*www.scnm.edu*

**NUTRITION**
The American Dietetic
  Association
216 West Jackson Boulevard
Chicago, IL 60606-6995
312-899-0040
*www.eatright.org*

**OSTEOPATHY**
American Academy of
  Osteopathy
3500 DePauw Boulevard
Suite 1080
Indianapolis, IN 46268-1139
317-879-1881
*www.aao.medguide.net*

American Osteopathic
  Association
142 East Ontario Street
Chicago, IL 60611
800-621-1773
*www.aoa-net.org*

**PET THERAPY**
Mayo Clinic
*www.mayohealth.org/
  mayo/9701/htm/pet_ther.htm*

**PHOTOTHERAPY/LIGHT THERAPY**
American Society for
  Photobiology
BioTech Park
1021 15th Street, Suite 9
Augusta,GA 30901-3158
706-722-7511
*www.photobiology.org*

Society for Light Treatment
and Biological Rhythms
842 Howard Avenue
New Haven, CT 06519
*www.sltbr.org*

**POLARITY THERAPY**
American Polarity Therapy
Association
Post Office Box 19858
Boulder, CO 80308
303-545-2080
*www.polaritytherapy.org*

**REFLEXOLOGY**
American Reflexology
Certification Board
Post Office Box 620607
Littleton, CO 80162
303-933-6921

International Institute of
Reflexology
5650 First Avenue North
Post Office Box 12642
St. Petersburg, FL 33733-2642
727-343-4811
*www.reflexology-usa.net*

Reflexology Association of
America
4012 Rainbow Street
K-PMB #585
Las Vegas, NV 89103-2059
*http://reflexology-usa.org*

**REIKI**
The International Center for
Reiki Training
21421 Hilltop Street, Unit 28
Southfield, MI 48034
800-332-8112
*www.reiki.org*

The Reiki Alliance
East 33135 Canyon Road
Post Office Box 41
Cataldo, ID 83810
208-682-3535
*www.furumoto.org*

The Reiki Pages
*http://reiki.7gen.com*

**ROLFING**
The Rolf Institute of Structural
Integration
205 Canyon Boulevard
Boulder, CO 80302
800-530-8875
*www.rolf.org*

**THERAPEUTIC TOUCH/
HEALING TOUCH**
Nurse-Healers Professional
Associates International
1150 Roger Bacon Drive
Suite 8
Reston, VA 20190
703-234-4149
*www.therapeutic-touch.org*

**TRIGGER POINT MYOTHERAPY**
National Association for
  Trigger Point Myotherapy
Post Office Box 68
Yarmouth Port, MA
  02675-0068
508-896-4484

**TRAGER**
The Trager Institute
21 Locust Avenue
Mill Valley, CA 94941-2806
415-388-2688
*www.trager.com*

**VISUALIZATION/GUIDED IMAGERY**
The Guided Imagery
  Resource Center
891 Moe Drive, Suite C
Akron, OH 44310-2538
800-800-8661
*www.healthjourneys.com*

**YOGA**
American Yoga Association
Post Office Box 1986
Sarasota, FL 34276
941-927-4977
*http://members.aol.com/
  amyogaassn*

**CAM WEB RESOURCES**
Alternative Health News
  Online
*www.altmedicine.com*

Ask Dr. Weil
*http://cgi.pathfinder.com/
  drweil*

Colorado Health Site
*www.coloradohealthnet.org*

Dogwood Institute
*http://galen.med.virginia.edu/%
  7Epjb3s/Complementary_
  Practices.html*

Falk Library of Health Sciences
University of Pittsburgh
*www.pitt.edu/~cbw/altm.html*

National Center for
  Complementary and
  Alternative Medicine
*http://nccam.nih.gov*

New York Online Access to
  Health (NOAH)
*www.noah.cuny.edu/
  alternative/alternative.html*

# Index